ARBELLA STUART

David N. Durant

ARBELLA STUART

A RIVAL TO THE QUEEN

WEIDENFELD AND NICOLSON
LONDON

Copyright © 1978 by David N. Durant

First published in Great Britain by
Weidenfeld and Nicolson
11 St John's Hill London SW11

ISBN 0 297 77442 5

Printed in Great Britain by
Butler & Tanner Ltd, Frome and London

To Nicholas and Diane, Jonathan and Andrew

CONTENTS

	Acknowledgements	xi
	Preface	xiii
1	So Far in Love	1
2	*Arabella Comitessa Levinox*	11
3	She Endured Very Well	20
4	Of Very Great Towardness	27
5	It Would be a Happy Thing	39
6	Good Lady Grandmother	50
7	I Pray you Send me her Picture	57
8	They Are Vanished into Smoke	65
9	My Jewel Arbella	74
10	Ye Drawing-Room Door	82
11	She Would Break Forth into Tears	88
12	Somewhat Troubled	97
13	Vapours on her Brain	105
14	Desirous to Free our Cousin	114
15	Living Very Retired	121
16	Why Should I be Ashamed?	130
17	Sumptuous and Profuse	139
18	Earnestly to Come Away	147
19	Arbella Goes Beyond Her	156
20	Make Good Music	163
21	Melancholy Humour	171
22	Grief of Mind	180
23	Highly Offended	186
24	Tricks and Gigs	195
25	No Other Way	202

CONTENTS

Abbreviations   211
Notes   212
Genealogical Tables   226
Manuscript Sources   229
Previous Biographies on Arbella Stuart   231
Bibliography   232
Portraiture of Arbella Stuart   234
Index   236

ILLUSTRATIONS

1 Arbella at twenty-three months (*National Trust. Photo Courtauld Institute*)

2 Margaret, Countess of Lennox (*National Portrait Gallery*)

3 Bess of Hardwick (*National Trust. Photo Courtauld Institute*)

4 Mary Queen of Scots and Henry Stuart, Lord Darnley (*National Trust. Photo Courtauld Institute*)

5 Charles Stuart, Arbella's father (*Photo National Portrait Gallery*)

6 Hardwick Hall (*National Trust*)

7 Sheffield Manor (*Bodleian Library, Oxford*)

8 Arbella at the age of thirteen and a half (*National Trust. Photo Courtauld Institute*)

9 One of Arbella's letters (*Bodleian Library, Oxford*)

10 A river nymph drawn by Inigo Jones (*Devonshire Collection, Chatsworth*)

11 Plaster overmantel with Arbella's arms (*National Trust. Photo Jill Langford*)

12 King James I (*National Portrait Gallery*)

13 Anne of Denmark, James's wife (*National Portrait Gallery*)

14 William Seymour, Arbella's husband.

ACKNOWLEDGEMENTS

Because I used the same research for *Arbella* as for *Bess of Hardwick*, my gratitude for assistance remains where it was placed before. I have continued to call on the help and generosity of the Trustees of the Chatsworth Settlement and the Librarian at Chatsworth, Tom Wragg and his assistant Peter Day, who as before have been unstinting in their aid. Likewise at Hardwick Hall, my friends Clive Baker, the Administrator, and his wife Kay have been as helpful as ever. And the staff of Hardwick must not be forgotten for they are one and all dedicated to that remarkable house. I am grateful too to the Marquess of Bath for allowing me to use the Longleat manuscripts and to the Librarian of Longleat, Miss Austin. For advice over the problems posed by portraits I am indebted to Robin Gibson, Assistant Keeper of the National Portrait Gallery and to Robert Gore, Historic Buildings Secretary at the National Trust. Once more my happy thanks to Jill Langford for her photographs and I am grateful to Pat Ceccarelli for her sound advice on child psychology. My sincere thanks are also due to all those unknown experts at Weidenfeld and Nicolson who saw this book into print but in particular to Barbara Gough who edited the typescript, Jenny Ashby, the copy editor, and Sappho Durrell who corrected the proofs with great sympathy. My gratitude is given to Anne Mitson who typed the final copy in so short a time. And finally once more I thank my wife Christabel, and my family who put up with me through yet another biography.

PREFACE

It has always seemed to me that when a reader has finished a biography there is the question of 'What happened next?' The life of the main character is neatly tied up, but what happened to the others? I had always planned to follow the story of Bess of Hardwick with that of her granddaughter, for the same research covered both women, and then to call it a day, for one cannot go on for ever. Here then is the story of what happened to some of the characters met with in my biography of Bess of Hardwick after her death, seen through the eyes of her granddaughter.

Throughout the book I have used the name by which she was known to her contemporaries, 'Arbella'. The later spelling 'Arabella' came from the latinization of the name and was only used by the Venetians in their reports to the Doge and Senate and never by her family. Her formidable grandmother was known as Bess by her second and third husbands, therefore, except where it is important to emphasize her rank and dignity, I have referred to her as Bess.

I have called Arbella a princess. But is this correct? Her position was ambiguous and Elizabeth kept it that way. She had no title. She was not even Countess of Lennox as Bess chose to call her at times. Yet at Elizabeth's Court she took precedence over all other ladies after the queen. She was the queen's nearest female relative and had Elizabeth nominated her as heir to the throne she would certainly have been called 'princess'. Officially she was known only as Lady Arbella Stuart, but foreign ambassadors often referred to her as the Princess Arbella. As for her own opinion on the matter we know nothing more than her mode of signature, a simple 'A.S.' or 'Arbella Stuart', and later the Stuart was changed to Seymour. I may have taken a liberty in calling her 'princess'.

Once more I must warn readers not to judge the Elizabethans and Jacobeans by our own standards, but to try to see them as their contemporaries saw them. Yet by attempting this we are immediately in difficulties, for we are conditioned by twentieth-century thinking and it is impossible to comprehend completely the sixteenth- and seventeenth-century outlooks. Health and death in childbed, are no longer special worries for the Western world, but they were matters of great concern for the Elizabethans and Jacobeans. So obvious to them indeed were these fears, that they seldom mentioned their concern. At marriage the wife's chances of surviving her first child were slim – marriage often meant the beginning of the end for a woman. Above all there was the ever-present Catholic menace, from abroad and within the country, threatening the souls of all good Protestants, for both sides were much concerned with the after life – it was a nearer reality – and death was never very far away. All these and countless other fears and worries affected their outlook. We must keep these points in mind when we exclaim at their eccentricities.

Arbella herself was certainly eccentric; she behaved in an extraordinary and self-destructive manner. The fate which overtook her was her own doing. And almost uniquely she had an earlier 'copybook' example in Catherine Grey to warn her of the inevitable consequences. Yet she still carried on her self-appointed course. I have often asked myself 'Why?' In this book I attempt to answer that question. I believe that her eccentricity was rooted in her childhood. But as the records of her upbringing are so few – for children were reckoned of no account – I have had to rely a great deal on the interpretation of the influences at work around her childish head. What effect they had on her, I will agree, is a matter for speculation, and that is how it will have to remain. But they provide the most plausible explanation to date to account for an eccentric whom even the Jacobeans could not explain.

SO FAR IN LOVE

In the late autumn of 1574 Charles Stuart, Earl of Lennox, and Elizabeth Cavendish fell in love at first sight. Charles was reported as being 'so far in love that belike he is sick without her'. And within a few days they were married. Elizabeth at twenty was a year older than her husband, and both might have thought that their marriage was entirely their own choice, but it had been heavily stage-managed by their mothers. Indeed it would have been unusual had it not been so; marriage in the upper society of sixteenth-century England was very much a business arrangement. What was unusual was that the young couple loved each other.

Charles and Elizabeth met for the first time and fell in love at Rufford Abbey, a house in a remote clearing of Sherwood Forest. It would be pleasant to report something of their days together but unfortunately little exists to record their instant affection. Likewise little remains of the abbey they knew: only the monks' undercroft and a roofless hall above it. In summer swallows wheel and scream through broken glassless windows and sparrows nest on the old roof corbels. The ruin now seems remote from any beings who once lived there, those who were born, grew up, fell in love, had babies and died there. Rufford Abbey today is a dead ruin giving no hint of the autumn idyll four hundred years ago.

Thus met and married the parents of Arbella Stuart, their only child. Their union was attended by thunderous anger from Queen Elizabeth when inevitably she had to be told. And throughout her life Arbella became accustomed to disapproval from her cousin the queen – it was the penalty for her royal blood.

Arbella's father Charles Stuart was descended through his mother Margaret, Dowager Countess of Lennox, from Margaret

Tudor, the eldest daughter of Henry VII. The royal princess Margaret was his grandmother, and he was in the line of succession to the throne of England. Arbella therefore was also in the line of succession and a royal princess – the only princess to be at the Court of Elizabeth. To the queen Arbella was an embarrassing reminder of her own mortality, a card in the diplomatic pack to be played in the game of European politics; to be offered in marriage to foreign princes but never allowed to marry. An ambitious husband might push her claim to the throne, then Arbella would become a rival and Queen Elizabeth would allow no rivals.

The marriage of Charles and Elizabeth would never have been allowed had the queen known of it – and so she was not asked. But once the deed was confessed then someone had to pay for the impertinence. It was old Margaret, the Dowager Countess of Lennox, who suffered the punishment; her own royal blood branded her as the culprit. As she went into the Tower she complained, 'thrice I have been cast into prison, not for matters of treason, but for love matters.'[1] Old Margaret's life had been a continuous struggle against the power of two thrones, those of England and Scotland, and she always lost.

But there was another culprit who got away with no punishment at all. Elizabeth Cavendish's mother was the competent, forceful and at times charming Bess of Hardwick, four times married and latterly to the great and mighty George Talbot, sixth Earl of Shrewsbury, joint keeper with his wife of the imprisoned Mary, Queen of Scots. Bess was a remarkable woman. She was born in about 1527, the fourth child of a Derbyshire squire, and had known early poverty when her father died. She was married for the first time around 1543 to Robert Barley the son of a neighbour, when she was about fifteen and he thirteen years old. The marriage was of no consequence and also short-lived; Bess was widowed within a year. She went as lady-in-waiting to the household of the Duchess of Suffolk, Frances Brandon, where she married her second husband Sir William Cavendish, already twice a widower. Sir William was a successful opportunist; he had been a useful servant to Henry VIII and was rewarded with church lands and high court position from which he had acquired considerable wealth.

Bess had married into money. Eight children followed of whom six survived.

After ten years of marriage, Sir William died and Bess was in the marriage market again. During the troubled years of the reign of Mary Tudor she had become a supporter and friend of Princess Elizabeth and at the latter's succession was given a court appointment which enabled her to meet and marry Sir William St Loe, a bachelor, Captain of the Queen's Guard, Chief Butler and owner of lands in Devon and Somerset. On his death in 1565 the lands went to Bess and her estates had now become substantial. So substantial that in 1567 she was able to arrange one of her greatest bargains, her marriage to the apparently enormously wealthy Earl of Shrewsbury. This was her last match and within eighteen months they were host and keeper to Mary, Queen of Scots, who was wished on to them by Queen Elizabeth. She remained with them for sixteen years.

Bess's great ambition was to found a dynasty and all her energies of building and money-making were directed to this aim. In marrying her daughter Elizabeth to Charles Stuart she was entering the highest arena of dynastic ambition; if she became grandmother to a boy, then there would be a good chance of him succeeding to Elizabeth's throne. Bess however escaped Elizabeth's anger. There was an understanding between the two powerful women which had been reached much earlier, after Bess had spent some nine months in the Tower. Elizabeth understood that Bess would never make any attempt to interfere with her authority. In marrying her daughter into the royal line she was only interfering with the succession.

It was left to Shrewsbury to break the news to the queen, which he did in a letter to the Earl of Leicester on 5 November before the marriage became fact, excusing himself, his wife and his step-daughter Elizabeth. Indeed Shrewsbury was in a difficult position – the marriage could be called treason. As he told Leicester for the queen's ears, 'the young man fell into liking with my wife's daughter before intended, and such liking was between them as my wife tells me she makes no doubt of a match, and hath so tied themselves upon their liking as cannot part. . . . this comes unlooked for without thanks to me.'[2] By 17 November the queen had received the earl's bad news and Margaret Lennox, her son Charles and his new bride Elizabeth were all ordered back to London to the Court to explain themselves. Bess was subjected to no such command; her loyalty was not questioned. The queen disliked Margaret Lennox, whose motives she suspected, and in her already formed opinion Margaret was the culprit – moreover she was a Catholic.

The marriage of Charles and Elizabeth was not brought about without considerable and secret planning. Early in October that same year, two great carts loaded high with furniture and baggage rumbled slowly out of London on their way north to Temple Newsam in Yorkshire. The transport was provided by the queen's Privy Council to assist old Margaret Lennox in her move from the London house at Hackney to her Yorkshire estates. On about 20 October the countess herself set out on the same route. With her went Charles Stuart, her one surviving son, brother to the murdered Darnley, husband of Mary, Queen of Scots. The journey had the appearance of an innocent change of residence, but there were some who suspected that Margaret Lennox had a more sinister motive for the expedition to her nothern estates. The queen had been distinctly wary when the countess had asked for permission to leave Court and make the journey. Elizabeth, suspecting something, had warned her cousin that she was not on any account to visit the Scots queen, a prisoner at Sheffield and Chatsworth. She had ordered Margaret not to go within thirty miles of either place. Margaret had answered that she was only flesh and blood and could never forget Mary's murder of her son Darnley. She would certainly not wish to see her daughter-in-law.

Old Margaret Lennox may be excused some duplicity. She had passed a long and unhappy life; out of eight children born to her only Charles had survived and he, whom she called 'my greatest dolour', was blessed with neither good physical health nor his brother Darnley's good looks. By 1574 Margaret Lennox was fifty-nine, not a great age by modern standards, but she termed herself an old woman and by contemporary measure she was. She had reached a time of life when she might have expected some respite from the cares of living, but nothing had been easy for the countess and added to everything she was in straitened circumstances.

Because of her stormy past and her insecure finances, Margaret Lennox was excusably a peculiar and difficult woman; she had little reason to trust anyone but herself.

The queen was not the only one to suspect Margaret's motives for moving north; the Spanish ambassador was interested and La Mothe Fénelon, the French ambassador, was near the mark in suggesting that *la Comtesse de Lenox* was proposing to continue her journey into Scotland to kidnap her grandson the little James, future King of England. This was a possibility only, but too far-fetched and dangerous to be a real threat; Margaret Lennox had another more simple plan in mind.

The progress of a countess on any journey was a slow business; her estate and rank required a large number of servants and they in turn generated baggage. The party would have been large, larger than the Lennox circumstances warranted; the daily mileage was small and the overnight stops many. One night on the way was spent at Northampton with the Duchess of Suffolk. The duchess was the widow and fourth wife of Charles Brandon, Duke of Suffolk, and although remarried to Richard Bertie grandly continued to call herself duchess.

That summer of 1574 Mrs Bertie had paid a visit to Chatsworth in Derbyshire, one of the houses of Bess of Hardwick. This meeting of the two ladies had been frowned upon by Queen Elizabeth, who did not like the possibility of strangers making a chance encounter with the Scots queen in the care of the Shrewsburys. Whether or not Mary was at Chatsworth at the time of Mrs Bertie's visit is not certain; certainly the Scots queen was there in mid-May but she had returned to Sheffield by 9 July. Mrs Bertie was likely enough carrying letters from Margaret Lennox. And Margaret, by making her overnight stop on the way north at Northampton, could collect Mary's replies. But letters were not the prime purpose of Mrs Bertie's summer visit to Chatsworth.

Bess of Hardwick still had one daughter unmarried in 1574, Elizabeth Cavendish, her second surviving daughter by her second husband Sir William Cavendish. In one respect only was Bess willing to forgo her dynastic ambition and this was in her loyalty to the queen; even this loyalty could be subdued if a single chance of strengthening her ambition could be engineered. And it is a near certain guess that Bess and Mrs Bertie were doing some engineering at Chatsworth.

Bess's husband was short of money and he had a costly family; his sons would require estates when they married; his marriage to Bess had required settlements on her sons; and the expense of keeping the Scots queen was to a great extent coming out of his own coffers. Bess had asked Shrewsbury to settle £1,000 on her daughter Elizabeth, to marry her to the Earl of Kent; he had refused, not perhaps out of perversity but because he did not have the money. Bess, as was the custom of her class and times, had tried to arrange a marriage for her daughter with almost every eligible bachelor on the market; the hindrance was Shrewsbury's inability to provide a worthwhile dowry for the girl. Bess had been in touch with the Berties on this very matter, for Richard Bertie had a son, Peregrine, whom Bess tried to secure for her daughter Elizabeth. As Shrewsbury later phrased it, Elizabeth had been 'disappointed of young Bartye'. The match may have been discussed and rejected that summer when the two ladies were together; rejected perhaps because Bess had other plans for her daughter.

Old Margaret Lennox left Northampton and continued on her way north, and Mrs Bertie went with her as far as Grantham on the road north. One more night was spent at Newark in Nottinghamshire, likely enough at the White Hart Inn, still standing in the corner of the colourful market place. The following morning a messenger arrived from Bess suggesting that Margaret Lennox and her party spend the next night at Rufford Abbey, another of the Shrewsbury estates, where Bess was conveniently poised with her daughter, contemplating the execution of her plan. No doubt Margaret was expecting the messenger, and Rufford Abbey was she said 'not one mile distant out of my way'.[3] This was perfectly true and also it was not within the thirty-mile radius of the Scots queen that she had promised Queen Elizabeth to avoid. Bess came to meet her guests on the road and escorted them triumphantly back to Rufford. Once at the abbey Margaret Lennox became sick; the rigours of the rough travelling, and the necessity to delay any departure until Charles Stuart and Elizabeth Cavendish had time to grow fond of each other, were the causes of Margaret's prostration. And the ploy worked better than either Bess or Margaret had hoped.

That the marriage had considerable advantages for Bess is obvious; what is not so obvious is why Margaret Lennox should have agreed to marry her son into a family which after all had come from small beginnings in one generation and which had no noble blood in its veins. Charles Stuart, with his mother's approval and connivance had, in a phraseology used three centuries later, married beneath himself. The reason is not hard to find and James of Scotland gave the answer – he wished it had not been a matter of money. Margaret was in severe financial difficulties, she had borrowed heavily and the payment of interest on the loans was eating into what income she was allowed from the Lennox estates in Scotland and England. By allying her son Charles with Bess's family she had her eye on what appeared to be the enormous wealth of the Cavendish and Shrewsbury families.

As far as the Cavendish family was concerned Margaret was quite right; Bess appeared to own a great deal of land, and with skilful management had added to what she originally had, but her wealth was tied up in her three sons Henry, William and Charles. Although her husband Shrewsbury was responsible for her maintenance, and custom dictated that he should provide a dowry for Elizabeth, there had been severe disagreement and the earl was being forced to make economies – one of his first was to restrict Bess's allowance in the belief that she could live off her own estates. Later he would say in reference to his own supposed wealth, 'My riches they talk of are in other men's purses.'[4] If Margaret was hoping to solve her own problems by marrying Charles to Elizabeth Cavendish then she was disappointed; Shrewsbury spared nothing immediately, and all she got from Bess was a loan. Undoubtedly the greatest benefit went to Bess, but then driving a hard bargain was almost a way of life for her. She had achieved for her daughter a brilliant marriage, and for both sides to gain the most from the match there had to be a son. The succession of the Crown was the pivot of Bess's hopes; in that hope she was cheated by fate.

In 1574 Bess's expectation of having a share in the succession was credible. The legitimate descendants of Henry VII through his daughter Margaret were the only serious claimants. Margaret Tudor's granddaughter Mary, the imprisoned Scots queen, held the strongest claim; she was also Queen Elizabeth's nearest relative. Mary was unfortunately a Catholic and unacceptable to the majority of Englishmen; although their respect for the law would have at first driven them to acknowledge her, riot and revolution would inevitably have followed – had not Elizabeth outlived her. Bess with her intimate knowledge of her prisoner would have realized that eventually Elizabeth would have to dispose of Mary, for the risk of keeping her alive was too great for the stability of the nation. In the event of Mary's death the only heir to Elizabeth's throne was Mary's eight-year-old son James VI of Scotland. Anything might happen to the child in the turbulent politics of Scotland, or he might be finished off by plague or other infection. Charles Stuart, married to Elizabeth Cavendish, was also in the same line of succession, but he was a sickly lad and not considered likely to survive. In 1574 the only legitimate successors to the English throne were first Mary, Queen of Scots, and second her son James, followed by the ailing Charles Stuart. Any children of Charles and Elizabeth Stuart would have equal claim with James, but James had the double advantage of being descended on his mother's side from Margaret Tudor's first husband, James IV of Scotland and on his father's side from Margaret's second husband, Archibald Douglas, sixth Earl of Angus.

Other more uncertain claims could be made for the descendants of Mary, the youngest daughter of Henry VII. Mary had married Charles Brandon, Duke of Suffolk, and her granddaughter Catherine Grey had perversely married Edward Seymour, Earl of Hertford. The marriage had been declared illegal by Elizabeth and the two sons Edward and Thomas Seymour were therefore illegitimate. From the list of claimants Queen Elizabeth could have named who she wished as her successor. Bess knew this full well and was taking a gamble on the children of Charles and Elizabeth being acceptable to Elizabeth, and other claimants might be carried away through the sieve of time.

As the old Countess of Lennox made her unwilling return to London following the queen's summons, her thoughts would have been on the succession problem and how seriously her royal cousin would take offence. From Huntingdon on 3 December she wrote to Leicester excusing the slowness of her journey, blaming floods and tired mules. Old Margaret may have waited to write to him until she could enlist the help of Mrs Bertie. Seven days later her party, including Charles and Elizabeth, was back at Hackney and Margaret wrote another short note to Burghley asking for his support. The French ambassador reported to his royal master that *la Comtesse de Lenox* had indeed arrived in London and that she was to face the queen at Court on 13 December. Fénelon also noted that Margaret Lennox 'was very fearful of the Queen's anger' – the royal rage was notorious. The countess appealed to anyone who might save her from the Tower, which she rightly felt was her inevitable destination. And Bess, who had supported the queen whenever she had commanded, was safe in Derbyshire out of all the turmoil and there is no evidence that she suffered anything but the mildest rebuke. For Margaret and her family the immediate result was that they were confined to the Hackney house while an investigation was made into all the circumstances of the marriage, for any sign of a popish plot involving Mary or for anything which might seriously incriminate the Catholic Margaret.

Charles Lennox's secretary was subjected to 'some kind of persuasion cunningly used'; Margaret's secretary Thomas Fowler was given similar treatment but no evidence emerged to indicate that the sudden marriage was anything other than an innocent affair, as Shrewsbury had claimed. Had Mrs Bertie been questioned, then there might have been a case to answer, but she was left unmolested and the dark plots hinted at by many were never proved. Once more Margaret Lennox had challenged the State and was required to pay for it.

How long old Margaret remained in the Tower is not known. On 14 March 1575 it was reported to Gilbert Talbot, Shrewsbury's son, that all the Lennox family were at Hackney and well, but whether this included Margaret is not clear. The birth of a child to Elizabeth Stuart must have been awaited by the two grandparents with anxiety. If it were a boy, then all the risks and the punishment suffered would have been worth while, but a girl would bring no

great pleasure. Some time in the late summer or early autumn
Arbella was born. As a girl, she displayed the same disregard for
the ambitions of others that she would show for the rest of her
life. Perhaps Margaret was released from her prison when the queen
heard with certain relief that Elizabeth Stuart's child was not a boy.
At all events Margaret was back at Hackney by 17 November when
she wrote to the Scots queen, adding almost as an afterthought, 'I
yield your Majesty my most humble thanks for your good remembrance and bounty towards our little daughter.'[5] This is the earliest
reference to Arbella's arrival and by then she must have been some
weeks old.

ARABELLA
COMITESSA LEVINOX

If any gods were present at Arbella's birth the gifts they brought were perverse in their qualities. She inherited her grandmother Bess's determination but not her ambition, old Margaret Lennox's gift of being at odds with the authority of the State and the Stuarts's wit and charm. In any girl not of royal blood these gifts would have ensured a happy and useful life, but like her grandmother Margaret she found the royal inheritance a bitter disadvantage – her royal blood rendered all her talents as nothing. Her inherited characteristics would bring about her eventual self-destruction.

It is probable that Arbella was born at Hackney, at all events she was at Hackney in the Lennox house for the earliest months of her life. At her baptism however her godparents were all on the Cavendish side; her uncle Charles Cavendish was one godfather and her aunt Mary together with her husband Gilbert Talbot, later seventh Earl of Shrewsbury, were the other sponsors. Indeed there were no Lennox relatives left to act as godparents, they were either blown-up, imprisoned or disgraced, apart from the infant James VI of Scotland, and to have chosen him or a proxy for him would have been to invoke the displeasure of Queen Elizabeth.[1]

No doubt it was in the minds of all that Arbella's birth would possibly be followed by that of a male heir, but in that hope there was disappointment, for after only eighteen months of marriage Charles Stuart died of a rapid consumption in early April 1576 and Elizabeth was not pregnant again. This must have been a set-back to the hopes of both Bess and Margaret but they were more than used to the bitter ways of fate and would have taken the matter philosophically. At a time when eccentric women did not excite comment, old Margaret Lennox was acknowledged to be 'peculiar' and in view of her previous history she must be allowed this attribute; she was also difficult. And in the matter of telling the truth either she or Mary, Queen of Scots – another difficult woman – was lying. For Margaret, when told by Queen Elizabeth not to see Mary on her trip north in 1574, had replied that she would never forget the murder of her son Darnley for which she blamed Mary. That would seem to be that. Margaret had no love for her daughter-in-law; but this was not so if Mary is to be believed. For in 1578 Mary told the Bishop of Glasgow that she had been on 'the very best of terms' with that 'good lady' for five or six years. But Mary's long incarceration in the castles and mansions of the Shrewsburys may have made her memory unreliable.

Whichever of these two difficult women one believes, it is still true that after the Lennox/Cavendish marriage, when the French ambassador La Mothe Fénelon was confounded in his forecast that the two women could never be anything but enemies, they became firm and loving friends. Margaret Lennox was useful to Mary because of her influence at Court and Mary to Margaret over the Lennox inheritance. And although both Bess and Margaret were forced to accept philosophically that there could be no Lennox heir other than Arbella, they could not and did not take the same fatalistic attitude over the just financial support of the young widow and her child. Margaret's friendship with the Scots queen and Bess's friendship with Queen Elizabeth were valuable in their coming struggle.

On the death of Charles Stuart the Scottish estates, which had been confirmed to him soon after his father's death in April 1572 by the young King James, were seized by the Scottish Crown. Margaret Lennox had written to Lord Ruthven, Lord Treasurer of Scotland, married to a Douglas – and Margaret was a Douglas – asking that Arbella should inherit the Scottish Lennox estates; she herself was in no doubt, but it was quite another matter to convince the Regent Mar who ruled for the moment during James's minority. The lands had been granted outright to Charles Lennox and his heirs for ever and there should have been no argument, but it was a dispute which dragged on for years, and long after Margaret was dead Bess was still trying to get the Scottish lands for her granddaughter Arbella. It was a battle which the indomitable Bess never won; for, notwithstanding the support of the English queen, the Scottish queen and many others whose authority was not recognized in Scotland, the Lennox lands remained with James to dispose of as he wished and he never disposed of them to Arbella.

Arbella's grandmother Bess never allowed the size of a problem to daunt her. The month after Charles Stuart's death Bess took herself up to Court to work on Elizabeth to push the Lennox claim with James in Scotland. Leicester, the queen's favourite, gave Bess the use of Leicester House in the Strand and sponsored her claim. The queen made a great fuss of her old friend and her expressions of delight may have been genuine, but inevitably the claim foundered on James's intransigence.

There is a portrait of Arbella painted at this time. It was likely enough commissioned by Bess and still hangs at Hardwick Hall where it must have been for the last four hundred years. It is clearly titled *Arabella Comitessa Levinox. Aetae Sue 23 Menses A.DÑI 1577* (Arbella Countess of Lennox aged 23 months 1577), and it must have been painted in the summer of 1577 after the death of her father. A chubby-cheeked, serious little Arbella stares out of her frame, her large blue eyes looking past us, her gold hair all but covered by a bonnet surrounded by pearls and diamonds set in gold; real pearls drip from the centres of embroidered flowers; around her neck hangs a magnificent gold chain and from it swings a shield showing a countess's coronet and the Lennox motto *Pour parvenir, j'endure*. The sitter might be taken for a child of any age, but she clutches in her left hand a doll in full court dress. The portrait is possibly not a very good likeness but that was not its intent; the emphasis is entirely on the magnificence of the dress and it is unlikely that Arbella possessed such finery at that age.

To our eyes the portrait of Arbella is touching, but that was not how Bess and her contemporaries would have seen it. It was unusual to have portraits painted of children and in any event portraits to Elizabethans meant something very different from the often simple photographic likenesses of today. This is not so much a painting of Arbella but rather of the Countess of Lennox in 1577; it conveys not her likeness but her rank and position in society and the deliberately emphasized finery displays her very high estate. All this poses a question: why was it painted?

In late July of 1577 Robert Dudley, Earl of Leicester and Queen Elizabeth's favourite, paid a visit to the Derbyshire health resort of Buxton ostensibly for the benefit of his gout. Mary, Queen of Scots had been trundled over to nearby Chatsworth, and Leicester and she conferred over a current rumour of a possible match between Mary and Don John of Austria. While Leicester was under her roof Bess used the opportunity to press Arbella's claim to the Lennox earldom; Leicester promised his help when he returned to Court and suggested that Bess should write a letter to the queen for him to take personally to his mistress. The portrait of Arbella was painted at about this time and it may have been intended for Leicester to take to the queen to reinforce Bess's letter. If so, then it would have posed problems for Bess too, for Arbella was in London, but Bess did not desire a likeness and any face would have sufficed as long as the indication of estate was there. It is more likely however that Bess took the portrait herself when she visited Court in September 1578, again to press Arbella's claim. The only certain point about the Arbella portrait is that it was painted expressly to further her claim to the Lennox earldom and the only person it could have been intended for was the queen herself.

With the loss of the income from the Scottish estates Margaret Lennox was left to support her widowed daughter-in-law and the little Arbella out of the Lennox estates in England; her means were made more slender by the payment of interest for debts incurred earlier. There was a debt outstanding to the English Crown – the Earl of Northumberland had originally lent money to Margaret, but his assets were seized when he was executed and consequently she now owed money to the Crown; another debt was owing to Bess, necessitating an annual payment of £500 over four years. This was Margaret's shaky financial position immediately after the death of her son. Elizabeth Lennox should have been given a dowry by the Shrewsburys on her marriage, but Bess had not told the earl anything until it was all but over and, as he put it, 'it was dealt in suddenly and without my knowledge.' Shrewsbury did not see why he should be called on to provide a dowry when he had never been consulted in the matter. In fact the earl was in financial trouble himself and it is doubtful whether he had the means available for his stepdaughter Elizabeth Lennox. Bess 'at last by brawling did get three thousand pounds', but it is questionable whether Shrewsbury handed the money over there and then, for certainly Elizabeth Lennox never saw a penny of the £3,000.[2]

With Arbella's father dead there was a danger that the wardship of the child would be sold by the Crown. The danger lay not so much in the immediate present but in the future, for any guardian taking over the wardship would not gain from revenues from lands, for she had none, but from the profitable sale by her guardian of her marriage later on. In fact it is unlikely that Burghley, the Master of Wards, would have let the wardship out of his own hands unless it went to Arbella's family. There is no direct evidence, but the inference is that Margaret Lennox was awarded the guardianship of Arbella, for the Shrewsburys made no move in the matter until five days before Margaret's death in 1578, when they could see the possibility of losing control of Arbella's upbringing and future.

It is a reasonable certainty that Arbella, at least until 1578, lived at Hackney; it is quite clear that Queen Elizabeth discouraged any visitors to the Shrewsburys. One of the earl's financial complaints among many was that he had been forced to set up his sons in separate establishments because Elizabeth would not permit them to live near the Scots queen. She would certainly not have permitted Elizabeth Lennox with her attendants to live under the same roof as the Scots queen – that would have given greater opportunity for passing secret messages. Besides both Bess and Shrewsbury had their hands more than full with Mary and the problems of her security, without the diversion of having a small family living with them.

Unconcerned in her early babyhood with the struggles and misfortunes taking place around her Arbella was lucky in one respect of her inheritance: Bess, Countess of Shrewsbury, was a remarkable woman who during Arbella's early years fought for her grandchild's rights with characteristic tenacity. If Bess could not win Arbella's due, then no one could; Arbella could not have had a better champion. And yet these two women, who were so closely related by blood and bound by a common cause, were utterly dissimilar. When Arbella had grown up and developed her own character, she and Bess fell into disaccord. But even after she had left Bess's care – with recriminations on both sides – she still returned from time to time to visit her invincible relative.

When Bess had married George Talbot, sixth Earl of Shrewsbury, premier earl of England, in the autumn of 1567, he was apparently the wealthiest of the queen's subjects, with castles, mansions and lands throughout Staffordshire, Shropshire, Leicestershire, Lincolnshire, Derbyshire and Yorkshire. For both parties the marriage made sense as their estates adjoined in many places and by his marriage to Bess the earl could expect to acquire all her lands to add to his own.

Both were about forty years of age and he too had been married before, to Gertrude Manners, sister of the Earl of Rutland, by whom he had sons and daughters. To ensure that her family benefited from her union with the Talbot estates, Bess and the earl arranged a double marriage between their own children some months after their own ceremony: Gilbert Talbot, the earl's second son, then aged sixteen, was married to Bess's youngest daughter Mary, who was no older than twelve; and Bess's eldest son Henry, aged eighteen, married the earl's youngest daughter Grace, who could not have been much more than eight years old. The joint wedding took place at Sheffield on 9 February 1568 and the two grooms were immediately sent on a protracted educational tour of Europe and to the University of Padua, until their brides should be old enough for childbearing.

George Talbot and his new countess had enjoyed their marriage for only eighteen months when Mary, Queen of Scots was thrust into their care. Mary had been forced to flee from Scotland after renouncing her right to the throne under duress in May 1568, and to the embarrassment of Elizabeth and Burghley the fugitive arrived in England. Elizabeth's response to her cousin's request for an army to help her reclaim her Scottish throne was to reject the plea, then to keep her under careful restraint and finally imprison her. In January 1569 Mary, Queen of Scots became the unwilling guest of the Earl and countess of Shrewsbury with whom she stayed a prisoner for the next sixteen years – years which were to be eventful and dramatic for all three.

The dreary days and nights of Mary's imprisonment passed slowly as her cause became more and more forlorn; with time to think, Mary indulged in ingenious plots and imaginative plans for escape, and as the years passed it became obvious to her that as long as Elizabeth ruled then her own inevitable fate would be eventual execution. This thought had occurred to Walsingham, Queen Elizabeth's Secretary of State, although it was not an idea Elizabeth allowed herself to dwell on. From Mary's point of view, if she was to avoid her inevitable fate, then Elizabeth would have to be done away with and Mary rule in her place. The plans of the Scottish queen became more and more desperate as time passed and the uncovering and foiling of their prisoner's plottings imposed an almost intolerable strain on Bess and Shrewsbury.

Into this unsuitable background of intrigue and plotting surrounding the unhappy Queen of Scotland, Arbella was precipitated by the sudden death of her grandmother Margaret Lennox. It is said that Margaret, apparently in perfect health, died at her Hackney home within a few hours of dining with the Earl of Leicester on 9 March 1578, aged sixty-three. If this account of her death is true, then it is suspicious, for only four days earlier the Earl of Shrewsbury had applied to Burghley for his interest in the wardship of Arbella – when Margaret, who was Arbella's guardian was brimming over with health!

The old countess had lived a momentously unhappy life. Born in 1515 Margaret was the daughter of Margaret Douglas, Dowager Queen of Scotland, eldest daughter of Henry VII of England, and through her passed the claim of the throne of England. The succession was the shuttlecock of politics and the cause of all Margaret's problems; she was also unwisely a Catholic. In her early years she had chosen a bad moment to fall in love with Thomas Howard, brother of the Duke of Norfolk and a near relative to Anne Boleyn. This was at a time when Anne, Henry VIII's second wife, was in disgrace, but had not yet been executed for adultery and incest in 1536. Both Margaret and Thomas Howard were put into the Tower for their presumption and they never met again for he shortly

afterwards died of a fever. In 1544 Henry VIII married her off to
Matthew Stuart, fourth Earl of Lennox, a Scottish noble of enormous prestige and related to the royal family; it was a political marriage designed at the time to strengthen the bonds between the two
countries. Margaret had eight children and none of them survived
her. The eldest, Henry, Lord Darnley, married Mary, Queen of
Scots in 1565, and this was despite Margaret's solemn promise to
Queen Elizabeth that she would not permit such an ill-omened
match – Elizabeth had no reason to trust her cousin. Again Margaret
was hurried to the Tower and only forgiven by Elizabeth when
Darnley was found strangled in 1567 at Kirk-o'-Field. Margaret's
third and final sojourn in the Tower was over the marriage of her
son Charles to Elizabeth Cavendish.

At Margaret's death the shuttlecock of politics fell into the court
of the innocent Arbella, and Margaret's problems were bequeathed
to her granddaughter. First and foremost was the question of the
English Lennox lands, which were immediately seized by Queen
Elizabeth on the pretext of the debt owing to the Crown from
the Earl of Northumberland's estate. In fairness Elizabeth gave
Margaret a state funeral and a monument of some magnificence in
Westminster Abbey, although this was something of a backhander:
Elizabeth was up to her old game of appearing to give something generously at no cost to herself – it was all paid for out of
Margaret's estate. And when James of Scotland attempted to claim
the English Lennox lands, Elizabeth used the excuse that the high
cost of the funeral and Margaret's debts had taken all – there was
nothing left. At the same time she reminded the Scots that they held
lands which rightfully belonged to the young Countess of Lennox.
Consequently there was nothing left for Arbella or her mother either,
their rightful substance having been taken by the two powerful states
of England and Scotland; like that of her grandmother Lennox,
Arbella's existence was threatened by the political jealousies of the
two kingdoms.

Fate had another buffet for the innocent Arbella. Margaret Lennox had left her jewels to her only granddaughter and these were
to be held by Thomas Fowler, the executor of her will, until Arbella
should be fourteen. But Fowler, notwithstanding a warrant from

the Scots queen to hand them over to Bess, left for Scotland with the jewels, which eventually found their way to James.

By 1578, when Arbella was only three years old, she had already suffered severe penalties because of her royal blood. The only champion left to her was her indomitable grandmother Bess and she too had reason to fear the overriding authority of the Crown.

3

SHE ENDURED VERY WELL

In the autumn of 1578 Bess returned to Court for the sole purpose of using her relationship with the queen to press the Lennox claim for Arbella. Old Margaret, before she died, had used her influence with the Scots queen, and Mary had made a will in 1577 in which she stated that she recognized Arbella's claim and called on her son James, the Scots king, to obey her in this. Twelve months later she gave the same instructions to her ambassador the Bishop of Glasgow. It was certainly Mary's intention that Arbella should have the Scottish Lennox lands but unfortunately Mary was impotent to enforce her commands; commands which James undutifully disobeyed. He revoked the earldom from Arbella on 3 May 1578 and the following month gave it to the next heir, Robert Stuart, Bishop of Caithness, who was elderly, childless and unmarried.

That was the situation which provoked Bess to visit Court that autumn. She had a strong ally in Leicester, the queen's favourite; at Buxton the previous year he had listened sympathetically, he had even presented Bess's case to the queen. On this occasion with the Court at Richmond he offered Bess the use of two rooms in his own lodgings which she gratefully accepted. Bess arrived at Court at the end of November. The visit had to be a short one as the responsibility of guarding the Scots queen prevented either Bess or Shrewsbury from being away for more than a week or two; her duty caused her return to Sheffield before the start of the great court festival of the twelve days of Christmas.

Elizabeth listened to her friend with sympathy and promised to do what she could over James's obstinacy, but in that direction Elizabeth was as impotent as her cousin Mary; her authority did not extend into Scotland. There was much writing of letters and evasive answers but they brought no result. Faced with this stalemate Bess's influence was not entirely without effect, for Elizabeth awarded Arbella an annual sum of £200 and £400 to her mother. It was a result which did not satisfy Bess for she kept the claim well heated during the coming years and stoked the fire whenever she thought the embers were dying and the matter was likely to be forgotten. The total annual sum of £600 might appear to have been sufficient to keep a mother and child, and in a less exalted position this would have been so, but Arbella was a princess of royal blood descended from Henry VII and therefore had to live in a fitting style, requiring a household and servants, which was not a cheap matter. Elizabeth considered the total of £600 quite sufficient and Bess did not, and as far as Elizabeth was concerned Bess would have to make up any difference if that was her conviction.

By Christmas Eve Bess had returned home bringing Arbella with her and, as strangers were not permitted at Sheffield Castle while Mary was beneath the roof, Arbella was dropped off at Chatsworth. Bess remarked to Walsingham, 'I came hither [Sheffield] of Cresto-line's eve and left my little Arbell at Chatsworth. She endured very well with travel and yet I was forced to take long journeys to be here with my lord afore ye day.' No mention was made of Elizabeth Lennox, but the inference is that she returned with Arbella to live at the expense of the Shrewsburys in Derbyshire; this would have solved the problem of living within the means awarded by the queen; and under her own roof Bess could also keep a strict eye on the child's upbringing and education.[1]

Arbella, when she arrived at Chatsworth that 'Crestoline eve', was nearly three-and-a-half years old, an impressionable age and not too young by contemporary standards to start her education. If Arbella was not to be the Countess of Lennox, then she might be queen if things could be managed that way and if both aspirations failed, then as a royal princess she would surely marry someone of rank. She would be required to know Latin, Italian and French; she would have to learn to dance and to play on the virginals and lute; to embroider and to write with a firm and elegant hand. All these accomplishments would be expected of her because of her rank and there would also be a good dose of Protestant reading thrown in.

This course of education contrasted with what Bess had received forty years before, when possibly all she learned was to read and write, but Bess was not thought to be destined for a great and glorious future. She probably never understood Latin, for the Latin adages from Erasmus which adorn her embroideries have no connection with the subject of the needlework. She never showed any inclination towards books, other than such suitable reading as the Bible, and Calvin on Job; nevertheless her addition was usually accurate. Bess's instruction came from what she had learned throughout her life, and Arbella was not to be allowed to gain her education in this haphazard way.

To modern eyes the Elizabethan's methods of teaching were horrific and their attitude to children must have stored up many psychological troubles in the minds of the young. It is true to say that with very few notable exceptions children were treated with no understanding whatsoever; they were considered of little account and learning was instilled by fear. 'Spare the rod and spoil the child', although written by Samuel Butler in 1663 was applicable much earlier – he was remembering his own childhood. 'If thou smite him with the rod, thou shall deliver his soul from Hell' was in the Bible and taken literally. 'The child whom the father loves most dear he does most punish tenderly in fear' was a precept firmly practised. In recalling her parents and their attitude Jane Grey noted, 'One of the greatest benefits that God ever gave me is that He sent me so sharp and severe parents.'[2]

Bess's attitude would have been no different from that of Frances Brandon. These were times when life was to be endured and happiness was not expected; torture was used without conscience. The public spectacles of hanging, disembowelling and burning were still enjoyed by many as an entertainment. The nobility when sentenced were mostly spared these degradations and were instead decapitated, while royalty had the privilege of private execution within the Tower walls; these were tributes to their rank and not due to any enlightenment. Pain was a common accompaniment to living and only the lucky avoided it; why then would any parent consider 'sparing the rod'? It would only coddle children for their later years, and to reinforce the rod was a battery of other implements to ensure that children would learn their grammar. Childhood was commonly a vale of tears to prepare for a manhood of suffering and pain. One is left to wonder how these children survived with a balanced outlook, and the truth, if it can ever be discovered, is likely to be that they seldom did.

But the suitability or otherwise of Elizabethan education apart, the whole background into which Arbella was dropped at Christmas 1578 was hardly likely to have had a good influence on any child's development. Bess and Shrewsbury had fallen into disaccord. Their differences were compounded of more than one cause. The strain of watching Mary was telling on Shrewsbury's health, and some of his servants had been arrested on suspicion of passing messages for the Scots queen, who throughout her stay with the Shrewsburys hardly ever stopped plotting and scheming her escape and Elizabeth's downfall.

Shrewsbury, although immensely loyal to his queen, had been allotted a task which was beyond his ability. The strain of his duty eventually brought about what would now be called a nervous breakdown. The cost of keeping the royal prisoner exceeded the allowance from Elizabeth and the difference came out of Shrewsbury's pocket. Indeed the man was in a very difficult position: Tudor politics veered with the strongest wind and if the wind blew hard enough Elizabeth could disappear and Mary take her place. What sort of chance would Shrewsbury have stood then if his treatment of Mary had been cruel or unjust? On the other hand he could not be too lenient with his prisoner or Elizabeth would suspect him of Marian sympathies. Elizabeth paid for Mary's court of up to thirty or so, but if Mary chose to let refugees join her then Shrewsbury turned a blind eye and supported the extra numbers until Cecil and Elizabeth, learning of the additional retainers, ordered the hangers-on out of the walls of Sheffield Castle.

In order to alleviate a looming financial problem Shrewsbury made an arrangement with Bess in 1572 which later caused him chagrin and distress, but again he was forced into the arrangement through the rising cost of his duty to the queen. When he had married Bess in 1567, a marriage settlement had been drawn up and though this document has long since disappeared it is possible to understand the major points by the 1572 deed of gift which superseded some of the clauses in the original settlement. On her marriage to Shrewsbury all Bess's lands which were not already settled on Henry Cavendish (her heir by her second husband Sir William Cavendish), and which she held until Henry became twenty-one in December 1571, became the property of Shrewsbury. This was the usual arrangement, and the lands which went to Shrewsbury were mainly those in Somerset and Gloucestershire which had come to Bess through her third husband Sir William St Loe. Bess was therefore giving up all her financial independence and in return, again according to custom, Shrewsbury at their marriage made over to his wife one-third of his unsettled income, to come to her at his death.

However Bess was in every way a dynastic matron and her great ambition was to found a family of Cavendishes on such wealth that they would last for a thousand years, an ambition fired by the memory of her early years when the power of the State through the Court of Wards had practically extinguished the Hardwicks. Shrewsbury never understood his wife's attitude and whenever he ran counter to her deepseated and unalterable ambition he was always surprised at the fury aroused. Also written into the marriage settlement was the provision that Shrewsbury would give to her two younger sons, William and Charles, the sum of about £20,000, when they reached the age of twenty-one. William would be of age at the end of 1573 and Shrewsbury could see this date looming before him. This would be followed a year later by the equally impossible figure on Charles's majority. The deed of gift which Shrewsbury made in 1572 and which he so unreasonably denounced later – simply returned to Bess her St Loe Lands, which were then settled on William and Charles, and Shrewsbury was excused from paying out to the two boys a huge sum of money he did not possess, and also Bess's long-standing debts. It was a sensible arrangement.

Sensible though the arrangement was in essence, it gave Bess back her financial independence and having regained this freedom she went back to her wheeling and dealing in lands, which she was superbly competent to do. Shrewsbury had the mortification of seeing his wife becoming richer as he became poorer. Had Shrewsbury realized that Bess was operating her markets solely for her sons and not for herself he would have been nearer understanding his wife, but he was not a man of intellect and could only suppose that Bess was siphoning away his fortune into her coffers. Nothing ever convinced him otherwise, and consequently his relationship with Bess deteriorated in direct proportion to her growing riches.[3]

As Shrewsbury's problems multiplied, so his health degenerated and he was less able to cope with his difficulties. His frustration was directed at Bess and from time to time he exploded into criticism and abuse of his wife, who in return answered in language which shocked even him. It must be said that through all their quarrels Bess never wronged Shrewsbury nor wished to be parted from him; Shrewsbury was guilty of both.

In August 1577 the arguments and wars between the two were suspended while they shared a common grief: their grandson the little George Talbot, only two-and-a-half years old and apparently in good health, suddenly died. George was the son of Bess's daughter Mary, married to Shrewsbury's son Gilbert. Bess, who was always one to give way to deluges of tears, was described by Shrewsbury in a letter to Walsingham as 'not so well able to rule her passions', which is about as near as he ever came to understanding his wife. Their shared tragedy caused them to forget their disputes and drew them together for a time. But by the time that Arbella came to Derbyshire in 1578, Bess had become richer, Shrewsbury poorer and his nervous disposition more pronounced. Consequently his antagonism towards Bess had returned.

If this disunity of background was not sufficiently detrimental to the upbringing of Arbella, further malignant influences on the child may have been created by Mary, Queen of Scots. Little direct evidence of what was happening to Arbella at this point in her life exists and any explanation must be speculative. If the order that Arbella was not to share the same roof as the prisoner had been adhered to, then any influence Mary may have had on the impressionable child would have been avoided, but the Shrewsburys prevailed on Cecil and the queen, and Arbella was allowed to live in the same household as the captive Mary.

The Scots queen has been depicted from many aspects and points of view; she has been described with sympathy and alternatively as a monster. The truth probably lies somewhere between the two opinions. Her upbringing must have contributed to her later behaviour, which by any standards is extraordinary – an example of an unbalanced outlook. From her first breath Mary was surrounded by falsehood and destruction from which in adult life she defended herself by using the same devices. She married Lord Darnley in 1565, which was unpopular and led to a revolt; she witnessed the murder of her secretary Rizzio while she was pregnant; and she was reputed to have had Darnley strangled in a close, outside the exploding and blazing house at Kirk-o'-Field in 1567. The latter event was considered diabolical by many inured and hardened to violence. Mary's behaviour was condemned by most Elizabethans as being beyond acceptance, and that is saying a great deal. The influence of this frustrated, disappointed and neurotic woman on Arbella at her most impressionable years, if permitted, must have been detrimental.

It is also possible that Mary, seeing in Arbella a rival to the claim to Elizabeth's throne of her son James, would have wished to have had little to do with Bess's granddaughter, particularly if this was likely to have irritated Bess. But nevertheless, whether Arbella was permitted access to the Scots queen or not, she was under the same roof and would have been fully aware that here was a queen in every sense, who was now a pathetic and restricted captive; a queen moreover who from her earliest years had been surrounded by intrigue and violence was now denied the violence but continued the intrigue. At best the daily scene would have displayed to Arbella all the disadvantages of queenship and none of the advantages, and at worst the personal influence of Mary on Arbella would have been deplorably malign.

4

OF VERY
GREAT TOWARDNESS

By 1581 Arbella had been living with her grandmother Bess for three years, time enough for her to get to know her aunt, the captive Queen Mary. The example of her unfortunate relative may have determined Arbella to avoid a similar fate, for throughout her life she never showed the least ambition for political power. There were other facts about Mary which must have impressed themselves on the child's mind, indeed the whole world around Arbella was conspiring to give her an unusual outlook which was with her for the whole of her life. Arbella's world was essentially female and from the day of her birth it had been dominated by powerful female personalities. First there had been her grandmother Lennox, who no matter how 'difficult' at least knew what she wanted. Old Margaret Lennox had died and Arbella was transferred to the ambience of her other grandmother Bess, another powerful figure who also knew what she wanted and how best to get it.

At the same time Arbella was placed in the small and peculiar orbit of the Scots queen. There were of course her uncles Henry, William and Charles on the Cavendish side, but these were shadowy figures, not permitted to live in the same house as Mary. They would have made fleeting visits, passing in and out of Arbella's vision without making a great impression. Arbella would not have remembered her father Charles Stuart, and her impressionable years were passed without a father figure to take his place: the substitutes were powerful and dominating female relatives. Unfortunately nothing is known about Arbella's mother. There are just a few letters and none of them tell us anything about her at all; she is another shadowy figure, perhaps dominated by Bess.

There was a common factor about the three women so affecting

Arbella's outlook which ran counter to the natural course of Tudor life, when women commonly died in childbirth and a man might be a widower two or three times during his lifetime. Mary, Queen of Scots had outlived three husbands, one of whom had been helped out of the world, and the third, Bothwell, had died in Denmark in 1578 insane; none of these cut an heroic figure. Arbella's grandmother Margaret had outlived her husband. The most remarkable of all was Arbella's other grandmother Bess who had already buried three husbands and by 1581 was well on the way to being rid of her fourth. Here were three powerful women who had defied the common-statistics and had survived their menfolk. To a small child aged six they must have appeared as invincible as they were dominating; Arbella could well have gained the impression that men were expendable.

And at the top of the pyramid of power and society was another example of an invincible woman related by blood to Arbella, Queen Elizabeth, who used men entirely for her own ends. The only man who might have made an impact on Arbella at the time was Shrewsbury, who gave an unfortunate impression, for he was engaged on a course of warfare against Arbella's champion Bess; this alone would have made him unattractive to Arbella. No matter where she looked in her own small world Arbella could only draw one conclusion, inevitable in the circumstances, that in her family women were all-powerful and men dispensable, an outlook which affected her entire life.

While Arbella was absorbing these lessons and drawing her own private conclusions, her mother Elizabeth Lennox became seriously ill. By 16 January it was feared she might die. On Sunday, five days later, Arbella's mother died at Sheffield, possibly at the manor, and she was interred in the Shrewsbury vault at Sheffield Cathedral. Shrewsbury, conscious of his duty, wrote immediately that same day to Burghley and to Walsingham (Leicester was out of favour over his secret marriage to Lettice Knollys). The point of the two letters was to advise the queen that now Arbella was left 'destitute' as he put it; he feared the £400 annual allowance for Elizabeth Lennox would be stopped. Shrewsbury mentioned that Bess 'so mourneth and lamenteth, that she cannot think of aught but tears'. She was indulging in the uncontrollable weeping which Shrewsbury found unattractive and tiresome.

It was in keeping with the attitude of the time that Arbella's re-action to her mother's death was not mentioned; she was a child and of little account. It was what she represented in the continuity of rank which mattered: she was a royal princess and her position required royal support. A week later Bess had pulled herself together and wrote to Burghley and Walsingham making the same request as Shrewsbury, warning Walsingham that her son William would follow up the letter with a visit. And William wrote to the queen directly asking that Elizabeth's allowance be continued with Arbella's. Again no mention was made of the child's reaction or feel-ings; her guardians were concerned only with her due.

Five days before Elizabeth Lennox died she made a will. It must have been dictated by Bess and agreed and signed by her daughter, because Elizabeth asked the queen to permit Bess to be Arbella's guardian, and then came round to the same urgent request that all the lands allowed to her which paid the £400 annually should be transferred to Arbella. Tactfully Elizabeth left her 'best jewel, a ring set with a great diamond' to the queen. Then she requested her 'friends' Leicester, Hatton the Lord Chancellor, the Lord Trea-surer Burghley, and Walsingham to continue their goodwill towards her 'smale orphant'. Finally she asked Bess to look after her money until Arbella was either married or sixteen, when she was to receive the residue.

Elizabeth's plea from the grave and the pressure kept up by almost the entire family eventually won nothing more for Arbella: her mother's annual £400 went back to the queen. But Bess had tried. In a long letter to Burghley dated 6 May 1582 Bess reminded him that Arbella was related 'in blood to her Majesty'; and to Walsingham she described Arbella as 'being well near seven years old and of very great towardness to learn anything and I very careful of her good education as she were my own and only child, and a great deal more for the consanguinity she is of to her Majesty'. But all this fell on deaf ears, and Bess was left to support her grand-child as she could well afford to do.[1]

Early in February after Elizabeth Lennox's death, Shrewsbury moved his prisoner back to Sheffield Castle from the manor and sent Bess off to her beloved Chatsworth; no doubt he was glad to get her off his hands. The claim for the Lennox earldom no longer occupied so much of Bess's energies; it was gradually allowed to be forgotten. In 1579 Esmé Stuart had arrived in Scotland from France. He was cousin to James's father, aged around forty and a polished operator. His mission was to counteract the English influence in Scottish affairs and his arrival alarmed the cunning Walsingham. James, now thirteen, quickly gave his trust and affections to his new cousin. The old Bishop of Caithness, the occupier of the Lennox earldom, was bribed with the earldom of March and he gave up the Lennox title and lands to Esmé Stuart.

Esmé's effect on Scottish affairs during the four years he was there was remarkable. He caused the downfall of the pro-English regent Morton, who was executed for the murder of Darnley – which pleased Mary, Queen of Scots – and by 1582 things had come to such a state that James, aged fifteen, was kidnapped by the Ruthven family, a pro-English faction, and Esmé was forced out of Scotland for ever by the end of the year. One is left to wonder how great a part Walsingham and his spies had in all this. Esmé was given a safe conduct to pass through England on his way to France in January 1583 and in passing had a curious and secret interview with Queen Elizabeth. He had been created Duke of Lennox and his possession of the title was so concrete that it was pointless for Bess to pursue the matter further.[2]

That Bess was able to prevail on Shrewsbury to support her claims for her family – as she had over the claim to the Lennox earldom, and again over Arbella's claim to her mother's £400 allowance – was due to a mixture of tact and charm, and when that failed the judicial use of a downright blazing row would usually bring her husband into line with her wishes. One of the symptoms of the earl's state of strain was to overreact and this is evident in many of his letters. However the earl's health had become more than just a family matter, for reports of his discontent with his countess had reached Court in 1579, when ironically their differences had for the time being been forgotten over their shared mourning for the little George Talbot. But as their distress receded into the past so the earl's overreaction to Bess's imagined provocations returned and Shrewsbury renewed hostilities towards his wife. His worries, both financial and family, allied to the strain of keeping watch over his prisoner had increased rather than lessened and were wearing the loyal earl down. One answer to the problems was to remove Mary from his care, but Shrewsbury's jealous concern for his honour would not allow him to admit failure to his queen. He regarded his honour as being something worth more than his life: it was a very tangible attribute never to be lost if it could be avoided.

Shrewsbury's peculiar state of mind is illustrated by his method of ridding himself of his closest ally and supporter, Bess. He simply saw her off to Chatsworth in June 1583 without any suggestion of finality in his adieu, in fact he said that he would send for her in a few days. Shrewsbury did not send for Bess and he started a vendetta against her and her sons William and Charles Cavendish by seizing rents from the estates which he had returned to them and harassing the tenants around Chatsworth. This culminated in what appeared to be an armed attack on Chatsworth in July 1584, when William took to the battlements and waved his sword at Shrewsbury's men. For this aggression the Privy Council put William in the Fleet Jail.

It was all utterly ridiculous, for Bess genuinely wished to return to Shrewsbury, but he had convinced himself that she was taking his money, and her steady increase in riches (since he signed that regretted deed in 1572), set against his own financial decline, was to Shrewsbury certain proof that she had been plundering his coffers. If he had been able to think sensibly for one moment he would have seen, though no doubt not liked to admit, that Bess was responsible in many ways for the safety of his prisoner. Shrewsbury was never very sensitive to what was going on around him and with Bess out of the way Mary was able to indulge in her schemings and plottings more freely than before. Neither was Shrewsbury acute enough to see that Bess's prosperity was mainly the result of her own astuteness.

Shrewsbury's harassment of Bess and her two younger sons became so extreme that she was unable to continue living at Chatsworth and was forced to become a refugee in Hardwick Hall, which she bought in 1583 after her brother James had died bankrupt in the Fleet Jail. There at Hardwick, with her financial support cut off by Shrewsbury, Bess started to make the large farmhouse into something more suitable for a countess and to accommodate the large number of attendants she was obliged to maintain. The building of Hardwick Hall was as spasmodic as her finances allowed. It is very unlikely that Arbella was with Bess during these acute years of her discontent with Shrewsbury; more probably she was with her aunt Mary and Gilbert Talbot.

More than once Shrewsbury complained of Bess's influence through her friends at Court and in this he was for once correct. In her struggle with Shrewsbury, Bess had the support of Queen Elizabeth, the Privy Council and Leicester, who all realized that the earl was behaving unreasonably.[3] However in the case of Leicester support and influence with his royal mistress on Bess's behalf was not a one-sided affair. The two were scheming together to ensure their own security and power after Elizabeth ceased to reign.

Although Bess's devotion to Elizabeth was supreme, it tended to weaken against her stronger devotion to her own dynastic ambitions. Leicester had fallen out of Elizabeth's favour over his love for and eventual marriage to Lettice Knollys. The whole affair was a court scandal, for Lettice had been married to Walter Devereux, Earl of Essex until his death in 1576 enabled her to marry Leicester. As well as being lady-in-waiting to Elizabeth she was 'one of the best looking ladies of the court'. But Leicester's love-life was haunted by Elizabeth his queen, who was pleased to bask in his brilliant admiration and undoubtedly felt affection for him, although she used him for her own very devious ends. Leicester's scandals had started in 1560 when his wife Amy Robsart was found dead at the foot of some stairs at Cumnor Place. He was then free to marry Elizabeth, but this raised enormous waves of resentment throughout the country and Elizabeth, always sensitive to what her subjects were thinking, altered course and allowed the marriage idea to cool off. In 1573 Leicester was rumoured to have married Lady Sheffield secretly. It was untrue, but it did not prevent Lady Sheffield from having a son by him, nor did it prevent her from marrying for a second time shortly afterwards. In 1578 Leicester secretly married Lettice.

Robert Dudley, Earl of Leicester was not above going behind the back of his royal mistress if he felt justified and the same can be said of Bess, so long as her gesture did not undermine the stability of the throne while Elizabeth occupied it. Lettice and Robert had a son, young Robert, Lord Denbigh, born in 1580, and little Robert and Arbella were betrothed or promised in marriage secretly sometime before 1584 when he would have been four years old and Arbella, his fiancée, eight. To Elizabethans marriage was not the romantic affair it has sometimes come to be regarded. Life was short and uncertain, and the only guarantee of a family's continuity was to marry young and have heirs as soon as possible to continue the line. But marriage had to be concluded between families of equal wealth so that ultimately the family became more powerful. The betrothal between little Robert and Arbella was such a match. Leicester was trading his power against Bess's wealth and Arbella's royal blood; their grandchildren could succeed Elizabeth at her death and Leicester obviously thought that he would be able to get his mistress's approval of the union.

The first rumour of this betrothal is in a letter from Lord Paget written to the Earl of Northumberland on 4 March 1584: 'the queen should be informed of the practices between Leicester and the countess for Arbella, for it comes on very lustily, in so much as the said earl hath sent down a picture of his baby.' The queen very likely already knew about it. The friendly letters, the favours to Bess and Leicester's visits to Buxton and Chatsworth were more than errands on the queen's business and furthermore there had been an exchange of portraits. But she trusted Bess and after all little Robert was only four years old – anything might happen before the marriage became fact.

Leicester visited Buxton in June of 1584 and found time to call on the beleaguered Bess at Chatsworth. Ostensibly he was mediating between husband and wife and wrote to Shrewsbury afterwards putting Bess's point of view very reasonably to the earl. After all it was in Leicester's interest to sort out the financial problems between the warring pair. The letter mentions Arbella as being at

Chatsworth although Bess had wished her to remain at Sheffield: 'my lord sending the little lady Arbella to me being a thing I desired much the contrary, that she might still be with my daughter Talbot'. At the least the comment indicates that Arbella was suffering from being shuffled about from one household to another and giving the child more insecurity against the background of her quarrelling guardians. Leicester would have seen Arbella at Chatsworth during that June visit although he does not mention this to Shrewsbury in his letter. He would have spoken to her and perhaps discussed her betrothal to Robert.

The scheme of marriage might have worked. Elizabeth raised no recorded objection, but once more her policy of procrastination paid off, for in the month following Leicester's visit to Chatsworth little Robert died and with him the high hopes of Leicester and Bess. It is a testimony to Bess's indomitability that she was arranging the betrothal through the time of her trouble and turmoil with Shrewsbury. It is also worth noting that she was only in a financial position to make the betrothal because of the earl's 1572 deed of gift; it gave her the freedom to make the necessary settlement arrangements without referring to or even discussing the matter with her husband. It was also the last time that Bess ever attempted to choose a husband for Arbella; there must have been a warning from the queen, for henceforth any prospective grooms were selected by Elizabeth.

Exactly where Arbella was living during this unsettling period can only be surmised from hints dropped and comments made in letters. Robert Beale, Clerk to the Council, writing to the Earl of Rutland in May 1584 from Sheffield Castle, where he had been called over the Scots queen's problems, makes another ambiguous statement:

The matter of the Lady Arbella's remayning with him [Shrewsbury] might have bin well brought to passe, if – as I heretofore wrote unto his lordship – the Countesse cold have [been] brought to have sought it at his hands in humble sort; for I see his mind so altered as that he will not be enforced by commandements, as thogh she hath more credit than he hath in court.

Obviously Beale has found Shrewsbury perverse and difficult, and what he seems to be saying is that Bess wished Arbella to stay with the earl rather than with her, and that since that was her wish the earl wanted the contrary. Arbella was being fought over. It is curious that Bess did not want her with her but the likely explanation is that she thought it inadvisable because of the harassments. Apart from the brief mention given by Leicester of Arbella actually being with Bess, it is unlikely that she remained long with her grandmother, for Shrewsbury forced his wife out of Chatsworth in July 1584 and Hardwick Hall was in no fit state to accommodate Arbella.[4]

From Arbella's later very obvious affection for her aunt Mary Talbot it would seem likely that the latter was in part responsible for bringing up Arbella when Bess was otherwise engaged, and there is no record at all of the child having been with her Cavendish uncles. Before Francis Talbot, Shrewsbury's heir, died in 1582, Mary and her husband Gilbert Talbot spent most of their time at his father's 'little house near Charing Cross'. Gilbert was useful to his father, he could represent his interests at Court when Shrewsbury was tied down in Derbyshire with his prisoner. He was not known as Shrewsbury's 'spy at Court' for nothing. When not in London, Gilbert and Mary lived at Goodrich Castle in Herefordshire, another of the Talbot properties. When, on the death of Francis, Gilbert became Shrewsbury's heir, he and Mary moved back to Sheffield and this is the period when Arbella is most reported as being with her aunt Mary Talbot. There must have been an easing of the queen's insistence that Gilbert should not live under the same roof as the Scots queen, and from the evidence of Mary's letters Arbella had comparatively easy access to the prisoner.

Arbella, when with the Talbots, was brought up with no children of her own age. John Talbot, born in 1583, was too much of a baby to be company for Arbella, likewise Elizabeth, who was born in 1582, and Mary, who was born in 1580. Also in the household was at least one other child, although at seven, Arbella would have thought of her fifteen-year-old cousin 'Bessie' Pierrepont as grown up. In her isolation the Scots queen had taken a liking to Bessie in 1571 when she was four years old; she called Bessie her 'bedfellow', made clothes for her and later took an interest in arranging her proposed marriages. It is possible that the lonely queen would have taken the same strong liking to Arbella had it been permitted.

But if the Scots queen's explanation of her quarrel with Bess is to be taken as the truth, then Arbella was the cause of the break. In March 1584, writing to the French ambassador Mauvissière, she said, 'nothing has alienated the Countess of Shrewsbury from me more but the vain hope, which she has conceived, of setting the crown of England on the head of her little girl Arbella, and this by means of marrying her to a son of the Earl of Leicester.' Here Mary is behaving at her worst towards Bess. By the time of the letter Shrewsbury had dismissed Bess to Chatsworth with the secret intention of never having her back again; with Bess out of the way there was no controlling the Scots queen.

Mary may well have encouraged Shrewsbury in his treatment of Bess; he was not beyond discussing his problems with his prisoner, nor she beyond fishing in troubled water. The letters of Mary to her friends display a rising tide of hatred towards Bess, and to Mauvissière she explained that Arbella was the cause; this may have been for the Frenchman to spread as gossip and yet Mary possibly had a point. If Robert Dudley had lived and married Arbella, any male heir they had would have been a strong favourite, in Elizabeth's eyes, as her successor. Arbella's place in the succession was equal to that of her cousin James of Scotland. In Arbella's betrothal to the young Robert Dudley, Mary had reason enough to feel betrayed by Bess.

It will never be known for certain who started the rumour that Shrewsbury was having an affair with his prisoner. Mary, in revenge, eventually accused Bess and with effect. Suspicion for starting the scandalous story points to Walsingham and his agents. Mary had been in secret contact with Philip of Spain over a plan for marriage to him, the invasion of England and Elizabeth's extinction, with the support of the Pope, to be followed by Mary taking her place on the throne of England. The Scots queen may have supposed her plans to have been secret but the earl's household at Sheffield was filled with spies and informers in Walsingham's pay. It was a simple matter to end Mary's negotiations by compromising her so severely that Philip would never consider marriage. When rumour added the birth of two children to Shrewsbury's credit then it became laughable, for Shrewsbury was a sick man suffering from overstrain, often unable to stand, crippled with gout and arthritis with a good deal of accompanying pain. Above all his loyalty to Elizabeth would have prevented him even contemplating enjoying Mary's affections even if he had been up to it physically.

Once Mary heard of the improbable rumours she was understandably distressed and the more so as she was powerless in the matter. To her false friend Mauvissière, who acted on the Scots queen's bidding when it suited the policy of his country, she wrote denying the whole story and added, 'it is my intention of involving indirectly the Countess of Shrewsbury.' Mary felt certain that William and Charles Cavendish had started the rumour, although this is the last thing that Bess would have permitted, for no matter how badly Shrewsbury behaved towards her she never sought revenge against him. But whoever started the story of Shrewsbury's and Mary's supposed intimacy, it can only be certain that Mary pinned the authorship on Bess.

The Scots queen was so successful in the counter-rumour spread by Mauvissière that it has been believed for four hundred years and certainly Shrewsbury believed it, as he was ready to believe anything against Bess. An indication that Walsingham was the generator of this titillating scandal is that it was never believed by Elizabeth or her Privy Council. In December 1584 Bess and her sons William and Charles Cavendish went through a charade of making a denial to the queen before a full Court. They stated with absolute truth that they had never started the rumours. And with that everyone had to be satisfied.

During all this turmoil Mary was dropping hints of sinister 'acts and practices' involving Bess. The fact of the matter was that Mary had written down a most extraordinary range of sexual activities concerning Elizabeth, which she claimed had been told her by Bess who, she wickedly said, had found the telling of it uncontrollably funny. Mary put these revelations in a letter addressed to the queen in 1584, but fortunately for herself she never sent it, for she would never have been believed. The now venomous Scots queen kept this letter up her sleeve to use against Bess as a final broadside; but she kept it too long and by the time apologies had been made at Court its efficacy, if any, had been lost.

It was Arbella's misfortune to have been introduced into this bubbling cauldron of venom at an impressionable age, and doubly unfortunate that Bess was unable to remove her granddaughter from the malignant influence of the Scots queen until she was successfully able to settle the problem of Shrewsbury's vendetta against her, with the help of Elizabeth and the Privy Council. But it took all the patience and forbearance of which Bess was capable until the major points of disagreement were settled by 1588, and by then Arbella was thirteen. The princess of royal blood had spent five years being brought up as best as could be managed in circumstances quite unsuited to an impressionable girl.[5]

5

IT WOULD BE
A HAPPY THING

During the last months of 1586, all England and most of Europe had their eyes on the Castle of Fotheringhay in Northamptonshire. Mary, Queen of Scots charged with treason against her cousin Queen Elizabeth, was on trial for her life. In 1584 Shrewsbury had gone to Court to ask that Mary be removed from his charge, and to use his influence to get matters between himself and Bess sorted out to his benefit. As far as the latter went he was unsuccessful but as the Privy Council and Elizabeth had already come to the conclusion that the Scots queen should be taken into closer care he had no trouble with the outcome of the former request, although it took Elizabeth until the next year, 1585, to make up her mind in the matter. Perhaps she would not have done anything then had it not been for the discovery of a plot or scheme devised by Dr William Parry to murder her. There is no reason to suppose that Mary had any involvement; nevertheless it was a warning of what a malign influence Mary was on Catholic politics.

Long before, Walsingham had made up his mind that Mary would have to die. As he was quite unable to get Elizabeth to consider such a necessary step for her own safety, he had to devise methods of getting rid of Mary himself. Sir Amias Paulet, into whose care Mary went after she left Shrewsbury's more considerate keeping, was a man on whose discretion Walsingham could rely when he would not have trusted Shrewsbury's. Cunningly Walsingham used a renegade Catholic, Gilbert Gifford, to draw a number of ardent Catholics into a scheme to conspire for Mary's release, and to place her on the throne after Elizabeth's murder. Anthony Babington, who gave his name to the plot, was led on by Walsingham's agents to write to Mary and to receive in return letters so compromising as to leave no doubt whatsoever of Mary's guilt.[1]

The trial, like so many trials for high treason at that time, was a foregone conclusion as far as the result was concerned. Shrewsbury, as a member of the Privy Council, heard the evidence at Fotheringhay and then the case was transferred to the Star Chamber in London. In essence Mary was being tried not only for her part in the Babington Plot but for her part in all the previous plots against Elizabeth: the Norfolk Plot, the Ridolfi Plot, the d'Aubigny Plot and the Throgmorton Plot as well. Even after the inevitable verdict had been passed, Elizabeth hesitated to sign the warrant for execution and eventually, having signed the document, in her devious way blamed her secretary William Davidson for the deed. Shrewsbury, in his position of Earl Marshal had to supervise the beheading of Mary, his prisoner for sixteen long years. It cannot have been easy for the man and, as he lifted his hand to signal the execution, he turned his head away, unable to watch this final act of extinction.

In her will Mary disinherited her son James. But Mary had no power in the last years of her life and certainly none after she was dead. More certainly she left to Arbella her *Book of Hours* which she had brought with her from France; in her own hand was written in it, '*Ce livre est à moy, Marie Reyne, 1554.*' During the years of her captivity she had filled its unprinted pages with poems and the names of friends.

Arbella's reaction to Mary's end was not recorded but it would have reinforced her determination never to take any part in power-plotting. Nevertheless her life even at this early age had already been involved in the politics of succession. Queen Elizabeth, unmarried and with no direct heir, had removed with one blow the head of her legal successor to the throne. Logically Arbella was next in line but holding equal claim with her cousin James of Scotland. If Elizabeth married Arbella off to a suitable foreign prince acceptable to the nation, then her succession, if it ever came, would be assured in a peaceful manner. But Elizabeth, ever devious, avoided making up her mind. Finality was something she could never live with and therefore there were times when it suited her to let it appear that Arbella was her chosen successor and at others, James of Scotland.

In March 1581 Elizabeth had considered Esmé Stuart as a husband for Arbella; this solved neatly the problem of the earldom of
Lennox, as Esmé had just been awarded the title by James. It would
not have solved the succession problem as Esmé was Catholic and
a leading member of the anti-English party in Scotland. In any case
he died in 1583 shortly after he had returned to France. Robert
Dudley, the little Lord Denbigh, had died too, in 1584 when he
was betrothed to Arbella. By the time she was eleven Arbella had
got through two fiancés.

In 1585 Arbella's marriage to James was mooted. It made sense
as far as the succession problem went, but Elizabeth let this opportunity pass – it made the succession too certain – and James lived
to marry Anne of Denmark by proxy in August 1589. James was
well aware of the peril to his own claim to Elizabeth's succession
should Arbella marry a husband ambitious to promote his wife's
royal blood. And in November 1587, the year his mother's head
was cut off, James tried to secure some sort of control over the selection of a husband for Arbella. His ambassador made the request
to Elizabeth that James should be proclaimed the rightful heir to
her throne and that Arbella should not be married without his advice
being sought and his consent given. This was far too much of a
commitment for Elizabeth, who gave one of her usual evasive
replies.

Arbella's first recorded visit to Court and meeting with Elizabeth
was in the summer of 1587. She had not been seen in London since
1578 when she was three and now she was returning, a royal princess
of twelve years with a strong claim to the succession. The visit was
not a purely social occasion, for Elizabeth was considering betrothing Arbella to Rainutio Farnese, the son of the Duke of Parma.

Parma was the Spanish Governor-General of the Netherlands
and general of the Spanish army fighting against the English army
and its Flemish allies. The war had been entered into with reluctance by Elizabeth and she bitterly resented the expense, yet, to
prevent Spain's domination of the Channel coast and to sustain the
Flemish Huguenots, she was forced to continue the support of her
allies with money and armies. By 1587 it was clear that Philip was
planning some sort of offensive against England – the building of

the Armada was reported to Burghley and Walsingham in December 1585.[2] Philip's plans were the direct result of the execution of Mary.

While Mary lived, the Pope and his ally Philip had had reasonable hopes of converting England from her heretic beliefs by engineering the murder of Elizabeth and putting Mary to rule in her place. With the death of the Scots queen this possibility was extinguished and other means had to be found to carry out what the Pope clearly saw as God's will. To make problems for Elizabeth, Mary had willed her English succession to Philip – in addition to considering himself the instrument of God's will, he was sustained by a righteous desire to seize what he regarded as his own. But to Elizabeth war was a wasteful extravagance to be avoided if at all possible. If by betrothing Arbella to Rainutio Spain might see the possibility of a peaceful conversion of England and become less determined to extinguish Protestantism by force, then to Elizabeth the proposition was worth a try. The scheme of betrothal was subsidiary to numerous other plans.

None of the official marriage negotiations carried out on Arbella's behalf took any note of her affections. This was the penalty of her rank – Bess's own first marriage had been so arranged and her Cavendish daughters had all had their marriages arranged for them. Among the wealthy marriage was a business deal, and to Elizabeth it was a political treaty. Arbella could expect no more and no doubt Bess had never encouraged her to have any romantic notions about marriage. The Rainutio proposal was plainly political and the London visit was partly to let Elizabeth meet her young second cousin but mainly to let Spain know that she was serious in the matter and that the right noises should be conveyed to Philip and Parma by their contacts at Elizabeth's Court. It was quite in character for Elizabeth to have hoped that the noises would be sufficient to hold off any threatened offensive without having to play her cards at all.

The whole scheme of Arbella's proposed betrothal has the mark of Burghley or the fertile, cunning mind of Walsingham. In December 1585 Parma, feeling threatened by the well-advertised English expeditionary army then being prepared for the Netherlands under the generalship of Leicester, had managed to send a letter to Elizabeth by a circuitous route intimating that he would consider proposals for a peaceful settlement. This overture had taken a backward knock when Mary was beheaded, and the proposal of Arbella's betrothal came at the tail end of a long chain of fruitless negotiation. On Christmas Eve 1586 Mendoza, the Spanish ambassador in Paris, wrote to his king suggesting the betrothal scheme. The Pope's support was to be secured by offering the duchies of Parma and Plasencia to the Holy See. Since 1584 there had been no Spanish ambassador in London; in that year Mendoza had been dismissed for his involvement in the Throckmorton Plot and was now ambassador in Paris. He was not a man to be trusted, but from Walsingham's point of view he was useful and a line of communication had been kept open between the two equally crafty diplomats.

There was a lot to be recommended in the marriage or betrothal plan, although there were drawbacks, as Mendoza pointed out to Philip without actually saying what they were. Rainutio had a claim to the English throne through his mother. Admittedly it was tenuous – she was descended from John of Gaunt, son of Edward III. It went back two hundred years and would not have been considered relevant in times of peace. But Elizabeth was searching for a way out of the costly war, and this remote claim added to Arbella's undoubted right would have made the marriage acceptable to England – if Rainutio's Catholicism could be played down a little. The proposed betrothal was the reason for Arbella's summons to Court.[3]

Elizabeth's Court was a brilliant pageant playing continuously around the queen. The background scenery was moved as required by attendant servants who every minute of the day played their part in the pageantry. The overture to serving the day-time meal of dinner occupied at least thirty officials for over half an hour. 'A gentleman entered the room bearing a rod and along with him another who had a table cloth, which after they had both knelt three times with the utmost veneration, he spread upon the table and, after kneeling again they both retired.' And that was only laying the table-cloth. The pageantry was a continuous spectacle. It occupied and kept employed a vast number of servants who were supporting actors for an equally vast number of courtiers, who likewise had set parts to play. A lady-in-waiting, who was in no sense a servant – it was an honoured post which Bess had once occupied – with a maid of honour would enter the dining chamber after the table was at last laid and, again with genuflections, would rub the plates with bread and salt, and so it went on.[4]

The Court was the most extravagant spectacle in England; it was also the centre and fountain of all worthwhile patronage. In consequence it drew to its bright lights the brilliant and clever, as well as the ne'er-do-well and the hanger-on in search of whatever could be picked up. Above all the pageantry and the scheming, the noise and the hubbub ruled the queen, to whom all paid homage with blatant adoration, encouraged by Elizabeth, who was surrounded, but never conquered, by her admirers and favourites.

In her vicious 'scandal' letter Mary had written a unique footnote about Elizabeth's Court which she had never visited and so could not comprehend. She was recounting what she claimed to have heard from Bess and her account has a touch of truth overflavoured with venom. When Mary told of Elizabeth allowing herself to be made love to by Leicester 'with all the familiarity ... of man and wife' not once but many many times, as well as Hatton and countless others, she overseasoned the poison brew to the point of incredibility.

However in recounting a time when Bess visited Court with her daughter Elizabeth Lennox, probably in 1578, Mary is more credible. The queen had let it be known that as her countenance shone with a blinding light like the sun, it was inadvisable for her Court to look her in the face and, when Bess and her daughter had approached Elizabeth, neither had dared look at the other for fear of bursting out loud with laughter at the extraordinary spectacle and the notion behind it. The element of truth is that many had likened the queen to the shining sun which dazzled those who dared to look. It seemed that no flattery of Elizabeth was too exaggerated to be accepted. Without doubt Elizabeth ruled over her fantastic Court in a mysterious way which baffled those who never witnessed the scene.

This was the Court to which Arbella came, when Elizabeth had moved out of London to hold her Court at Theobalds, Burghley's house in Hertfordshire. Arbella came without Bess, who had stayed behind in Derbyshire. Bess had other things on her mind. The queen and her council had made one great effort to bring Shrewsbury to heel and with considerable skill had forced the reluctant earl to take Bess back again. After a reunion at Court the couple had left for Wingfield Manor at the end of April. But the happy state had not existed for long and Shrewsbury retired to Handsworth Manor near Sheffield to console himself with Eleanor Britton, a rapacious lady of his household. Arbella was introduced to Court, probably by her aunt Mary and Gilbert Talbot, sometime between the Shrewsburys' departure from London in April and the end of August.

Arbella's uncle Charles was also at Court that summer; he and his brother William were representing Bess's interests and keeping their mother in touch by their letters. Charles, in a long letter to Bess, sums up the political factions very neatly. Essex, Charles reported, was gaining over Leicester 'marvelously' for the queen's favours. 'Sir Walter Raleigh is in wonderful declination yet labours to underprop himself by my Lord Treasurer [Burghley].' Lord Cumberland and his brother, whom Bess was later to take to the Court of the Star Chamber, had been trying to get crown lands in the Peak Forest but Elizabeth had awarded them to Bess as reward for her travails over Shrewsbury. From Charles's gossipy comments the royal Court was, as he put it, 'in that height'. Clearly Elizabeth was enjoying her favourites competing for her slightest concession.

... the lady Arbella hath been once at court [Charles told his mother] ...her Majesty spoke to her but not long and examined her nothing touching her book. She dined in the Presence but my Lord Treasurer [Burghley] bade her to supper, and at dinner [in the 'Presence'] I dining with her and sitting against him, he asked me whether I came with my niece or not. I said I came with her, then he spoke openly and directed his speech to Sir Walter Raleigh greatly in her commendation as that she had the French, the Italian, played of instruments, danced, wrought [with a needle] and wrote very fair, wished she were fifteen years old. And with that rouned [whispered] Mr Raleigh in the ear, who answered 'it would be a happy thing'. At supper [the evening with Burghley] he made exceeding much of her, so did he the afternoon in his Great Chamber publicly.

Charles then described especially for his mother's benefit the gallery which Burghley had lately built off his great chamber at Theobalds, 126 feet long and the roof 'with a great fret like the low gallery at Chatsworth'. The great chamber he explained was 60 feet long, 22 feet wide and 20 feet high. Clearly Bess had never seen Burghley's mansion and had never marvelled at the structure in the great chamber: 'at the nether end a fair rock with duck and pheasants and divers other birds which serves for a cupboard, the old trees are still there.' Nor had she seen the ceiling which at night glowed like the midnight sky with a moon and stars shining brightly. These were devices which must have been a constant wonder to all his friends. This was the great Lord Treasurer playing open house to the queen, when technically it became hers, and it must have cost him a great sum of money, for they were certainly there on 10 July and still there on 13 August before leaving for Greenwich.

Arbella, brought up in the knowledge that she might one day be queen, even though she would not have wished to be, could have had her head turned by the sudden change from the sombre, tense background of her Derbyshire life to the colour and lively music of the Court at Theobalds. She was dining in the afternoon with the queen, and Burghley made compliments about her to Raleigh. Here we are as much in the dark as Charles and Bess as to what was whispered. Later that day she supped with Burghley at his own court; these were honours from the highest, accorded to her to generate reports for Philip's ears in Spain, in the hope that the great invasion he was planning for England – even as the Court feasted at Theobalds – would be called off in contemplation of Arbella's marriage to Rainutio.

After Arbella's visit was over the French ambassador wrote to Henri III of France on 27 August telling him of the remark Elizabeth made to him about Arbella, 'Look to her well: she will one day be even as I am,' a statement made for Philip's benefit as much as anyone's. So spun the wheels of diplomacy, catching in Arbella's flying gowns, threatening to enmesh her life for ever. Had she been Bess she would have sacrificed herself willingly for Elizabeth, but like her other grandmother she probably preferred to keep as clear of the machinery as she could. Philip was not distracted by these ploys and the urgent matter of Rainutio's betrothal died over Philip's lack of enthusiasm; it was only revived later after the crashing defeat of Spain's Armada.'[5]

And so the court whirled round Arbella's young head, intoxicating her with its life. Essex, then the brightest star, was, as Charles so truly said, gaining over Leicester, who anyway was to die in the following year 1588. Robert Devereux, Earl of Essex, was twenty-one when Arbella met him for the first time. At some time he caught her fancy and it is as likely to have been on this first visit as on any other. He was attractive, lively, courtly and exciting, but he had an inbuilt flaw like Raleigh, Drake and so many other Elizabethans, he lacked emotional stability. Essex had no sense of proportion and like others he ended his life on the block, a traitor to his queen, in 1601. But this was far in the future and could not be foreseen. All the same Arbella, by entertaining any admiration for the queen's favourite – even if that admiration was not returned – was risking her future at Court. Elizabeth would have no rivals.

Earlier in the year Arbella had been with her aunt Mary, and Gilbert Talbot, at Shrewsbury House in Chelsea, one of the Talbot properties. It was probably in late June that John Harington paid her a visit in Chelsea. Harington was a godson of the queen, an honour shared with Arbella's uncle Henry Cavendish and a score of others. He was a true courtier who was witty and talented but who never obtained any political office. He was later knighted by Essex in 1599 in Ireland – one of many honours which roused Elizabeth to fury that her favourite should assume the rights of consort by making knights in the battlefield.

Harington relates that during his visit to Arbella she made him read 'the tale of Drusilla in Orlando, and censured it with gravity beyond her years'. 'Drusilla' was a story in Ariosto's poem *Orlando Furioso*, published in Ferrara in 1516. Clearly this vast epic on the wars of Charlemagne was part of Arbella's curriculum, selected for the perfection of its style. But Harington was reading this in Italian, for it had never been translated into English, and Arbella could comprehend and comment on it 'with gravity beyond her years'. The Drusilla episode, featuring in the tale of Morganor, is sad and romantic. Drusilla was 'a lovely lady' who found that men tended to die around her; she completed her story by taking poison for the love of her husband, a dramatic conclusion not dissimilar to Arbella's own end.

In Harington Arbella would have had a good guide to the finer points of 'Drusilla', for he was even then translating the entire work into English. It was published in 1591 and must have been far advanced by 1587. An anecdote about Harington tells that he translated the Rabelaisian tale of Giocomo for the pleasure of his court friends, but the work fell into the queen's hands and she was offended (probably untrue for Elizabeth liked a ribald story). As a result Harington was ordered from Court until he had translated the entire epic, which he did. Harington's other claim to fame is that he made and perfected a perfumed privy.

The Court was still at Theobalds on 13 August and left shortly afterwards. At all events Arbella's visit was over at about that date, and her small amount of plate was packed up on the twenty-first of that month and sent up to Derbyshire, along with that of her grandmother. Somehow Arbella had acquired a few pieces, including 'a bason and ewer, parcel gilt' for washing her hands in at mealtimes: 'two beer jugs, gilt with covers; one great bowl, gilt with a cover; two livery pots, parcel gilt; eleven spoons; six plates; one gilt spoon; three plain white candlesticks; and two stone jugs trimmed with silver and gilt'.

She returned to Derbyshire, to her school-work and her books, those 'silent councillors' she called them; they had become her only companions, as she had left her aunt Mary behind in London with all the noise and gossip of the Court.[6] Arbella had to forget the dancing and feasting for another year, or until her future was decided in far-away capitals. She returned to a lonely residence, perhaps at Wingfield Manor, for Bess had no accommodation for Arbella at the old Hardwick Hall. Wingfield Manor was a solitary fortified mansion filled with memories of the Scots queen's imprisonment. On her first visit in 1569 Mary had complained of the stench of the overworked garderobes; her last visit had been only three years earlier in 1584, on the last journey from Shrewsbury's keeping to her eventual execution at Fotheringhay. The servants would have remembered Mary's visits and their memories of her would have been as haunting as ghosts.

6

GOOD LADY GRANDMOTHER

It is certain that had Arbella been a court beauty many flatterers would have told us so; instead there is only one comment from the French ambassador de l'Aubespine, who had called her 'sufficiently handsome in the face', which really was no compliment at all. The conclusion must be that Arbella was neither plain nor beautiful but something falling between the two. A portrait of Arbella painted in 1589 when she was thirteen and a half does not tend to confirm de l'Aubespine's opinion.

It is difficult at this distance in time to assess what was thought of as beauty in the late 1580s, for standards have changed constantly throughout the intervening four hundred years. However, in the spirit of court flattery for Elizabeth, a long nose like the queen's was a feature much admired, and the genuine portrait of Arbella shows her with just such a flattering nose and with features similar in some ways to her father's portrait painted when he was ten years old, now hanging at Holyrood palace. Arbella's portrait shows her with fair hair which could be called mouse-coloured, not at all like Bess's reddish tints or her aunt Mary's auburn curls. She has a wide mouth, round chin – rather weak – and an unfortunately vacant expression. One is left with the impression that if this is how Arbella really looked then not even a Frenchman could have called her 'sufficiently handsome'. It is more likely that Arbella was not as plain as this portrait makes her and that in life her personality was shown by a constantly changing expression and vivacity of humour. Both characteristics have been lost by the brush of the ungifted painter. A later portrait, which hangs in Marlborough House, called *Arbella*, is, if of her, perhaps a better likeness, for this shows a woman in her mid-thirties who could be said to be attractive: she has the suggestion of a smile and no longer has the distressing vacancy in her eye.

The only first-hand evidence of what Arbella was really like must obviously come from her letters, and while these tell nothing of her appearance they show a lot of her character. Arbella wrote a good letter with informative asides totally unlike the very dull letters her grandmother Bess wrote. Arbella's show an amusing wit and an observing eye. Her English is surprisingly lively and readable: it has a balance and composition inspired by her reading of Latin and Italian works. Arbella's prose is a credit to her anonymous tutors.

The earliest letter to survive was written to Bess on 8 February 1588, the year of the Armada. It was addressed from a house called Fines. Unfortunately the letter has vanished for the present, and until it reappears it cannot be established whether the transcriber made an error or not, for no trace of the house exists and it certainly had nothing whatsoever to do with either Bess or Aunt Mary Talbot. And yet the letter gives the impression of having been written from a household of Mary Talbot to Bess at Hardwick Hall. Bess is addressed as 'Good lady grandmother'. Arbella then explains that she is sending with the letter a pot of jelly made by her servant, and the ends of her hair cut on Saturday, which was the sixth day of the moon. This opening paragraph suggests some sort of superstitious rigmarole being carried out – not uncommon – as a harmless insurance against mischance and ill health, which the church and medical profession were powerless to prevent or cure. Arbella shows a morbid interest in a recent sickness of her little cousin Mary, then aged eight. Excitedly she explains that 'Mary had three little fits of an ague, but now she is well and merry'. What was done to the little Mary, Arbella does not say.[1] Manifestly her cousin's fits had been the event of the week, but they must have been harmless, for Mary lived to marry the third Earl of Pembroke.

In the summer of 1588 Arbella left her Derbyshire fastness for another visit to Court. Unfortunately the references to this visit were all made fifteen years later and are therefore not so reliable – it was the summer of the Armada and there were other matters to think about. The visit resulted in Arbella being banished from Court for three years. She was again with her aunt Mary and Gilbert

Talbot; her grandmother Bess was still tied down with the trouble over her finances and Shrewsbury, although the queen's firm intervention had improved Bess's circumstances. Arbella gave her version of the visit in the course of a highly emotional and very long letter written in 1603 when she was in deep trouble. 'How dare others visit me in distress', she wrote of the 1588 visit, 'when the Earl of Essex, then in highest favour, durst scarcely steal a salutation in the privy chamber, where, howsoever it pleased her Majesty I should be disgraced in the presence at Greenwich and discouraged in the lobby at Whitehall.' That was one account, highly coloured to prove another point, but since it is from Arbella herself then it must be taken as the most authentic. Another account also written in 1603 was from the Venetian secretary Scaramelli in London, reporting to the Doge and Senate in Venice.

Fourteen years ago she [Arbella] was brought to the Court by the Queen, who made her one of her ladies-in-waiting; she was then quite young, and displayed of such haughtiness that she soon began to claim first place; and one day on going into chapel she herself took such precedence of all the Princesses who were in her Majesty's suite; nor would she retire, though repeatedly told to do so by the Master of Ceremonies, for she said that by God's will that was the very lowest place that could possibly be given her. At this time the Queen, in indignation ordered her back to her private existence without so much as seeing her before she took her leave, or indeed ever afterwards.

The Venetian account was given to discredit Arbella over a later matter and as it was written from memory at a distance of fifteen years, and not fourteen as he thought, by a foreigner who would not have been very attentive at the time, his details are likely to be less accurate than those Arbella gives. Indeed on two points he is wrong: the queen did not banish her 'for ever afterwards' but for three years only; and as Arbella was the only royal princess it is difficult to understand who could have taken precedence over her. The only common point on which both accounts agree is that Arbella was disgraced and sent from the Court. But then a great many things were going on behind the scenes that summer, before the Armada arrived in the English Channel, which would account for Arbella's dismissal from Court as a card to be put back in the

pack. The queen, by lighting on Arbella's familiarity with Essex
– the current royal favourite – had as good an excuse as any to get
rid of Arbella, and a typical one at that.[2]

The queen and her Privy Council knew from the many varying
pieces of information being received that some sort of offensive
against England was being planned by Philip. They also had a very
good idea that an Armada was being planned, but the details were
so varied that it could not be said with certainty what course the
offensive would follow. To divert this expected onslaught a number
of peace feelers had been put out to Parma, who, perhaps to gain
time and lull Elizabeth with false hopes, gave these overtures consideration. As some of these negotiations were carried out in complete secrecy by spies and others, little has survived. In the early
part of 1588 there were no less than three members of the Privy
Council each in touch with Parma in their own secret ways, all independent of each other and in complete ignorance of what the others
were doing.

Possibly the queen herself knew only part of what was in hand.
The reason for these goings-on was simply that Leicester was dis-
trusted by both Walsingham and Burghley as being unreliable (In
that, suspicion proved them correct.) Burghley was laid low with
gout which gave Walsingham a chance to proceed on his own initiative. There was another privy councillor involved, the Comptroller
of the Queen's Household Sir James Croft, whom Walsingham
suspected was a Catholic sympathizer or even a supporter of Spain.
It has been said that Croft was earlier in the pay of the King of
Spain. He may have been, but there is no reason to doubt his loyalty
to Elizabeth, and his earlier association with Spain may have been
a blind to cause Philip to believe he had Croft's support. But such
is the way of secret diplomacy that any documentary evidence of
the matter either way is unlikely to be found.

In mid-February a peace commission to Parma had been sent
by the queen, with Burghley's help. The commission went without
the blessing of Walsingham, who feared that he might be appointed,
or Leicester, who shared the same fear. Neither could see any profit
to be won and it was a failure from the start. Parma kept them waiting at Calais for weeks, and Croft, the only enthusiastic member,

defying his two co-commissioners, went off on his own to see Parma
– in spite of the fact that he spoke only English – taking with him
Burghley's younger son Sir Robert Cecil. Again what happened
comes from an account written fifteen years later. The Venetian
secretary in a letter of May 1603, reporting to the Doge, alleged
that

at the very height of the Spanish preparations against England in 1588,
she [Queen Elizabeth] of her own initiative despatched into Flanders
Robert Cecil, a little hunchback, and then in private life, but very wise;
and he in simple travellers garb, but with credentials from her, whispered
to the ear of Alexander Farnese that the Queen would give Arbella as
wife to his son Rainutio, and with her the succession to the throne.

This too is an unreliable account but it is very likely that, during
the course of that abortive visit by the commission, Robert Cecil
did try to tempt Parma into peace with the offer of Arbella's
betrothal. It had certainly been discussed before, and if Parma could
have been wooed to found a separate Flemish princedom it would
have been a tempting offer. But for the moment Parma was not to
be so beguiled and Croft, who had exceeded his instructions either
through zeal or misunderstanding of the language, was ordered to
return to England. He was imprisoned in the Tower for a year, leaving the rest of the commission to be overtaken by the events of the
Armada. Even if the Venetian account is only partially true, then
Arbella's visit to Court in 1588 was in connection with the futile
peace negotiations, and the involvement of Arbella came from the
initiative of Burghley and the queen, since Croft and Cecil were
acting on their behalf. Arbella had again been played by the queen
as a diplomatic card.

By the end of June it was clear that the commission was getting
nowhere at all and the offer of Arbella in marriage was of no consequence. It may very well have been that with Arbella no longer
of any significance Elizabeth became irked by her presence at Court.
She could never abide the thought of anyone taking her place, and
Arbella's partiality for Essex and her childishly assumed airs gave
Elizabeth a reason for getting her cousin out of the way in a testy
manner, while England under its queen prepared to meet the

enemy. Elizabeth bore Arbella no ill will, for exactly twelve months later she asked Gilbert Talbot how she was.[3]

On 5 July 1588 the Court left Greenwich for Richmond and Arbella's visit probably ended. And, since Burghley had been absent and sick, she wrote a short postscript to a letter written by Gilbert and Mary Talbot and addressed to Burghley from 'our poor lodging in Coleman St, 13 July 1588'. Arbella wrote in French and wished him to be restored to full health and happiness. Why the Talbots should have been staying in Coleman Street is a mystery when they had three London houses at their disposal. The description of a 'poor lodging' should not be taken literally as it was a common disparagement, used according to the mood of the writer. Burghley, that April contorted with gout, had written 'from my solitary cottage ... being utterly lame in my back'. It was a matter of how the writer wished to be seen. While the Court moved out to Richmond and from Richmond to St James's, the Armada made its slow and stately approach towards England. Arbella returned once more to Derbyshire, banned from Court until Elizabeth saw fit to summon her again.

As Arbella travelled north that July, the Spanish fleet entered the Channel. The bark *Talbot*, Shrewsbury's own ship of about 200 tons with ninety men aboard, was serving in the westward fleet under Drake. This ship had been something of a loss to Shrewsbury in recent years and more than once he had considered selling it. The bark had joined a number of privateering adventures which had not paid off. On this last trip it gained Shrewsbury not even glory but it let him out of further expense for it was used as one of the fire ships set in among the Spanish fleet as it lay at anchor outside Calais on the night of 28 July. The earl was entitled to £900 in compensation for its loss.[4] En route to Derbyshire Arbella might have seen the militia bands of the county raised by Shrewsbury and mustered for the emergency; or the sheriff and his men taking a suspected recusant to Derby Jail. Otherwise in landlocked Derbyshire there would have been no hint of the possible invasion, and Arbella returned to her school-books and her tutor.

Arbella's grandmother Bess was then living at old Hardwick Hall, which she was trying to make habitable as far as her finances permitted. It is possible that the extraordinarily haphazard manner in which this old building was added to by Bess was in part due to the earl's interruptions of her revenues, and she may have been finishing work already begun by her brother James, unable to complete what he had started. His life is a grandiose story of financial decline: he had expensive ideas well beyond his means and it would have been in character for him to have undertaken the building of a Hardwick Hall far in excess of his ability to pay for it. At the time of the Armada Bess had begun to complete the top floor of the central block of the old hall, and was living in considerable discomfort. This was no place for Arbella.

Again it is possible that Arbella returned to Wingfield Manor, and certainly she was there on 5 November that year. Nicholas Kinnersley, one of Bess's gentlemen servants and steward of Wingfield, wrote to Bess confessing that Arbella was out of hand and had not looked at her school-books for six days. She was eating well but discipline had broken down, and the only remedy was a long visit from Bess to knock the wildness out of her – 'Lady Arbella was merry tonight at 8 o'clock.' Earlier in the letter Kinnersley related some mysterious visits from Shrewsbury's men enquiring where Bess was and what she was doing: 'Late at night a boy came from Sheffield and talked with them in the stables, he returned next day.'[5] This probably indicated no more than that Shrewsbury was trying to find out where Bess was so as to avoid meeting her, but the secret comings and goings must have contributed to the atmosphere of unease in a house already haunted by the memory of the Scots queen. Wingfield was an old house and no doubt complained in the night: the echo of a distant banging door, mice scattering behind the panels, a creaking stair tread, were sounds to evoke the past.

7

I PRAY YOU SEND ME HER PICTURE

After the brief mention of Arbella at Wingfield in November of 1588, she vanishes again and there is no first-hand report of her for three years. The possibility is that she was living with her aunt Mary until Bess was able to build sufficient accommodation for her at old Hardwick Hall, but that is speculation. Wherever she was, it is certain that she was not at Court during this time; and when Mary and Gilbert Talbot attended Court it is probable that Arbella returned to Wingfield.

During this period of Arbella's rustication, James of Scotland completed his wooing of Anne of Denmark and was married to her at ceremonies held simultaneously in Edinburgh and Denmark on 20 August 1589. After a first attempt to land his bride had failed – owing to an obvious intervention of witchcraft when a great storm had prevented Anne and her party from making the passage to Scotland – James gallantly braved the black arts and went to fetch her himself, by way of Norway. Another marriage ceremony was celebrated in November with the couple at last returning safely to Scotland on 1 May 1590.

After James had been rebuffed by Elizabeth in his understandable attempt to secure some sort of control over Arbella's marriage, he tried to exercise control in other ways. He became anxious about the serious proposal involving Rainutio Farnese, for the marriage carried with it the promise that Arbella should succeed Elizabeth. James was alarmed by the prospect of losing his place in the succession to Elizabeth's throne. Having failed in his bid to have a direct control in the matter he sought to damage the negotiations by putting out his own candidate Ludovic Stuart, son of his earlier favourite and now Duke of Lennox. He floated the suggestion in

1588 and again in 1589. Another rumour in 1590 was that Arbella was to marry Henry Percy, Earl of Northumberland. James was moreover no friend to Arbella; he had treated her rather shabbily, for he had kept the Lennox jewels which had been left to Arbella by her grandmother old Margaret Lennox. They had found their way to James by way of Thomas Fowler, but it took the English ambassador three attempts in 1590 to learn the truth of the missing heirlooms.

It was during these three years of Arbella's life that the full-length portrait of her which hangs in the long gallery of Hardwick Hall was painted, if the information on it is correct: *Arbella Stuart, Countess of Lennox aged 13 and a half. 1589.* The sixth Duke of Devonshire, who had a great love of Hardwick and who tried to live there during the bitterly cold winters of the 1830s, added a number of titles to the portraits at Hardwick which had no more serious backing than his own opinion; although in the case of this portrait the attribution appears to be contemporary with the painting. But 1589 was a time of Arbella's life when nothing at all was happening which could have been the reason for having the portrait made. Arbella was not at Court; the betrothal plan to Rainutio was shelved for the moment and there were no official suitors in the offing. A likely explanation is that Bess, who had finished the small gallery on the third floor of old Hardwick in April 1589, had the portrait made to hang in her new little gallery. Bess was the only one left with the determination to call Arbella Countess of Lennox when all others had let the claim drop, and the title was in keeping with the grand idea of gallery portraits.

The finances of Arbella's grandmother had suffered less from Shrewsbury's interference after the queen's intervention and had so improved that by the middle of 1590, or even slightly earlier, she was confident enough of her income to undertake a new building venture. She commissioned Robert Smythson, the architect of Wollaton Hall and Worksop Manor, to provide plans for a new Hardwick Hall to be built within a few hundred yards of the old, which was even then unfinished. When Bess had bought the Hardwick lands in 1583 after her brother's bankruptcy, they had been purchased in the name of her second son, Arbella's uncle William, and although Bess kept a life interest it was to all other intents William's after Bess's death. William had married Anne Keighley in 1581 after being knighted the year before; they already had a growing family by 1589, and he had been returned as a member of Parliament since 1587. However William and his wife Anne had no house of their own other than a London house which they probably rented. Henry Cavendish had his own establishment at Tutbury Priory, Charles Cavendish had been provided with Stoke Manor and lands in the 1570s, but William, despite his growing importance, was expected to share the same roof as Bess.

In planning the extensions to the old Hardwick, Bess had provided two suites of state apartments, presumably for the use of William and herself. But in the new Hardwick Bess was providing not only a home for herself and William but a suitable mansion for the dynasty she had founded and which was to be carried on by William and his heirs. It is often claimed that in building the new Hardwick, Bess was planning a palace for a future Queen Arbella. This cannot be so for it was built on William's land and, although it has a magnificent suite of state apartments, these were intended for William and his heirs to entertain their royal guests in. The rest of the new Hardwick was fitted out in a far from royal style and it was never big enough to be a royal palace. By 1590, if Bess entertained any ambition that Arbella might be queen, then she was not to be the one to provide the palaces. Hardwick Hall was built for William on William's land and for William's heirs.

It seemed that almost as soon as Bess had got the foundations of her new house dug out, Shrewsbury realized that he could never get the better of his astute but estranged wife. With the realization came his final defeat, for he died on 18 November 1590 and released to Bess the income from the Talbot lands settled on her at their marriage over twenty years earlier. Unfortunately the Talbot estate had not recovered from the costly business of being host to Mary, Queen of Scots; from debts run up by Francis Talbot who had died in 1582; from the marriage settlements of three daughters; from having to maintain three sons in their own separate establishments; from the exactions of Bess over twelve years until Shrewsbury cut off all allowances to his wife; and latterly from the debts of Gilbert.

These costly liabilities would have ruined almost any other estate but in this case they had only served to drain away all available cash. Although Bess had every right to expect an income of about £3,500 a year from the Talbots, it was difficult to get this out of Gilbert without litigation – probably he found himself as unable as he was unwilling to pay.

Some six weeks before he died the earl gave out a sibylline prophecy. His words were faithfully taken down by one of his servants. He feared that Arbella would 'bring trouble to his house by his wife and her daughter's devices. Both of them work with Dr Brown of London, a cunning fellow. They are dealing with one of the heralds about pedigrees which must be kept from him. Gilbert Talbot is much ruled by them.' Was this the result of gossip gleaned from the stables of Wingfield Manor? It was certainly inspired by Shrewsbury's fixed hatred of Bess, nevertheless some of what he forecast came to pass, but only after Bess's death and nineteen years after his own death. In 1610 Arbella was to 'bring trouble to his house' in a way even he could not have foreseen.[1]

Arbella's banishment from Court came to an end in the autumn of 1591, and her return to the unique and exciting world of the royal Court was once more dictated mainly by politics and in part by family matters. By then Arbella was sixteen, the age when she might have expected to have been married; however a betrothal of Arbella was under consideration. The war in the Netherlands continued as before and, although the defeat of the Armada had been a set-back for Philip, he was not deterred. Parma, his general in the Spanish Netherlands, was not prosecuting the war with sufficient energy. Possibly Parma was easing his offensive while the matter of Rainutio's marriage to Arbella was once more being considered. Walsingham had died in the spring of 1590, leaving Burghley free to pursue the original peace plan of 1588 which he had formulated before the arrival of the Armada. The secret offer to Parma of English support for a separate princedom in the Netherlands and Rainutio's marriage to Arbella with assured succession to Elizabeth's throne was now proving attractive to Parma.

Around this second marriage proposal swirl the fog and half-twilight world of secret agents, of letters in cipher and silent contacts made in Amsterdam in the darkness of night. Occasionally the shrouds of secrecy lift to show tantalizing views of agents and spies 'toing and froing' between London and Flushing. After Walsingham's death Robert Cecil inherited his network of secret agents under Thomas Phelippes, Walsingham's confidential secretary, who headed the carefully built-up system. It was not a spy network in the modern sense but a rather more haphazard system built up by recruiting agents through blackmail, bribery and other less direct methods. The agents were seldom fired by a spirit of patriotism; Walsingham cunningly used the temptations of revenge against an enemy, or the promise of freedom from imprisonment to recruit his unreliable informants. Unless Walsingham, or after him Cecil, had a secure lever with which to handle their agents, the information supplied was often suspect.

Cecil it will be recalled had been involved in the 1588 marriage proposal to Rainutio when he made a personal visit to Parma on that very matter. It was easy for Cecil to reopen the proposal where it had been closed, or it may have been Parma who made the first move – all in the strictest secrecy. On 31 October 1591, three weeks before Arbella left Derbyshire with her grandmother for London, Phelippes wrote to Thomas Barnes, 'the practise of a marriage [has been sought] between Arbella and the Duke of Parma's son, which is given out to be his errand to England'. Phelippes then remarks that he is surprised that Barnes had not reported this to him and concludes with a titillating sentence which sends the imagination racing: he refers to 'Morley, the singing man', who 'employs himself in that kind of service and has brought divers into danger'. Interestingly something can be said about both Morley and Barnes and they are typical of Phelippes's agents in that their history is not particularly savoury.

Barnes was one of the most shadowy of contacts. One cannot be quite certain whether he was a double agent for Phelippes or Parma – perhaps it depended on who paid the highest fee. He had been involved in the Babington Plot which had been engineered by Walsingham to bring about Mary's end, and the part he played in that episode may have been on Walsingham's behalf – or it may not! At all events Barnes had gone to the Tower for his involvement and after his release had spied on his old contacts, becoming one of Walsingham's three principal agents. In return for his freedom he may have agreed to act for Walsingham, but like all matters surrounding Walsingham's secret networks it is never possible to know for certain what was behind seemingly simple happenings. Barnes may have bartered his services for his freedom, or he may have been Walsingham's creature from the beginning, and the session in the Tower only a cover-up to establish an identity. But in 1591, when he was in Flushing, Barnes appears to have been working for Cecil.

Phelippes was surprised that Barnes had made no report on Parma's attitude to the proposed betrothal. Indeed he should have been surprised, for both he and Cecil knew about this anyway from another source: he had been told by John Ricroft what was going on at least eight weeks earlier. Ricroft had been 'busy getting the picture of Arbella to carry to the Duke of Parma, and has Mr U's letter to aid him therein to Mr Hildyard'. It was surprising that Barnes in Flushing knew nothing. Clearly he was not doing what Phelippes paid him for – unless the other side was paying more.

The other agent, Morley, on the other hand was not so involved in spying; if Barnes was a professional, then Morley, the 'singing man', was an amateur. Thomas Morley was an organist at St Paul's and later Gentleman of the Chapel Royal, a courtier and musician of note who dabbled in occasional spying in what was a fatally amateur fashion.

At least one other channel of communication was open between England and Parma. Another shady character, Thomas Moody, was operating in the same matter of marriage, entirely independently of Cecil and Phelippes. Moody had offered his services to Sir Thomas Heneage, the Vice-Chamberlain, in October 1590 asking for employment in France or Spain. This man was a servant of Sir Edward Stafford who had been the English ambassador in Paris. In 1587 there had been a very amateurish plot to get rid of Elizabeth – possibly another sub-plot laid on by Walsingham to persuade Elizabeth of the danger of letting the Scots queen live. Sir Edward Stafford's younger brother William had been implicated and in a confession had involved Moody, who had recently been released from the Newgate Jail for debt. Stafford framed Moody by saying

that he had undertaken to place a bag of gunpowder beneath Elizabeth's bed and set it off – not a very likely tale. After this curious
episode Sir Edward Stafford took Moody with him to France as
a servant; again this whole thing seems an incomplete story for, if
Moody had been attempting to blow up the queen, it is hardly likely
that the then ex-ambassador would have taken him on as his servant.

By 1590 however Moody was in need of work, hence his letter
to Heneage, but it was not Heneage who took him on. In October
1591 Moody was in Flushing and wrote to 'Poly', the code name
for a correspondent in London: 'I beseech you send me word,
whether you be not made acquainted with matters that one Barnes
hath been handling, touching the Lady Arbella. I pray you send
me her picture, for that there is someone very desirous to see it.'
And on 2 April 1592 an informant, in a letter probably addressed
to Sir Robert Cecil, reported to him Moody's activities: 'Michael
Moody, Sir Edward Stafford's servant, is employed beyond the sea
to practise with Arbella about a marriage between her and the Duke
of Parma's son; he was sent for once before for her picture, and
has been thrice to England in this year.'[2]

Plainly there was more than one person in England promoting
Arbella's marriage with Rainutio. Barnes was acting for Phelippes
and Cecil, and his must have been the official government channel.
Who then was 'Poly'? The Cecils had every reason to distrust Essex
and there is a very strong suspicion that 'Poly' was one of the confidential servants of Essex. 'Poly' was in ignorance that the Cecils
knew what he was up to; these two statesmen were far sharper than
Essex. It is likely that Elizabeth knew what both Essex and Cecil
were doing and since they were acting along parallel lines there was
no point in stopping them.

Both parties therefore were asking for Arbella's portrait and her
presence in London was needed for the painting before it could be
taken to Flushing for Parma's consideration. No one was better able
to paint the likeness than Nicholas Hilliard, the court painter, or,
as Ricroft called him, 'Hildyard', and for convenience it would have
to be a miniature so that it could be taken secretly in a pocket or
baggage. While Arbella had been passing her days in the wilds of
Derbyshire, unknown to her the contact with Parma had been made.

Cecil's spies and agents had carried the messages and Parma's reaction had been favourable. Politics dictated that Arbella should be summonsed by the queen out of her life in limbo since there was a possibility that the princess could be a queen with her consort Rainutio ruling over an independent Spanish Netherlands and, after Elizabeth's eventual death, what then? Bess can be forgiven if she let her ambitions soar. It was the nearest that Arbella ever came to a throne, but Bess, a realist, would have done well to have tempered her enthusiasm; long acquaintance with her queen should have told her that royal politics were never what they appeared and the end was never where it seemed. Surprisingly neither Bess nor Arbella has left any comment on this interlude. It was a time of excitement for Arbella, and possibly Bess's greatest moment. To both it must have seemed an historic summons.

8

THEY ARE VANISHED INTO SMOKE

On 18 October 1591, Arbella, with her grandmother Bess, set out from Hardwick to make the trip to London. Bess was now sixty-three and she realized that this would be her last visit to London and the royal Court. With the possibility in the offing that Arbella would be assured the succession of Elizabeth's throne and consequently Bess's family connected in the closest way with the Crown, the journey had the aspect of a triumphal procession. It was a large party which set out to accompany the dowager countess on this last prestigious progress and, as the visit was planned to be a long one, it had taken a great deal of organizing. Accompanying Bess and Arbella were her uncles William and Charles Cavendish, their wives and their servants. Arbella took her own personal maid Mrs Abrahall. In addition to this already large company were Bess's own servants, ladies-in-waiting and personal maids, with a cook and a brewer as well as a small staff of household attendants which brought the total to around forty people. They went by two heavy coaches, the ladies travelling within while the rest of the party went on horseback.

The journey took all of seven days by the old route of Market Harborough, Dunstable and Barnet and it was a slow progress owing to the heavy, lumbering and uncomfortable coaches; about twenty miles a day was all that could be expected. As they approached the important market towns, bells rang out to welcome the travellers, and overnight when they put up at inns the party was entertained by waits and music. The triumphal procession must have taken on the feeling of a festival occasion. It was a sedate and slow journey which finally ended on arrival at Shrewsbury House in Chelsea, conveniently on the river. This was to be their headquarters for the eight months of the extended visit. To feed the household, sheep and oxen had been driven up from one of Bess's estates in Leicestershire; to accommodate the large party the stables had been converted into dormitories, and the horses and livestock grazed in the fields surrounding the village; to pay for the high costs of the visit, revenues had been diverted to Chelsea from some of Bess's distant estates. This was to be a visit to be remembered by all who took part.

Bess's purpose was not only concerned with Arbella and the proposed marriage to Rainutio. There were other matters which Bess had to attend to apart from the interests of her grandchild's betrothal – the perpetual problem of Arbella's finances for example. Bess felt that by right it was incumbent on the queen to provide for the only royal princess in keeping with her rank – £200 a year in Bess's opinion was not enough. In Elizabeth's eyes Bess was quite able to provide for her granddaughter, as indeed she was, and it was also due to Elizabeth's help that she had emerged triumphant from her tangle with Shrewsbury, and with her considerable finances intact. But Bess was never one to see things that way and, although no doubt graciously thankful to the queen, she would also have felt that Arbella's rank carried the right to a royal allowance. With the prospect of the marriage then certainly Elizabeth would have been unable to avoid this issue and she would have been called upon to provide estates for Arbella's support – but only if the marriage became fact.

In addition to these matters concerning her granddaughter, Bess was also in London to speed the settling of the legal rumpus raised by Gilbert Talbot over the payment of her own marriage settlement. She was also planning the most extravagant shopping expedition of her life. The Cavendish dynasty, which she had founded on such vast wealth, had now been provided with the beginnings of a great house, but there were not enough splendid hangings to cover its walls, neither was there suitable gold and silver plate to welcome the expected royal visitors; what Bess had possessed had been sold when Shrewsbury had been at his most harassing. Bess wanted to buy the necessary equipment to provide the sumptuous background which would surely be needed for royal entertainment. (In fact the only royal person ever to visit Hardwick was the Princess Victoria before she became queen.) It must have been in Bess's mind that a Queen Arbella would bring enormous advantages to her dynasty. The prospect of this final glorious achievement would have been exciting even to such a down-to-earth character as Bess.

That Christmas the Court was at Whitehall, a huge royal palace with all the appurtenances for impressive ceremonial. It was also the most public of the royal palaces, for the main road from Westminster to the City ran right beneath the Holbein Gate. For entertainment it had a tennis court, the famous tiltyard, a cockpit and the privy gardens with an extraordinary decoration of thirty-four animals on top of thirty-four brightly painted pillars. For the Elizabethans with their childish delight in devices, within the privy gardens and surrounded by the pillars was a sundial which told the time in thirty different ways, and to catch the unwary a strong multijetted fountain which could be suddenly set aspraying. The queen's own apartments in this vast palace overlooked the river. Here was her bedchamber with a bed in multicoloured wood and next door a bathroom perhaps entirely walled with mirrors. England may have been an island out of the mainstream of the Renaissance but in Elizabeth's palaces there were many delights which surprised foreign visitors into admiration.

Shrewsbury House at Chelsea was convenient for the Court at Whitehall. It was only a short distance up the road to London, or better and more comfortably impressive, by river to the water gatehouse at the palace. But before Bess, Arbella or any of the party could make their début at Court something had to be done to renew their country dresses. Yards of black taffeta were bought for Bess – a suitable colour for one widowed four times – trimmed with black cobweb lawn. Blue and white starches were bought to stiffen the lace collars of the new fineries. Fifty yards of velvet, as much again of damask and forty yards of satin must have included a gown for Arbella, but the colours were not stated and there were so many other ladies in Bess's court that it is often impossible to distinguish what was bought for Arbella. One would like to know for certain if a 'Pair of bracelets set with diamonds, pearl and rubies' which cost £21, and a heavy gold chain worth £26 were intended for Arbella's re-entrance to court.[1]

The refurbished ladies would have made their visit to Court in time for the twelve nights of celebrations which started on Christmas Day; this was the great party of the year and plainly Bess had timed their arrival so as not to miss it. Plays would have been put on in the banqueting hall, a temporary structure built only ten years before; dancing, music and gaming were all mixed up with the official business of state. The French ambassador brought M. de Plessis to consult with the queen on 2 January; a warrant was issued on 28 December directing the Lord Treasurer to deliver munitions to be taken to Holland for the war; petitions were received and considered; leases granted and secret reports came in to Robert Cecil; orders were made by Burghley. These were matters concerning the business of the nation which allowed the queen no rest. The social life of the Court swirled around the throne and somewhere in all this Arbella was lost to sight and unreported.

The royal princess was now sixteen years old and, one must hope, of some maturity for her age. Later she recalled this visit, 'What fair words I have had of courtiers and councillors, and so they are vanished into smoke.' A cynical outlook, but a necessary one in a court where so much was intended for impressive display with little depth or meaning.

It is likely that the secret discussions concerning the marriage were not carried out during that first court visit, but postponed until later in the year. It was only in July that Hilliard was paid by Bess for 'the drawing of one picture, forty shillings' and Rowland Lockey was paid £1. From the prices paid, this work would appear to have consisted of a miniature by Hilliard and a copy by Lockey. The artists were paid on 27 July but the painting would have been executed in the spring. By the time Hilliard and Lockey were paid for their work the miniature would have been well on its way to Parma in Flanders. But until Parma had given his answer there was little point in making the finer points of the arrangement between Elizabeth and Bess; there would have been nothing to do but wait.

How far the negotiations had progressed is impossible to say. There was of course one great stumbling block, that of the difference of religion between the two young people. Rainutio was a Catholic

and Arbella had been brought up in the spirit of Erasmus and all
things Protestant. Never throughout the forty years of her life was
there any hint of other beliefs. But, no doubt with a compelling
necessity to find a reasonable peace formula, Elizabeth, Burghley
and Cecil would have found a way round this, satisfying to the conscience of all concerned. Arbella was often to be the misplaced hope
of dissident Catholics in that she could be married off to a suitable
Catholic prince and eventually rule over an England reunited with
the Church of Rome. They may have been encouraged in this hope
by the fact that Arbella's aunt, Mary Talbot, with whom she spent
so much time in her early teens, became a Catholic, to the embarrassment of her husband Gilbert. But, notwithstanding any influence of her aunt Mary, Arbella never diverged from the sound
teachings of Bess and the carefully selected tutors.

Arbella only made occasional visits to the Court during that
memorable spring and summer of 1592. What otherwise occupied
her is not evident; certainly she would have spent a lot of time
attending on her grandmother at Chelsea. But, with the twelve
nights of celebrations over, the Court had moved to Westminster
by the end of January and by the end of February was at Richmond.
It is unlikely that either Arbella or Bess followed the Court on these
peregrinations. There was a constant coming and going of important
visitors to Shrewsbury House, while at Easter, which fell on 26
March, Arbella and her uncle Henry Cavendish took communion
at Chelsea. Bess's personal maid Mrs Digby had a baby at the end
of February and Arbella gave £2 as a christening present.[2]

Nevertheless, although on the surface it may have given the impression of a dull life to Arbella, Chelsea must have been infinitely
preferable to the isolation she had endured in Derbyshire. There
was for example the diversion of clothes. Anything could be bought
in London and although there was no other way to buy gowns than
to purchase the materials and have them made up by Tasker, Bess's
London tailor, the discussions of the design and materials would
have been exciting distractions for Arbella. Just after Easter a few
yards of velvet were bought with some lace for collars or trimmings
and canvas for the lining of the skirt of a gown. The impression
is that, more often than having a completely new ensemble, these

ladies of the highest rank were content to alter and bedeck what they already had and were happy enough with the effect.

Meanwhile the Court had left London and gone off on one of Elizabeth's progresses. Arbella did not go and this is the likely period for the painting of Hilliard's portrait. In early April Sir Thomas Gresham at Osterley entertained the queen and her Court. From there she moved to Wimbledon, then to Croydon and by the end of April was installed at Greenwich for the whole summer.

In the first week of May Bess went comfortably downriver for a three-week stay with the Court at Greenwich. With her went Arbella, William Cavendish and Arbella's aunt Jane Kniveton (who was Bess's younger half-sister), together with servants, in four boats. Whitsun was early that year and the visit coincided with the celebrations. Bess was certainly choosing the times of her visits carefully – again there would have been perhaps a play and certainly music and dancing. This is the most likely time for discussions between Bess and the queen about the main details of Arbella's betrothal scheme; some sort of reaction would have been received from Parma even if he had not by then received the miniature. On 9 May Burghley recorded the despatch to Flushing of a messenger who could very easily have been involved in these secret negotiations.

Bess acquired a pair of velvet shoes, a pair in Spanish leather and another pair in neat's leather, together with a pair of 'pantables' or overshoes for herself. Since none of the court shoes were stated to be for herself and there were three other women including Arbella in her party, it is a fair assumption that one pair at least was for Arbella.[3] The parties and the music came to an end and on 25 May Arbella, with Bess and her ladies, returned upriver to Chelsea in an episcopal barge lent to them by Richard Fletcher, Bishop of Bristol. Fletcher had been attentive to Arbella's grandmother since her arrival at Chelsea, even sending the gift of a kid in April. He was a widower and perhaps had his eye on the wealthy widow. If so, then he was disappointed, for Bess never married again.

These good times must have passed quickly. The days were full of minor events and on 11 June Bess with her party, including Arbella, set out for her last visit to the Court at Greenwich and to say a subject's goodbye to her queen who, as far as Elizabeth allowed herself to have friends, had been a friend to Bess. Once again there was a flurry of activity to brighten up old clothes. One of the ladies of the party – it could easily have been Arbella – had a gown trimmed with red baize, while almost certainly for Arbella there was a powdered ermine gown. The visit lasted until 19 July when Bess said her final goodbye to the queen. Leaving Arbella at Court in the care of her relatives, she sailed up the Thames for the last time with six boats, to begin her return to Hardwick and home in Derbyshire by early August. Arbella probably stayed on at Court until it moved to Bisham in mid-August; it was important for the peace moves that Arbella should be seen at Court and enjoying the queen's favour.

While Arbella had undoubtedly been enjoying the life at Court, a Jesuit priest from Spain, an Englishman by the name of George Dingley, had been arrested at about Easter-time. Dingley had been trained at a college for English priests in Valladolid, expressly for the purpose of returning to England to teach the Catholic faith and to administer the sacraments. Dingley must have been amazingly naïve, for in February he had landed by boat on the Thames and 'lay all night under a hedge'. It must have been fearfully cold. Next day Dingley arrived in London still wearing his Spanish clothes, muddy and very travel-stained. With the Spanish war continuing, anyone with an eye to see would have been suspicious of this apparition. He spent a month with Lady Throckmorton until the arrival of a search party, which forced him to leave by the back door.

Inevitably and eventually Dingley was arrested and months later, on 24 and 27 August, made a written confession to Burghley. As a priest the man was harmless and he certainly never came to England to act as a spy in any accepted sense of the word, but in his very long confessions, when he was clearly anxious to tell everything he knew and more besides, he told Burghley of a plot hatched out by the arch-recusant Sir William Stanley, then living in Spain and advising Philip on English politics. Two dissident Englishmen, John Simple and Anthony Roulston had 'promised to convey her [Arbella] out of England by stealth' and they with their prisoner had been expected in Brussels. Dingley said that his confession was

voluntary. He was probably telling the truth throughout – he had
nothing to lose by telling of a plot which had failed and of the two
principals who were by then safely back in Spain. Other points
which can be checked in the confessions are true; seemingly he was
a simple man as well as naïve and the revelation of the kidnap plot
must be accepted as truth. Dingley was an honest man, whole-
hearted in his faith, who had been meddling in matters which he
did not understand, apparently quite unaware of the danger he was
running.[4]

But whether Dingley was harmless or not, his revelations were
taken seriously and Burghley took no chances with Arbella's safety.
Bess had been back at Hardwick for some seven weeks, and had
resumed the building of her new house (which had been suspended
during the eight months of the London visit), when she received
a letter from Burghley, obviously prompted by Dingley's confessions. Meanwhile Arbella had returned from London and was
lodged uncomfortably with Bess in the unfinished old Hardwick
Hall, less draughty now that the windows had been glazed. Burghley
instructed Bess to keep Arbella under the closest watch against kidnap attempts, and her reply throws a cold light on the conditions
of their living.

I will not have any unknown or suspected person to come to my house.
Upon the least suspicion that may happen here, I shall give advertisement
to your Lordship. I have little resort to me; my house is furnished with
sufficient company. Arbell walks not late; at such time as she shall take
the air, it shall be near the house and well attended on; she goeth not
to anybody's house at all; I see her almost every hour of the day; she
lieth in my bedchamber.

A complete contrast to Arbella's full life in London. To judge
by Bess's next comment they had not been having an easy time even
in so remote a fastness as Hardwick. A year earlier, she explained,
a priest had been found staying about a mile from Hardwick. Bess
had him arrested, although he was shortly released when it was seen
that he was harmless. There had been trouble with a tutor for
Arbella: 'one Morley who hath attended on Arbell and read to her
for the space of three years-and-a-half, showed himself to be much

discontented since my return.' The discontented Morley had been dismissed and replaced by another, but not without giving rise to further suspicions. Bess had mentioned nothing of these alarms to Arbella.[5]

In all truth Hardwick at that time was no place to observe easily the comings and goings of strangers – there were too many workmen about on the building. By 15 October Bess and Arbella had removed to Chatsworth and a safer haven. Meanwhile across the Channel events were following a course which brought to nothing the purpose of Arbella's recent visit to the bright lights and music of the Court. Parma had aroused Philip's suspicions that he was back-pedalling on the war effort and Philip was about to replace him with a more vigorous general when Parma died. For 22 November Burghley completed an entry in his diary of events: 'The D of Parma dyed at Arrass.'[6] With him died any hopes of immediate peace in the Netherlands and any hopes of Arbella's marriage with Rainutio, who without his father's power became useless.

Once more one is left to guess what Arbella's thoughts would have been about this betrothal; possibly as a young girl she was excited at the thought of marriage to a foreign nobleman and the continuation of the court parties. Arbella had not yet shown any of her later determination to avoid collaboration with the State. For the moment she was prepared to go along with her grandmother's policy of complete obedience to the queen's wishes, which had paid Bess so well.

9

MY JEWEL ARBELLA

Parma had not been the only one on the Continent to interest himself in Arbella. The Jesuits were also interested, but their concern understandably stemmed from their theological dogma. In England the differences between Catholics and Protestants had been settled more or less for the moment to the satisfaction of the majority of countrymen. It was Elizabeth's flair that she was able to tell the mood of the nation with astonishing accuracy, and she recognized the necessity for a delicate balance and compromise. Across the Channel things were not settled so easily. The teaching of Martin Luther had spread across Europe in the sixteenth century to the discomfiture of the entrenched popes, who were strongly opposed to any reformation of the Christian Church and consequent weakening of their power.

The Catholic answer to Lutheranism was the Counter Reformation, and there followed a long succession of wars, international and civil, which by 1590 left a Europe divided between northern Protestants and southern Catholics. France was at war with itself and divided between the two theological poles, although Henri IV had become a Catholic. The Pope as spiritual leader of the Counter Reformation fortunately had no army of his own, and relied upon Philip of Spain to supply his deficiency. In the rest of Europe the Pope could not find substantial backing; Italy was simply a collection of Catholic kingdoms and not a united nation. With France undecided, Spain was left as the only strong Catholic country in Europe, a country made economically stronger by the Indian gold looted from the Americas and carried at hazard across the Atlantic.

But even this alliance between the Pope and Philip had its differences, for Philip was shouldering the main burden of the struggle and was perhaps more interested in extending his own empire than that of the Pope. Furthermore since 1536 Spain had nurtured the Society of Ignatius Loyola, a society of Jesuits whose missionary work had followed the banners of the Conquistadors and were then spread all over the known world. By the 1590s the Jesuits had become the most powerful single body in the Church of Rome. In fact so strong was the power of the Jesuits that, although acting as a spearhead of the Counter Reformation, they were not always in agreement with their pope. At St Peter's in Rome the Pope often found it difficult, if not impossible, to impose his wishes on his Spanish allies. On one point they were in agreement: England must be brought back, by some means, from the heathen darkness.

Queen Elizabeth with her northern Protestant faith was the chief obstacle in the way of the Catholic allies. Once Elizabeth was removed, so Philip was advised by emigré Englishmen, then the great Catholic majority would ensure that England became Catholic. This was what Philip wanted to hear; consequently it followed that if Philip could land an army in England to help the Catholics overthrow Elizabeth, then all England would be united behind his soldiers. In the meantime the Jesuits kept the true faith alight in England by sending over priests such as Dingley, to give strength to those who were expected to welcome Philip's armies. Who then was to be put in place of Elizabeth? Or, if she died of natural causes before Philip could depose her, who was to take over the rule of the new Catholic England? James of Scotland was plainly out of the question for he was as Protestant as Elizabeth.

The answer to this problem was given in a twenty-six-page book in Latin published on the Continent in 1594, *A Conference About the Next Succession to the Crown of England*, dedicated to Leicester. It was written under the name of R. Doleman, who was actually Richard Verstegan, an English Catholic who had fled from London in 1582 when his secret printing press was discovered. Doleman was thought to be a pen name for Father Parsons, co-ordinator of English Jesuits, but his part was only the minor one of correction and rewriting. The *Conference* had an immediate and almost overnight success and was read by everyone who mattered, for it set out to do what Elizabeth refused to do – name a successor. Doleman,

or Verstegan, argued through all the possible claims dismissing
them one by one because of bastardy, bigamy and other legal impediments.

Arbella was a problem to him. As her claim was beyond doubt
he assailed her cause by inventing spurious illegalities. Delving into
the past and without providing a shred of proof, he went back to
Henry VIII's eldest sister Margaret, married to James IV of Scotland.
Soon after James died, Queen Margaret had secretly married Lord
Stuart of Annerdale – so he claimed – and he was still living when
she married Archibald Douglas, Earl of Angus. Margaret and
Archibald were of course Arbella's great-grandparents, and through
them came her claim to Elizabeth's throne; by producing the Lord
of Annerdale out of the air Verstegan was trying to show that
Arbella's grandmother was illegitimate.

He showed equal invention when he discussed the claim of the
Seymours through Catherine Grey; she too was illegitimate –
apparently her father had a wife living when he married Frances
Brandon, Catherine's mother. By one means or another the *Conference* found fault with all claims until it finally came to Philip's
son the Infante of Spain, an inevitable conclusion. In England of
course the falsity of the arguments could be understood but it aired
the discussion of succession which Elizabeth refused to allow Parliament to debate. Doleman made plain what was already known: that
James of Scotland and Arbella had equal claim and that if Elizabeth
would accept the marriage of Edward Seymour with Catherine Grey
– which she did not – then Lord Beauchamp, their eldest son, was
in the running too.

Doleman's untimely reminder to Elizabeth of this problem of
succession, which she would rather have kept out of mind, was an
irritation to her. The sight of Arbella at Court would have been
a further irritation since the girl was so closely involved. With the
wish to have the problem out of mind went the determination to
have Arbella out of sight. After her return to Derbyshire in 1592
from the whirl of court life, Arbella was replaced in the limbo where
the queen preferred her to be. She was out of sight and out of mind
until a suitable political gambit arose in which her marriage could
be used to advantage. Arbella therefore remained in Derbyshire

with her grandmother, who was resolutely completing her building of the new Hardwick Hall. Resolute Bess certainly was and nothing was allowed to interrupt her scheme to found a dynasty as near eternal as she could ensure it – a dynasty secured on a base of enormous wealth.

While Bess was building Hardwick, England was struck by a succession of very wet summers which ruined crops from 1594 to 1597, and famine resulted on a scale which brought unimagined disaster throughout the country. Riots were threatened and suppressed in different parts of England – riots protesting against the rocketing price of corn – and cargoes of expensive wheat were imported to help support an inadequately fed population. During these famine years Bess's revenues fell by twenty-five per cent and characteristically she increased her payments to the 'poor at the gates'. But the fall of a quarter in a total revenue of £9,500 made no difference to her dynastic ambition:[1] nothing was allowed to interrupt the building. She was aging and she wished to live in the splendour of the new Hardwick she was creating.

The possibility that Arbella might become queen was not one of the main concerns of Bess's ambitions. She would certainly have admitted the enormous advantages to be gained by her family, but the possibility was never an essential part of her schemes. As long as Elizabeth lived and the succession was left an open question, Arbella's claim remained a glowing presumption in Bess's mind. But with the death of Parma, and the end of the dream of immediate power for Bess and her family, came the end, for a time at least, of any thought of Arbella's income being provided by the queen.

Bess could no longer leave her granddaughter unprovided for and she succeeded in taking care of her in a way which was typical of her and her ways of business. Her old friend Sir Francis Willoughby, who had been one of her supporters during the struggle with Shrewsbury and with whom she shared a partnership in an ironworks at Oakamore in Staffordshire, was in financial trouble. Sir Francis was an unusual man even in an age of unusual men. He came from a family which had been established for centuries in lands near Nottingham, with other holdings in Staffordshire and Leicestershire; they were in no sense new arrivals. But like many old landed families the Willoughbys were feeling the pinch, and the reason was that Sir Francis had been blessed with a handful of daughters each of whom had to be provided with a suitable dowry. This had reduced his revenues. He had also overstretched himself by building an enormous renaissance palace, Wollaton Hall near Nottingham, one of the surviving wonders of Elizabethan England. This was another example of dynastic ambition; more remarkable in that he had no male heir to leave his palace to, nor to inherit his more mortgaged lands, a problem he got round by marrying his eldest daughter to a relative and making her husband his heir.

To recoup his failing fortunes the enterprising Sir Francis had embarked on a succession of commercial projects which had resulted in spectacular losses. The projects included an experiment in woad-growing; glass-making; extending his coal-mining interests; and of course his ironworks. Sir Francis's trouble was that he put his trust in servants who let him down and had no trust in his family who would have been more loyal. By 1594 he was deeper in debt. He had been discussing raising a loan from Bess for some time, and the delay in concluding the protracted business was because of the difficulty of finding Willoughby estates as collateral which were not either already mortgaged or tied up in dowries for his daughters.

Finally agreement was reached and in May 1594 Bess lent Sir Francis £3,050 at an interest of £300 annually, secured on lands worth £15,000; and Sir Francis was further in debt with little chance of redeeming the mortgage. It was typical of Bess that having no need of the bargain herself – for she had more than enough land – the whole transaction was carried out in Arbella's name and the mortgage, when it inevitably fell in, resulted in the lands becoming Arbella's. With an outlay of £3,050 Bess had therefore secured an income of £300 for her granddaughter and eventually lands worth five times the capital sum she had paid out.

Further gifts of capital followed in the closing years of the century. In 1599 Bess gave Arbella over £1,140 to buy lands at Skegby in Lincolnshire and by 1600 Arbella's £200 from crown lands allowed her by the queen had been augmented to a total from all sources of around £600–£700 – the sum which Bess considered would have been appropriately paid by the queen. Arbella had been provided with a separate substance and was being given by her grandmother the opportunity to be independent.[2]

There had been earlier references to Arbella's finances. Bess kept a separate account, although it has not survived, and obviously she knew what there was for her granddaughter. In 1583, when Arbella had been eight years old, one of Bess's servants, possibly her steward, had been told to give Gilbert Talbot £100 for Arbella; and in May the same servant was to deliver £100 of Arbella's money to Mary Talbot. At midsummer that same year another £100 of Arbella's money was delivered to William Cavendish. There were also payments of similar sums to or for Arbella in William's own accounts. But this was neither Bess's nor William's money; these sums were the half-yearly revenues awarded to Arbella by the queen and the money was collected by whoever happened to be in London and paid over to whoever had been out of pocket for Arbella's upkeep. In January 1594 Bess paid over to her granddaughter £2,000. At the same time William handed over to Arbella £1,360, which they entered in the accounts as being paid to Arbella as her mother's will ordered – a total of £3,360. These sums, however, very likely constituted the dowry for Elizabeth which Bess screwed out of Shrewsbury and which Arbella's mother never received, and which should, by her will, have been paid to Arbella in 1591 – a sum of £3,000. The extra £360 may be explained as a mean payment of interest for the three years delay.[3]

Bess's generosity towards Arbella did not stop with large capital gifts. Over the years of the 1590s there was a stream of smaller gifts. In May 1594 she lent Arbella £350, 'to be repaid when my Lady shall command it'. Likely enough Bess never did command it. On the same day she gave Arbella £100. Other presents were an annual New Year gift of £20, and, to underline her musical accomplishments, 'given to the Lady Arbella to pay for a set of vials £20' in December 1595. But it was not only money; for in January 1594 Bess recorded, 'Taken out of my jewel coffer as followeth: a bone lace with thirty pearls for a coronet given to my jewel Arbella'. This was it seems a head-dress incorporating a coronet decked with pearls which must have been worth a great deal of money, for pearls were

highly prized for their scarcity value. In August 1599 she noted,
'Given to my daughter Arbella to buy her a pearl to enlarge her
chain £100', which gives some idea of their value. An entry of £40
on New Year's Day 1594 leaves one to guess: 'towards the buying
of certain household stuff given away by her mother'. There is no
mention of why or what it was Elizabeth had given away but Bess
had not forgotten over the twelve years since her daughter had
died.[4]

By 1601 Arbella was twenty-five and, having received the
payment of the £3,000 due to her from her mother's estate and the
income provided by Bess, she was becoming more independent; she
had at last become responsible for her own small staff or household.
Unfortunately nothing remains to show what size of mini-court
Arbella maintained as an appendage to Bess's larger court. On two
occasions Bess paid two of Arbella's servants: in May 1594 when Mrs
Abrahall, her personal servant, left Arbella's service, Bess gave her
£5 and another £5 for her two-year-old son; and a month later Bess
paid Thomas Hood, one of Arbella's gentleman servants (possibly
her steward), £26 13s. 4d – a very generous wage and far in excess
of that of Bess's highest-paid servant.

But although Arbella had officially come of age and was paying
her own household, and furthermore had been given a separate
financial existence, she was still kept in close propinquity to Bess.
It must have been iritating to remain tied so close to her aging grandmother. In this respect her life was not so very different from that
of any other girl of similar high rank, but the differences which
would have rankled were that she was not allowed to go to Court
until sent for and by twenty-five, had it not been for her royal blood,
she would almost certainly have been married and free of the close
restrictions she was living under. Otherwise her lot was not at vari-
ance with custom. When a girl came of age, if not by then married,
she would wait at home under the care of her parents or, if orphaned,
in the care of grandparents, until a husband of equal wealth and rank
had been selected for her.

Bess's letter to Burghley in 1592, when there were fears for her
granddaughter's safety, shows how close was the surveillance over
Arbella: 'at such time as she shall take the air, it shall be near the

house and well attended on.... I see her almost every hour of the day; she lieth in my bedchamber.' Then she had been seventeen and just returned from Court: she was prepared to accept the restrictions. By 1600 Arbella was eight years older and, although Bess and she had moved into the newly finished Hardwick Hall, she would have felt very differently about her bondage.[5]

10

YE DRAWING-ROOM DOOR

By 1600 Arbella could look back over the eight years since her last visit to Court with little satisfaction. They had passed without any event of importance to her. From her chamber in the old Hardwick, she had watched her grandmother's new Hardwick go up until in 1597 they had moved into Bess's new mansion. This was an occasion celebrated by the music of four amateurs from among the household servants. Two of these musicians, James Starkey, Bess's chaplain-in-ordinary, and John Good were to be closely involved in Arbella's coming crisis. Another of the musicians, Richard Abrahall, was one of Arbella's gentleman servants and son to Mrs Abrahall who had left Arbella in 1594.

Those eight years had been passed under the ever-watchful eye of her grandmother. The time had been spent in moving sometimes for short periods to Chatsworth or South Wingfield, then back to Hardwick. It was a lot which, although unenviable, was to be expected by any girl of her rank; the trouble, as Arbella saw it, was that it had gone on for too long. She had been sent back to Derby-shire to await a royal summons which had not come. However there were compensations which would not have been expected in many other households. Bess had become an important figure in the area and was remembered at Court. She gave good rewards and as a consequence was an attraction to any band of entertainers who might pass up or down England.

It is very likely that Arbella saw Shakespeare's plays performed in Bess's houses; the queen's players visited Chatsworth in 1593, and were at the old Hardwick in 1596 and the new Hardwick in 1600. If not the queen's players, there were many visits from other actors, paid performers and servants of other noble households willing to offer the diversion of an evening's entertainment in return for food and drink, a warm night's rest and a small reward. Admiral Lord Thomas Howard's players followed close after those of the queen at the new Hardwick in 1600, when the high great chamber would have been used. Lord Ogle's troupe also visited frequently (Ogle was Charles Cavendish's father-in-law). The players of the Earls of Huntingdon and of Pembroke also came to the new Hardwick Hall to perform their dramas. These were diversions of a high quality, such as would have been seen at Court, and in this respect Arbella was lucky, for a less famous grandmother would have attracted less famous players – or none at all.

Like the queen, Bess encouraged music. Arbella herself played and could join in the appreciation of performances by her uncle Henry's own musicians who, not withstanding Bess's distaste for her eldest son, made frequent visits to Hardwick. Other performances were given by musicians of the Earl of Lincoln and Lord Mounteagle. On one evening there had been what amounted to a concert by the singing of the waits of Nottingham and the musicians of the Earls of Rutland and Essex. That was in the autumn of 1599 in the new Hardwick. It was not often that such a feast of music could be arranged but in 1596, in the old Hardwick, the waits of Wakefield and a total of four trumpeters, including one from the Earl of Essex and another from the Earl of Northumberland, had made the old hall rock with their brassy notes. More often the music came from the waits or singers of the local townships – of Doncaster, of Pontefract and of Newark – or from John Bridges, a local trumpeter who first played at Hardwick in 1595 and thereafter made almost regular visits. Sometimes the music was made by amateurs among the household: at Christmas in 1596 a small group played 'at ye drawing room door' in the old hall; on another occasion Starkey, Good and Parker were given the enormous sum of £1 for their singing.[1] These diversions were the compensation for living at Hardwick and must have been prized by Arbella, the performances appreciated and perhaps discussed afterwards with those who took part.

Arbella's greatest privation was perhaps that she had no company of her own age and rank; she had no one with whom to share her

fears and hopes. She seldom saw her aunt Mary Talbot now that
Bess had quarrelled with Gilbert over the payment of the marriage
settlement. Her uncle William and his wife Anne had shared life
at the old hall except when they were in London, which they frequently were. In 1596, when William had been Sheriff of Derbyshire, the house had often been filled with the comings and goings
of the important men of the county. But by 1600 Bess had completed
the building of Owlcotes, just four miles away and in sight of Hardwick from the roof walk, and when William and Anne and their
children had moved to their new home, they took a lot of the bustle
of life from Hardwick with them.

There had of course been the novelty for Arbella of moving into
her new apartments at Hardwick. Her bedchamber was probably
what is now known as the lawn bedchamber, because it overlooks
the wide sweeping lawn on the east side of the house, although there
would have been no lawn in Arbella's time. The room is in the
south-east turret and connected to her grandmother's suite of
rooms. It is a smallish room on the first floor where all the family
rooms lay, lit by two of the vast leaded windows for which Hardwick
is so well known. This is a room which has Arbella's own coat of
arms above the fire-place and its significance in Bess's mind is indicated by its position in a small shield above the larger Hardwick
display. Off this chamber and down two steps was an unheated outer
room for Arbella's personal servant, which contained no more than
a bed. Even Arbella's chamber had little more than a bed in it, perhaps just a stool and a cupboard, and the leaded windows must have
taken much of the heat from the fire. She was to call this room her
'quandom study'.

She did not sleep in it, for her own bed was in her grandmother's
room – a four-poster with a pretty canopy in blue and white with
a matching fringe and over the bed a cover in a checker pattern
embroidered in crewel, a thin worsted yarn. Bess's bedchamber was
cluttered with personal impedimenta – an assortment of three desks,
chairs, stools, six coffers and an iron chest – not to mention Bess's
own four-poster in which she would lie cocooned against the cold
Derbyshire winters beneath layer upon layer of bed-clothes. To
share the bedchamber must have been as unwelcome to Arbella as

it was to her grandmother. Now that Arbella was twenty-five, with her own small income and her own servants, she was finding it difficult to see eye to eye with her relative, although she always showed her full and due respect.

For Arbella there was only one way to escape from the confined life she was forced to endure, and that was by marriage. But Elizabeth had not sent for Arbella during those eight long years, and at twenty-five this chance of escape seemed to be receding. By 1600 there were reports of the queen's decline. Elizabeth had suffered a serious attack of smallpox in 1562 which had all but finished her off, but in 1563 gastric trouble caused her another serious illness which recurred from time to time. Although at sixty-seven she was six years younger than Bess, she did not enjoy so robust a constitution. By 1600 these untoward attacks had served to make the queen an old and failing woman, while Bess, who had been spared any serious reported illness during her life, was showing no signs of failing health whatsoever. Naturally the state of the queen's health gave rise to private discussion of that forbidden subject – the queen's successor.

After the failure of the marriage proposal between Arbella and Rainutio Farnese in 1592, the Pope had come forward with his own candidate in 1596. By suggesting Cardinal Farnese, the brother of Rainutio, the Pope had it in mind that the marriage would bring about a Catholic Arbella and thus a Catholic England. He was even prepared, as a gesture of his sincerity, to release the cardinal from his vows of celibacy, so far could the rules be broken if exigency demanded. This papal candidate is unlikely to have received any serious attention at all from Elizabeth; the Pope's motives were too transparent.

Since the queen refused to name a groom for Arbella or a successor for herself, rumour filled the vacuum. In 1599 Duke Mathias, the brother of Cardinal Archduke Albert of Austria, was suggested to Robert Cecil. After the death of Parma, Archduke Albert, married to the Infante of Spain, had taken over the Spanish Netherlands and the prosecution of the war. A marriage to the brother of this powerful governor-general so close to the throne of Spain was a political possibility and received some serious consideration by Cecil, who had stepped into his father's shoes in Elizabeth's councils when Burghley died in 1598. That Cecil considered this offer at all caused James great consternation in Scotland.

In fact when it came to the point – and it was a point which Elizabeth fought shy of – there was only one possible successor, and that was James of Scotland. His religion as a Protestant was impeccable; his descent from Henry VII was irreproachable; furthermore he was married and had a male heir, Prince Henry. Cecil was well aware of the claim and had long since made his contacts with James; Elizabeth in her heart recognized it too but, procrastinating as ever, by refusing to name her heir she gave herself room for political manœuvre. It is curious that most of England also believed in the succession of James, but for a different reason: Thomas Wilson, in his *The State of England Anno Dom 1600*,[2] dismissed Arbella to second place after James because of the bastardy of her father – Verstegan's *Conference* had plainly started something.

Over those eight long years Arbella had time to look back over the suitors who had been put forward or whose names had been associated with hers. Esmé Stuart, proposed in 1581, was dead in 1583; little Robert Dudley, Leicester's son, betrothed secretly in 1583, had died in 1584 – Leicester himself was dead four years later. Admittedly Esmé Stuart's son Ludovic had been mentioned in the context of a marriage to Arbella and had survived, but this had not been an official proposal. Rainutio Farnese too was still alive, but his father Parma was not, and by marrying someone else Rainutio had thus perhaps escaped a dangerous association. The signs of her own malign influence were there before her when she reviewed these hopes, now extinct. But she survived, like her grandmother who, already long past the expected lifespan, was well on the way to doubling it, and had buried four husbands.

Arbella had plenty of time to brood over these omens as she wandered through the new Hardwick, through its matted long gallery and the high silent state rooms on the second floor, ready to receive royal guests who never came. On the lower floors there was the busy life of the servants, the stone-flagged great hall – the domain of the yeomen – echoing with laughter and voices only subdued when called to order by the usher. The purpose and end of all the life at Hardwick was centred on the old countess living quietly in her apartments on the first floor away from the hubbub of the hall, sometimes receiving her visitors in her own withdrawing chamber, or on more important occasions using the great state suite on the floor above, and she herself dedicated to the foundation and maintenance of her dynasty. Arbella was apart from all this bustling and single-minded purpose, living half in reality with Bess and half in the images of her mind. Arbella's thinking was based on the reading of ancient classics, which is evident from her letters containing constant allusions to Plutarch and Pliny, and the lives of the ancient gods.

Arbella had played the part which Bess and Elizabeth had assigned to her, and it had brought her nothing. Now at twenty-five she was as closely kept and restricted as ever she had been for eight long years. As far as Arbella was concerned, if obedience to authority – a course recommended by Bess – brought this constrained existence, then the time had come for her to follow the path of her other grandmother, Margaret Lennox, a path leading to revolt against authority and to escape from the claustrophobia of Bess's cluttered bedchamber.

Working out this resolution in the quietness of her mind, Arbella took time to reach her inevitable conclusion. And yet, had she thought the matter out further, she would have seen that Elizabeth's reign was drawing to an end and that with her passing would come Arbella's own freedom and return to life at Court; she would have presented no threat to James Stuart once he was crowned King of England. But this would have been balanced reasoning and perhaps Arbella was not able to reach a sensible conclusion in the isolated world of her grandmother's court. Perhaps she really feared that she would become Elizabeth's heir, and if she did not know all the facts she could have been encouraged in that. Arbella had everything to gain from letting time pass and yet she concocted a plan of escape from Hardwick which was the most dangerous she could have conceived – dangerous, unless she believed implicitly in her destiny to survive.

11

SHE WOULD BREAK FORTH INTO TEARS

For Arbella the first years of the new century passed much as the closing years of the old, without any event of importance to her. For her New Year gift in 1600 she gave the queen 'a scarf or head-veil of lawn cut-work, flourished with silver and silk of sondry colours', and in return she received a gilt plate worth about £9. As a fine point of protocol it was very slightly heavier than the plate given to Bess by the queen. Although the time was uneventful it was nevertheless passing remorselessly: the queen, refusing to accept the fact, was obviously aging. This concentrated the minds of those who had an interest in altering the religion of England, and those who wished to have a hand in the power game of the succession. Even those with little personal interest in these matters added to the uncertainty by speculation on the succession, which quickly became rumour.

At Brussels in the spring of 1601 Robert Cecil was said to be intent on becoming king by marrying Arbella. At the same time there were rumours that the Prince of Condé, nephew to Henri IV, was to marry Arbella. This was probably a match which was given serious consideration by Elizabeth, who was striving for a means to ally England with France against Spain; the marriage would have provided for such an alliance. An anonymous author wrote a long argument, in Italian, favouring the proposed marriage; he was clearly intensely interested in the subject. In March 1602 the Duke of Nevers made a visit to England and the Court. The inextinguishable Father Rivers smelt out a reason for the occasion: it was, he said, to discuss a marriage with Arbella. The duke's visit, which was treated as an occasion for trundling out the full apparatus of state, helped to further the friendly attitude towards France which Elizabeth was

promoting. To quash rumours about her failing health she favoured
Nevers by dancing with him, a pastime of which she had always
been fond, but of which she had more recently become a spectator.
But these were only rumours of marriages and Arbella remained
isolated in Derbyshire and was not summoned by the queen.[1]

An event which must have moved Arbella was the ill-starred
revolt by the erratic Essex in 1601. He had fled from Ireland in
1599 after his failure to subdue the Irish – failure continued to be
the fate of any who became actively involved in the peculiar history
of that race – resulting in his being put under house arrest in London. Essex, unable to believe that his punishment could have been
inflicted by Elizabeth, came to the private conclusion that he was
being penalized by Cecil and other factions against him in the Privy
Council. He became paranoic in this belief and decided to rid his
queen of the self-interested councillors surrounding her. Essex was
partially right. Cecil neither trusted him nor wanted him in the
queen's councils, and for long had been seeking a way to get rid
of him; but in a way far more subtle than Essex imagined.

Cecil allowed him copious rope with which to hang himself. This
brilliant courtier was in disgrace with Elizabeth for no reason other
than his own shortcomings. Elizabeth's disfavour was genuine and
not much influenced by Cecil, but if she had listened to him earlier
she would have had her favourite's head off long before Cecil's
desire became fact. It took the treasonable matter of the Essex
revolt, which in typical swashbuckling fashion its leader misjudged
and mismanaged, to convince Elizabeth. Arrests, trials and execu-
tions followed, reprisals which Cecil used with great cunning to
remove most of his enemies for ever. On Ash Wednesday 1601 Essex
was beheaded for his treason, and with three blows of the axe Cecil's
arch-enemy was eliminated. Cecil of course was right. Had Essex
lived on after Elizabeth's death he would only have brought trouble
and revolution by interfering with the succession and, as Cecil well
knew, he stood a better chance of settling Essex under Elizabeth
than he would under James. Two years later when Arbella herself was
in dire trouble, she remembered Essex and his death; she must have
nóted the date to remind herself of the end of an admired friend.[2]

In 1601 Arbella's grandmother, with more realism than the

queen, made her will and had the contents of her houses listed in
a great inventory. Bess left to Arbella her 'cristal glass trimmed with
silver gilt and set with lapis lazuli and agates'. It must have been
a magnificent thing. Also she left her 'one sable, the head being of
gold set with stone and a white ermin sable the head likewise of
gold enamelled and set with stone and all my pearls and jewells
which I shall have at the time of my death except such as shall be
otherwise bequeathed'. This was quite a treasure trove and in addition she left Arbella £1,000. It was all in all a generous bequest
for her favourite grandchild.

Arbella was leading a life isolated from her own generation; she
had become a solitary person. The activity of the household surrounding her grandmother was no place for introspection and
Arbella had withdrawn more and more into herself and the company
of her 'silent councillors' in her 'quandom study'. In the household
of her grandmother was James Starkey, styled in 1599 as ordinary
chaplain in the household; he was just one of several priests who
occupied positions in the hierarchy surrounding Bess. At a time
when church attendance on Sundays was compulsory, it saved a
lot of time and trouble in a remote household like Hardwick, which
was two miles from the nearest church, to have its own chapel with
resident priests.

In fact these clergy fulfilled other functions. Henry Jenkinson was
one who acted as paymaster for the building of Hardwick; Roger
Harrison, resident priest at Chatsworth, was co-opted as rent collec-
tor and bailiff for the surrounding estate. These well-paid priests
holding sinecures were not allowed by Bess to do nothing; they were
involved in the running of what had become a very profitable and
successful corporation with Bess as its first 'president' and William
Cavendish as 'managing director'. Starkey had come to Hardwick
as early as 1593 to act as tutor to one of the sons of William Cavendish, possibly William, the future second Earl of Devonshire, born
in 1590. In the new Hardwick Hall there was a room called the 'Nur-
sury' in the 1601 inventory, and it is likely that this room, off which
was the small bedchamber of Bess's half-sister Jane Kniveton, was
a schoolroom where Starkey would have acted as tutor to little
William.

William Cavendish had taken Starkey into his household with the promise of a living and a parish, but the living which had been granted was then taken away. William had a deserved reputation for meanness and after many years had passed Starkey was still without his promised living; here was a man with a grievance. Starkey's exact age is unknown but it is likely he was a contemporary of Arbella and therefore around twenty-seven years old. Arbella with no companions of her own age and class enjoyed a kind of friendship with Starkey.

Pondering her fate Arbella slowly came to the conclusion that if there was to be no escape from Hardwick by the queen's means then she would have to arrange it for herself. Plans must have formed in her mind and been dismissed until an acceptable one presented itself, but this took time. In the meanwhile, for safety, she sent her jewels and money, which Bess had threatened to take from her, to Yorkshire; but whom she could trust so implicitly in Yorkshire Arbella never revealed.

In 1602 at Easter, which fell in the first week in April, Arbella told James Starkey that she had 'thought of all means she could to get from home, by reason she was hardly used in dispiteful and disgraceful words'. Here was a confidence and, unusually, Arbella was revealing herself to another, but she had a reason. In every respect Arbella had a right to better treatment from her grandmother, who no doubt had not observed that her granddaughter had become a grown woman and deserving of some respect, but unmarried women had few rights. Arbella confided in Starkey that she could not endure 'being bobbed and her nose played withall'. These were punishments given to disobedient children. At twenty-seven it is no wonder that Arbella found her existence insupportable. Starkey observed that her attitude 'seemed not feigned, for oftentimes, being at her books, she would break forth into tears'. Likely enough Starkey's opinion was correct, and Arbella was not putting on an act. She had no need to, for the tears were those of frustration.

Starkey's pity was won and he offered to deliver letters and messages for her when he went to London, for Starkey himself was planning to leave. He had found Hardwick and the meanness of William Cavendish unbearable. Earlier there had been some talk when Starkey had his initials put on the cover of a bible. He had intended 'Ja.S.', for James Starkey but there had been a mistake and it had come back with 'J.A.S.' The restricted company of the gentleman servants in the remoteness of Hardwick had taken this to mean James and Arbella, Stuart or Starkey. The smallness of the talk would have encouraged this sort of idle gossip which had disturbed Starkey, but plainly there was nothing in it at all.[3]

Some time that summer Starkey left Hardwick, but without any letters from Arbella. She had even bribed him with the offer of a living when she had one to dispose of – that was looking very far ahead, since for the present she had nothing to give – but Arbella did not use her messenger; either he backed out, or perhaps she had not reached her final decision. Arbella did not reach her conclusion until December when, without her grandmother's knowledge, she asked one of the household, John Dodderidge or, as he was sometimes called, John Good, to take a message to the Earl of Hertford's solicitor Kirton at Amesbury. Dodderidge took fright at this for fear of losing his job, but Arbella pressed him, saying that she would take care of that, and he reluctantly agreed to act as Arbella's messenger.

Dodderidge or Good, although not one of Bess's gentleman servants, was certainly more than just in the yeoman category. He was a trusted servant who had witnessed Bess's will in 1601 and, unusually, he had the use of a chamber at Hardwick, most likely in the old hall. Exactly what his position was cannot be discovered, but he had been awarded a lease on one of Bess's farms at Kirkby in Nottinghamshire – a sure sign of a trusted employee – and furthermore his son Francis was having his school fees paid by Bess. He was employed by Bess in helping to fit out the interior of Owlcotes for William Cavendish, and Bess's household accounts show him on three occasions as being associated with James Starkey. Dodderidge therefore was a valued and trusted servant to Bess and by going behind his mistress's back he had a great deal to lose. On the other hand he was aware that Bess was nearing the end of her life and therefore his future prosperity was in doubt. He would also have heard reports of the aging Queen Elizabeth, and may have reasoned from insufficient information that Arbella could offer him a future.

By agreeing to act as Arbella's messenger he may well have thought that he could, given luck, back two mistresses.

Dodderidge got cold feet when Arbella explained nearer Christmas that she wished him to take a message not to Amesbury but to the Earl of Hertford, proposing herself in marriage to Edward Seymour, son of Lord Beauchamp, and grandson of Hertford. As she had never even met the boy who was then aged only sixteen, this was in no way a love-match, but only a means for escape. Dodderidge, even in the remoteness of Derbyshire, realized the significance of this proposed betrothal. It was a proposal which would never have had the agreement of Elizabeth. Of all the families in England, the Seymours were the last with whom Arbella should have involved herself, for Hertford was the son of the disgraced Protector Somerset. He had married Catherine Grey without permission and if Elizabeth had accepted the legitimacy of the union then their son Lord Beauchamp would have had a claim to the succession. Young Edward Seymour, the eldest son of Beauchamp, if married to Arbella, would have provided heirs with a very strong claim to Elizabeth's throne. On the face of it Arbella's choice seemed an inexplicable madness which, had it gone further than that, would have doomed both parties to the Tower.

However, given Arbella's extraordinary outlook, encouraged by her upbringing and the events which had affected her young life, the choice is not so exceptional. Arbella had come to believe that she would survive any crisis brought about by a marriage proposal. In her solitary and introspective life she had become convinced that by means of this proposal to Edward Seymour she would actually escape from Hardwick and her grandmother's oppression. By proposing herself to Edward Seymour she would end the restraint she was enduring and before it came to the actual marriage Edward might die, and with his death would end any cause for punishment.

Of course Arbella was confident that she would survive and as a widow she would have independence at last. She may also have been encouraged to delay her plan by the state of the queen's health, for if Arbella delayed enough and got her timing right, Elizabeth would die off in the middle of the arrangements, which would alter almost every point to Arbella's advantage. Certainly she had no

ambition to succeed Elizabeth, as might be suggested in her proposal to marry Seymour. Never throughout her life did she display
the slightest inclination towards power; the lesson she had learned
from the constant struggles of Mary, Queen of Scots and her grandmother Margaret Lennox were examples enough to convince
Arbella.

However one looks at the marriage which Arbella was proposing
to the Seymours, one is inevitably drawn to the conclusion that
Arbella was eccentric and her reasoning faulty. She could have proposed herself to almost any other family in England without risk
of more than a passing rebuke and yet Arbella chose the most explo-
sive combination she could find, confident in her own survival –
had she felt otherwise she would never have made the proposal.

Since Dodderidge was being suborned behind Bess's back, the
arrangements for his journey had to be seemingly innocent. Dodderidge requested permission to visit relatives, and he asked one
of Bess's gentlewomen several times before his request was granted.
Meanwhile Arbella was arranging to use one of her uncle Henry's
horses. Henry Cavendish was always glad of an opportunity to
outwit his mother, but he did not arrive at Hardwick until Christmas
Eve and it was Christmas Day by the time Dodderidge had been
provided with one of Henry's horses. After dinner he was away
heading for London with what must have been an uneasy mind.

Dodderidge had memorized Arbella's message and her instructions. He was to go straight to Hertford's house at Tottenham and,
having gained the earl's attention, was to say to him:

It is best known to your Lordship what your desire was of a marriage
betwixt your Honour's grandchild, the Lord Beauchamp's eldest son and
my Lady Arbella. The matter has been thoroughly considered on by some
of her friends, for they think that your Lordship do not take an orderly
course in your proceedings, for it was thought fitter that my Lady
Arbella should have been first moved in the matter and that the parties
might have had sight the one of the other to see how they could like.

Thus Arbella excused herself for making the first move by referring
back to an earlier proposal said to have come from Kirton, with
Hertford's backing. If there ever had been such a proposal then it
was a very strange one and quite out of keeping with what is known

of Hertford, who throughout Elizabeth's reign kept a very low profile and was careful to do nothing to engage the queen's attention. Dodderidge was to continue his memorized message saying that, if the Earl of Hertford agreed, the young Edward Seymour was to be sent up to Hardwick with some old man, under the pretence of wishing to sell land – a bait which Arbella knew her grandmother would not ignore.

Having so gained their entrance into Hardwick the two were to prove their identity to Arbella by bringing with them a picture or handwriting of the Lady Jane Grey 'whose hand I know.... she sent her sister a book at her death ... or of the Lady Catherine or Queen Jane Seymour, or any of that family which we know they and none but they have.'[4] Arbella was harking back a long way down the echoing corridors of history and turning over her grandmother's early friendship with Jane Grey's mother Frances Brandon. There must have been letters still at Hardwick written by those so long dead. And although in the 1601 inventory there was no mention of any portrait of Jane Grey, there had been one at Chatsworth in 1566 and in 1789 John Byng in his Torrington Diaries noted one.

Arbella must have been confident that this direct approach would receive Hertford's serious attention. Again had she thought further she would have known that since marriage was very much a business contract with each side bringing an advantage to the other, Hertford would have given her proposal no consideration on that ground alone. Arbella had no rich estates to offer; all she had was her embarrassing royal blood which to the Seymours would have been a liability, since they had trouble enough with their own illegitimate royal blood.

So Dodderidge rode on to London with Arbella's message in his head, taking five days over the trip to arrive at the Hertford house at Tottenham at three in the afternoon on 30 December. He asked for Gilbert Prynne, the gentleman steward and head of the earl's establishment. This in itself was suspicious, for yeoman servants commonly made their business known to the porter at the gate. Dodderidge had refused to do this and furthermore once he met Prynne would say nothing except to the earl himself. These double suspicions made Hertford receive Dodderidge with Prynne and another of his gentleman servants, Edward Daniel, as witnesses in his dining chamber; he may have been dining or have just finished. Arbella's messenger delivered the memorized details kneeling in front of the earl.

As the words ran on, filling the ears of the suspicious listeners, Hertford 'mightily distasting and disliking, grew impatient' and interrupted Dodderidge with 'many bitter reprehensions'. The ominous words 'Thou art prepared for punishment' must have terrified poor Dodderidge. The message was taken down in writing and Arbella's courier was then locked up while the significance of his eruption into the New Year celebrations of the earl's household was considered. Dodderidge was questioned again that evening and finally locked away with one of the earl's servants to pass a very sleepless night.

After more questioning the next morning – questions sharpened with threats to try to draw out any hidden truths – Dodderidge was sent under guard to secretary Cecil at Court, with all the confessions he had made in the previous hours. Fearfully Dodderidge must have gone through the London streets, still on Henry Cavendish's horse, to meet what fate he could not know. With him too went a letter he had written to Arbella: 'My reception here is contrary to all expectation.' But she never received it, and while on that first day of the New Year Dodderidge was being questioned yet again at Court and finally being put in the Gatehouse Jail, Arbella was dutifully obeying her grandmother, expecting all the time to see an old man accompanied by a youth arrive shortly at the gates of Hardwick, who would lead her on the way to freedom.[5]

12

SOMEWHAT TROUBLED

In proposing herself to one of the Seymour family, Arbella was displaying an eccentric attraction to that family, prompted by arcane memory. Bess herself had been unfortunately involved with an earlier Seymour marriage which had apparently been the reason for her spending seven months in the Tower in 1561. Arbella must have heard the story from her grandmother more than once and the telling of it had given in Arbella's mind some romantic attachment which overruled common sense.

Fifteen years before Arbella was born Edward Seymour, Earl of Hertford – to one of whose grandsons Arbella was offering herself in marriage – had fallen in love with Catherine Grey, sister of the tragic Jane Grey and daughter of Bess's great friend Frances Brandon. Catherine, like Arbella, was descended from Henry VII, and Edward from Edward III through his mother, therefore marriage without the queen's approval was out of the question. Her approval was unlikely, since any heirs of the union would have strong claims to Elizabeth's succession through the double transfusion of royal blood and so create problems after Elizabeth's death. The reasons against the marriage between Catherine and Edward Seymour had been identical to those now barring Arbella's marriage to Edward's grandson and, although some forty-three years separated the two events, Elizabeth's opposition would have been just as strong. Arbella was apparently deliberately following the same pattern.

Both Catherine and Edward had been warned of the consequences of marrying and yet in the autumn of 1560, when the queen was away from the Court at Westminster hunting at Eltham, they married secretly at Hertford House. A few weeks later Edward went to France leaving his bride at Court and pregnant. Finally, unable to keep her secret any longer – it had become obvious to some – Catherine blurted out the frantic truth to her mother's old friend Bess, who 'fell into a great weeping' and was no help at all.

Inevitably the secret came out. Catherine was put into the Tower and Edward was summoned from France; he was arrested when he landed at Dover. Bess also went into the Tower for having taken no part whatsoever. Yet when she was released seven months later, a debt of £5,000 owing to the Crown was reduced to £1,000; Bess may have felt that the money was well earned. But Catherine and Edward were not released. Inside the Tower Catherine had her baby, Edward Seymour, and it was to his son that Arbella was proposing herself. The Privy Council deliberated at length and at last declared the marriage illegal and Edward guilty of seducing a royal virgin – they had been unable to find the priest who performed the marriage and the only other witness, Edward's sister, Jane Seymour had died. The culprits were sentenced to life-imprisonment.

At first the young lovers had a certain amount of freedom within the Tower walls and Catherine replied to the council's verdict by having another son born to her in prison; an error which did their cause no good. Eventually, some eight years after the marriage, Catherine died in captivity and Edward, no longer a danger to Elizabeth, was released. Thereafter he spent his lifetime proving the legitimacy of his two sons by Catherine, a pastime which drove his second wife to hysterics. Catherine had never grasped the significance of her Tudor descent. Arbella must have understood this point, but chose to ignore it with grand eccentricity.[1]

Therefore in 1603 Arbella must have been supremely confident that her schemes would work and yet, apart from the likelihood of Hertford refusing to consider her proposal, there were other serious weaknesses to her plot. It was unlikely that a young man, inexperienced as he would have been, could have hoodwinked Bess with the cock-and-bull story of having land for sale. Also there is the small mystery of a statement by Arbella that Kirton had married a daughter of Sir William Cavendish by an earlier marriage. Sir William had eight children before he married Bess and of those only two survived, Catherine who had married Thomas Brooke, and Anne who had married Sir Henry Bainton. Neither had married

Kirton. Arbella's plot for escape was so shot through with faults that even if one part had gone to plan it would have been brought down by the failure of another part. But Arbella was confident as she awaited Dodderidge's advent to Hardwick. It was not of course Dodderidge who returned.

Sir Henry Bronker, queen's commissioner, was on his way to Hardwick by 3 January. Robert Cecil, efficient in his service to the queen, had sent a man ideally suited to this difficult task requiring infinite tact. Bronker had been personally briefed by the queen, and his mission was to find out exactly what had been going on at Hardwick: whether Arbella's proposed betrothal was part of some deep Catholic plot to overthrow Elizabeth, or just simply a hare-brained scheme cooked up by Arbella without her grandmother's knowledge. It would have been a simple matter to have summoned Arbella to London for close questioning, but it is a credit to the understanding between Bess and the queen that neither Cecil nor Elizabeth suspected nor believed in Bess's involvement. The trust between the queen and her illustrious subject was complete.

Bronker arrived at Hardwick on 7 January. His later report to the queen told her, 'On Friday I came to Hardwick and found the house without any strange company.' He was taken up the long, dramatic flight of stairs leading to the second floor and the great state apartments. There he was received in the long gallery by Bess, 'where she was walking with the La: Arbella and William Cavendish'. Bronker's reception by the three must have been one of curiosity mixed with apprehension. The purpose of this important messenger from the queen was unknown to any of them, although Arbella may have had an awful feeling that something, somewhere had not gone right. Bronker played down the significance of his mission by telling Bess that the queen's business had brought him to the area and that he had been ordered to call at Hardwick to give Elizabeth's gracious favour to her old friend. This white lie had the effect of easing Bess's apprehension and with what must have been considerable relief the seventy-five-year-old countess went down on her knees, or attempted to until Bronker stopped her; then, 'drawing her on with compliments towards the further end of the gallery to free her from the young lady', he gave Bess a letter from the queen.

Whatever was in the letter did not give much comfort, neither did it explain the purpose of Bronker's visit. He noted Bess's 'change of countenance' in reading the queen's letter. Her apprehension and bafflement must have returned although she may have guessed that since Bronker's visit was not concerned with her business then it must involve Arbella; that thought would have increased her apprehension. Bess was to be kept in ignorance of Bronker's purpose until the following day. Finally he asked Bess if he might talk to Arbella alone, and Bess would then have had a dawning realization that Arbella was in deep trouble. At this she protested her innocence – but innocence of what she could not know.

Arbella was taken by Bronker to the other end of the gallery far out of earshot of Bess and William. By way of small talk and to draw out Arbella, Bronker told her of the queen's goodwill and of her thanks for that New Year's gift; and that she would like to hear how she was. To give Arbella a chance to explain herself he told her that the queen would be pleased to consider any need if Arbella would tell him what it was. Quite what Arbella's feelings were at this point does not need much description; she must have been aware that things had gone very wrong indeed. If, as Bess and the queen came to believe, Arbella had been scheming outrageously in order to bring the queen's attention to herself and hopefully thereby to secure her removal from Hardwick, then with Bronker's arrival and his questions she would have revealed her plans. As Arbella did not follow this simple course the conclusion must be that her proposal to Edward Seymour was intended and that the discovery of her schemes by the queen was not part of her plan; Bronker's questioning of Arbella was not something she had expected.

Arbella was given yet another chance to tell Bronker what she knew but she failed to grasp it although, as Bronker observed, 'it seemed by the coming and going of her colour that she was somewhat troubled.' Even when asked if she had been in touch with the Earl of Hertford, Arbella denied that she had. At this point, having told one lie, she had to continue with her denials and even when Bronker produced Dodderidge's confession and showed it to her Arbella's denials continued. She was plainly terrified out of her wits and did not really know what she was saying. Eventually under

Bronker's patient questioning Arbella cracked, but seeing that he would get no sense out of her that day Bronker told her to write down her confession that night and let him have it next morning.

The confession which Arbella gave him next morning was, as Bronker said, 'confused, obscure and in truth ridiculous'. The night of reflection had been no help to Arbella. Possibly she had not slept at all and Bess had been pressing her to know what all the trouble was about. Her grandmother could be terrifying when angry or provoked, but Arbella told Bess nothing, although she did reveal something of her concern to her uncle William. Seeing that no sense could be got out of Arbella, Bronker wrote out what he knew and got her to sign the paper; with that he had to be content. Before Bronker left on the Saturday he gave Bess a full report. He explained to Cecil that he had to do this, as William would have told her anyway. So leaving behind him two women so different in outlook and ambition, both of whom wished desperately to be parted from the other, Bronker rode away. The scenes and recriminations would have started as soon as he was down the hill of Hardwick and out of sight.[2]

Bronker's return to London was not so speedy as his journey north. He was delayed at Northampton by a nasty fall which shook him so much that he rested to recover, and meanwhile sent a full report to the queen with a copy to Cecil. In Bronker's opinion there was little in the matter but foolishness on Arbella's part, no deep plotting, no Catholic involvement and no harm intended to the queen. He left out any real explanation of Arbella's motives – possibly he never understood what was driving her to these bizarre actions. An undated letter from Arbella, addressed to the queen, was possibly brought back with Bronker and sent with his report. In it Arbella admitted all that she was accused of, probably at Bronker's dictation, and apologized.

Bronker eventually limped into London on 13 January and wrote to Cecil from his house in Lambeth Marsh. 'I came here this morning but very secretly, as you advised me.' Meanwhile Cecil's investigations were being made with thoroughness. David Owen of Penymeath near Caernarvon, who was mentioned by Dodderidge in his confession as having been involved in an earlier marriage proposal between Arbella and Hertford's grandson, was examined by the sheriff. Owen claimed that the idea had originated not with Bess but with Hugh Owen, brother-in-law of the Earl of Northumberland, and that he himself had had nothing to do with it at all. David Owen had been a gentleman servant in Bess's household for some twenty years and by 1601 had retired to a quiet life in Anglesey. He had witnessed Elizabeth Lennox's will in 1581 and his son Richard had gone to Hardwick as Arbella's page in 1601. One is left to wonder what this earlier proposal of marriage was about if the inspiration had come from neither Bess nor Hertford.[3]

At Hardwick Bronker's visit had provoked a drama which brewed up into a crisis after he left. Arbella, now that she had confessed her stupidity, would not have known what her fate might be; she knew almost nothing about what had taken place in London. All she could have known was that Dodderidge had made a confession, but how Dodderidge was taken and how his confession was made was something she did not know. No doubt Arbella let her mind run through all the awful possibilities: Hertford could have been arrested, Dodderidge imprisoned; even then she might be the subject of a charge of treason for attempting a betrothal without the queen's approval. The worst prospects were frankly appalling. Her greatest concern would have been for her grandmother's anger. Bess too knew the consequence of treason in connection with unpermitted royal marriages – she had spent seven months in the Tower. Never one to take kindly to her dependants planning their own course of action opposed to hers, she would not have viewed Arbella's plotting in any kindly way at all, particularly as it jeopardized her own relationship with the queen. Bess had written to Elizabeth the day after Bronker had left Hardwick, exonerating herself from all knowledge of Arbella's folly and asking the queen to take her ungrateful granddaughter off her hands, a proposal which Arbella would have supported.

Exactly what went on at Hardwick during those days and nights was never completely told. Bess, who gave complete allegiance to the queen in all things, was at loggerheads with Arbella who, for what may have been the first time, was asserting herself – but in a direction opposed to Bess's creed. Arbella had secretly and deliberately gone against the queen's wishes; she was no longer content to await the queen's selection of a husband and had taken matters into her own hands. From Bess's point of view such behaviour in her grandchild would have been unforgivable. But, if Bess had reflected, she would have seen that her granddaughter's action was not so very far removed from her own, when she married off her daughter Elizabeth to Charles Stuart without the queen's permission, although the motives were utterly different. The two women, so very different in outlook and temperament, had clashed head on in their basic beliefs. In seeking to get Arbella off her hands Bess was, as always, being a realist, since there was now no chance of their community.

On 15 January Arbella wrote a letter to John Hacker of East Bridgford in Nottinghamshire. Hacker was a man who could be classed as one of Bess's gentleman servants; although not in attendance on his mistress he was often called upon to help over legal matters and Bess's business in his own county. It was very unlikely that he would have helped Arbella. She asked Hacker to contact her aunt Mary Talbot and request her to come 'with the like speed she would do if my lady grandmother were in extremity'. Arbella's lady-in-waiting Bridget Shirland managed to get out of Hardwick; she too had written to Hacker from the house of Hercules Clay, another of Bess's loyal gentleman servants, at Sutton-in-Ashfield, about six miles from Hardwick.

Hacker never received either of these letters, which is strange because, although it would have been an easy matter to intercept Arbella's letters at Hardwick, was Bess so powerful that her net spread so far? Someone else was intercepting Bridget's letters to him and not only that, but making false non-committal answers. In addition a letter that Bridget wrote to Edward Frank and two to Mr Bradshaw were intercepted and prompted forged replies. She had asked Frank, the constable of Heath, a village near Hardwick, to bring letters to Sutton which he had lately brought from London and also for news of the goings-on at Hardwick. In one of her letters to Bradshaw Bridget had enclosed a letter for Bronker and told Bradshaw to take it with all speed to London.

The three to whom Arbella and Bridget were appealing for help

were the least likely to involve themselves in the troublesome affair
as they were loyal servants of Bess. However in each case the 'messenger that was to have carried the ... letter returned with a feigned
answer', and the feigned answers were in the handwriting of Bess's
steward Timothy Pusey. Bridget's letters all went to Cecil. Bess had
some very loyal servants who had to live with Bess after Arbella
had gone and they knew very well on which side their bread was
buttered.

The answer to Bess's plea to be relieved of the trouble and anxiety
of keeping charge of her grandchild eventually arrived from Cecil
and the Vice-Chamberlain Sir John Stanhope, writing on the
queen's behalf. Arbella was to be left at Hardwick, but in order to
gain some respite Bess was to appoint 'some discrete gentlewoman to
be in her company and some honest gentlemen to attend her among
the rest'. This was an unrealistic solution, as Bess would have recognized. The ministers went on to say that the queen was pleased with
the way she had dealt with Arbella and content that Bess herself
was completely innocent of any involvement. The letter concluded
that Arbella had fallen under the influence of some 'base companions', the chief of whom was Dodderidge. The reply offered no
solution to the problem at Hardwick and it gave comfort to neither
Bess nor Arbella. The two women were now acting against each
other, for Arbella had forfeited her grandmother's sympathy. Both
shared an equal determination to thwart the other, Bess relying on
realistic reasoning, and Arbella on haphazard instinct dictated by
her strange philosophy and belief in her proven ability to emerge
from a situation unscathed. The battle was only beginning.[4]

13

VAPOURS ON HER BRAIN

Arbella responded to Cecil and Stanhope with apparent submission. In an undated draft letter to the queen she thanked her, apologized for causing trouble and accepted the suggestion that she had concocted the whole plan to draw attention to her plight. But this explanation which the Court had supplied placed Bess in something of a dilemma. She must have known what her granddaughter's true intention had been – to marry without the queen's permission – and that it was treasonable. However much Bess disagreed with some of her family she never wished treason on them; she even spared Henry Cavendish that fate. And yet by accepting the official explanation from Cecil and Stanhope she would remain the guardian of her rebellious granddaughter. By now seventy-six Bess was undoubtedly feeling the strain of the recent untoward events, hence her request to be relieved of Arbella's keeping. As far as the queen was concerned an innocent interpretation had been found, the culprit had apologized and that was the end of the matter. This was not to be. Arbella, like her grandmother, did not give up easily; it was only the end of the first round.

Arbella opened round two at the end of January 1603. She had been regaling her grandmother with some incredible story of a true lover who was not Hartford's grandson. Quite rightly Bess got Arbella to put the whole story down in a letter to be sent to Stanhope and Cecil. What Arbella wrote was six long pages of rambling obscurity. In the opening paragraphs she promised to tell the true reason for her proposal to Hertford and characteristically went on to do nothing of the sort. She had a lover, but not Hertford's grandson; it was one whose 'credit ... [was], as he right well deserves, great with her Majesty'. If the letter had not been so long, it might have been ingenious. What Arbella suggested was that if she were permitted to visit the Privy Council in London, then and only then would she reveal who was this paragon standing so high in the queen's estimation, and suitable in every way. On and on rambled the letter until the message all but got lost in the undue repetition. It was a resourceful plan to escape from Hardwick.

No doubt Bess brooded over the letter. But, although Arbella's character was so different from her own, we can be certain that Bess, having seen to her granddaughter's upbringing for over sixteen years, knew very well what was behind all the flowery phrases used to explain an imaginary lover. With this letter to Cecil and Stanhope went another from Bess dated 2 February. Still keeping up the pretence that Arbella had been led astray by others she wrote, 'she hath set down in her own hand this declaration so fraught with vanity. Such as it is I have sent it hereinclosed, but I could not by any possible means prevail with her to set down the matter plainly, as I desired she would in a few lines. These strange courses are wonderful to me.' And so after this opening shot of round two Arbella waited at Hardwick for the reply to come from the queen, a reply which she hoped would request her presence in London, and escape from Hardwick.

Both Arbella and her grandmother were united in the desire to be parted. After Arbella had confessed to the queen she wrote to Cecil and Stanhope on 6 February. This time her letter showed a realism which was unusual for Arbella. Bess may have persuaded her granddaughter of the dangers of becoming involved in consultations with the Privy Council; Arbella might confess to some folly which would result in her being locked away in the Tower. This second letter asked that Bronker should be sent to Hardwick when Arbella would give an explanation to him of who her secret lover was. Both Arbella and Bess had found Bronker sympathetic and if Arbella wanted to see Bronker then that would suit Bess's purpose; she herself would at the same time be able to explain the necessity of removing Arbella from Hardwick. Bess had a flair for getting her antagonists to combine interests with her – she had often employed this tactic in her distressing disagreements with Shrewsbury.

Arbella has been accused of becoming hysterical during these weeks of tribulation. Possibly she was; her behaviour was certainly eccentric. As she told Cecil and Stanhope in the letter dated 6 February, she was twenty-seven years old, 'yet it be not her highness's pleasure to allow me that liberty ... which many infants have to choose their own guardians, as I desire to do my place of abode.' But there was more than that. Arbella was indeed twenty-seven and during her life she had never had any serious romantic attachment of depth, as far as is known; she was forced to lead the life of a nun, and a nun without the soothing balm of a conscience dedicated to emotional spiritualism. For the sake of politics, the queen had compelled Arbella to an existence which her whole body and mind rebelled against and rejected.[1]

At about the time when Arbella was so busy writing, the scene of the drama switched to London in an unexpected manner: James Starkey, Arbella's erstwhile helper, hanged himself. He left a confession of his earlier involvement and asked Arbella's forgiveness. He also asked God's forgiveness for taking his own life and pleaded his own innocence in Arbella's schemes. Starkey had been mentioned in Dodderidge's confession made on 2 January and he may have been pulled in for questioning; certainly something was troubling his mind. The suicide was sufficiently interesting to be noted by de Beaumont, the French ambassador, in a letter to Henri IV, and also by the Venetian secretary in London when writing to the Doge and Senate (although he sent a very garbled account, it was in the main correct). With an eye to the succession after Elizabeth this Venetian reported that Arbella was

now a young lady of twenty-eight years of age, of great beauty and remarkable qualities, being gifted with many accomplishments, among them the knowledge of Latin, French, Spanish and Italian, besides her native English. She has very exalted ideas, having been brought up in the belief that she would succeed to the crown. She has always lived in poverty, far from London, in the charge of a Puritan governer and governess.

He stated that Starkey's body was found in Arbella's own house, which was not correct.

By now Arbella's actions were becoming irrational. On 16

February she wrote to Edward Talbot, who was at the time with his father-in-law Lord Ogle at Bothal in Northumberland. To be certain that Edward got the letter she had previously sent a copy to her aunt Grace, wife of her ally Henry Cavendish, asking that it be forwarded to Edward. Arbella's letter told Edward that 'councillors are acquainted with both our bad hands.' She was hinting that Edward was implicated in her plotting, but this was not possible, for of all the Talbot sons Gilbert was the only one to allow himself to become involved with Bess and her family; Edward had always kept well out of the family trouble-spots. He must have been surprised to receive Arbella's letter, particularly as she asked him to make the long journey from Northumberland to London to deliver a message to the queen. Irrationally Arbella never told him what the message was. Edward forwarded both letters to Cecil who must have been as mystified as their recipient had been.

Then Arbella went on hunger strike. She made a vow to neither eat nor drink at Hardwick until she heard from the queen. By now it was 15 February, only fifteen days since she had written asking to see Bronker again, and no reply had been received. However the delay was normal, as a messenger would take three days to reach London. In expecting to receive such a speedy reply Arbella was being unrealistic but not so in forcing the pace by her refusal to eat; that at least would have got her out of Hardwick. Bess had written to Cecil telling him of the latest turn in events: 'Arbella hath a doctor of physic with her for a fortnight together, and enforced to take much physic this unseasonable time, but finds little ease.' Then she added the penetrating comment, 'I see her mind is the cause of all.' She finished her letter with a postscript,

Arbell is so wilfully bent that she hath made a vow not to eat or drink in this house at Hardwick, or where I am, till she may hear from her Majesty, so that for the preservation of her life I am enforced to suffer her to go to Oldcotes two miles from here. I am wearied of my life.... And I earnestly pray you to send Sir Henry Bronker hither.

Oldcotes was William's house of Owlcotes. On the same day that Bess was writing that letter Cecil wrote from the Court at Richmond telling her that Bronker was on his way.

Sir Henry Bronker made a more leisurely return to Hardwick than his first hurried journey. He arrived with a list of thirty-three questions, no doubt devised by the Privy Council, and Arbella was brought back from Owlcotes on 27 February, a long interval from when Cecil had told Bess that Bronker was on his way. Bronker's list, with Arbella's answers was dated 2 March. Her replies to these serious questions verge on the farcical, for she revealed that her lover who was so dear to her and so high in the queen's estimation was none other than the already married James of Scotland. If Bronker made a written report on this extraordinary visit, then it has not survived, but it is more likely he made a personal report to Cecil.

He left Hardwick the following day, 3 March, taking with him a letter from Bess for Cecil and Stanhope, enclosing another from Arbella written when Bronker was still at Hardwick. The letter was almost as pointless as her answers had been, and Cecil's comment written across the back of one of the pages plainly shows that he was as confounded as anyone else who reads them today: 'I think that she hath some vapours on her brain.' Bess's note to Cecil contained the heartfelt complaint, 'A few more weeks as I have suffered of late will make an end of me.' Whatever Cecil's private thoughts and comments were, it was Bess who was left to cope with the peculiar actions of her granddaughter.[2]

After Bronker's departure Arbella bombarded him with more letters; two dated 4 March were taken to London by Mr Chaworth, one of Bess's gentlemen, a third on 6 March was followed by yet another on the following day. Arbella wrote nothing on 8 March but made up for this with an eighteen-page letter on the 9 March. All of these were forwarded by Bronker to Cecil, whose answer to Bess classified Arbella's letters as being in a 'very strange style'. The letters were a mass of well-written and disordered phrases. Of all the letters she ever wrote, those which she sent to Bronker at the height of her distress and frustration contain the most revealing statements about herself. Her dislike of men was displayed in one of her letters of the 4 March: 'I told you there was no trust in man', and again in her letter dated 7 March: 'for all men are liars. There is no trust in man, whose breath is still in his nostrils.' But the most revealing comment of all was in her long discourse of 9 March: 'they are dead whom I loved.'[3]

Arbella's appeals to Bronker, to Cecil and Stanhope for her freedom were now falling on deaf ears; these men had a more serious matter on their hands. The queen, whose health had always been good, had caught a chill early in February and by the end of the month she had pneumonia – it was the beginning of her end. Cecil and Stanhope would not trouble their queen overmuch with the trivial matter of Arbella's freedom; it could wait until the queen recovered or, if not, then for her successor. By 18 March Elizabeth was 'already in a manner insensible, not speaking sometimes for two or three hours, and within the last two days for about four-and-twenty holding her finger continually in her mouth with her eyes open and fixed to the ground'. It was plain to all who saw the queen that she was dying.

It is likely that news of the queen's last illness had reached Hardwick. She had been unwell when Bronker left London for his second visit on 2 March, but not seriously so. He would have given this news to Bess and for subsequent reports she would have been informed by letters brought from London by what seems to have been an almost constant stream of messengers. Arbella was oblivious to the queen's state of health; her personal dramas were absorbing all her energies.

In an overlong letter of 4 March to Bronker, Arbella described something of the close surveillance under which she was kept and the conditions at Hardwick.

... and though my ears were battered on one side with a contemned, and in truth contemptible storm of threatenings with which my lady my grandmother thought to have won my resolved heart ... [I] went my way without so much as looking behind me.... And vowing I would never answer to those names by which I was called and recalled and cried out upon ... I took my way down with heavy heart, and, being followed [by Bess and others] ... we had another skirmish, where you and I sat scribbling till twelve of the clock at night. But I finding myself scarce able to stand on my feet, what for my side and what for my head, yet with commanding voice, [I] called a troop of such Viragoes [her waiting ladies] as Virgil's Camilla [did] that stood at the receipt in the next chamber, and, never entreating them to give or take blows for my sake, was content to send you the first news of this conflict.

In her very long letter of the 9 March Arbella reveals a keen remembrance of Essex, the day being, as she points out, Ash Wednesday, the anniversary of his execution. The attachment may have been only in her imagination; nevertheless she had been banished from Court in 1588 and when she mentions the disgrace in this same letter her comment is without rancour. Perhaps she may have felt her banishment was justified.

While Arbella was despatching her letters in volleys she was also making another plan for escape. She was opening round three. Secretly she had been in touch with her uncle Henry Cavendish, Bess's 'bad son'. He was the most likely to be willing or able to help Arbella. Although out of favour with his mother Henry was still received at Hardwick; even his illegitimate son and heir Henry had been graciously received by his grandmother. It is likely that Arbella was able to tell her uncle of her wish to escape, during one of his visits rather than by an incriminating letter; somehow a plan was made.

The day after she had written her longest letter to Bronker, Arbella (in Bess's own words) 'about 12 of the clock came forth of her chamber, went towards the gates, as she said, intending to walk, but being pursuaded it was dinner time did stay'. Unknown to Bess the first part of the escape plan had failed. Had Arbella walked through the gates as planned she would still not have escaped, for Henry and his helper, a Catholic, Stapleton, had not done their reconnoitring properly. The two, with several servants, had gone to Ault Hucknall, the nearest village to Hardwick, at ten o'clock that morning, intending to keep watch on the gates of Hardwick from the tower of the church, but the tower was locked and they had been unable to get the key. After this set-back, and while they were at the vicar's house, a message arrived from Arbella by her page Richard Owen and 'old Freake', her embroiderer. This may have been sent by Arbella after she had been unable to walk out of the garden, for one of the men was heard to say, 'She cannot come out this day.' There were, claimed a witness, 'a hundred horsemen' dispersed in groups about the village. This may be a countryman's exaggeration, but Bess estimated forty, still a formidable number, and one horse was provided with a pillion hidden beneath a cloak.

With the failure of the plan Henry and his men did not give up; the Cavendish family seemed to have this streak of determination so evident in Bess. Again in Bess's words, 'about two of the clock in the afternoon, there came to my gates my son Henry and one Stapleton.' Henry Cavendish in wishing to embarrass his mother was sailing very close to the wind of treason, for Stapleton was known to be a Catholic. It was one thing for Henry to annoy his mother and aid his beleaguered niece, but to involve himself with Stapleton over such a matter was being very foolish indeed. Bess allowed only Henry and his man to pass through the porter's gates: 'I would not suffer Stapleton to come within my gates, for I have disliked him of long for many respects; it is about eight years since I saw him.' Although Bess was a very old lady there was nothing wrong with her memory. It was in October 1594 that Stapleton had been at Hardwick for two nights when Bess had last seen him, and she had not forgotten.

Henry was permitted to see Arbella, probably in Bess's withdrawing room. They had spoken scarcely a dozen words together before they both went downstairs, out of the main hall door, across the forecourt garden to the gate, where the porter loyally refused to let them pass. Bess's servants were in a difficult position and must have had her firm instructions. Probably Arbella was indignant. Messages passed between the lodge and Bess in the main house, but it was to no avail. As Bess said later, 'I did not think it good she should speak with Stapleton, and wished her to forbear it, for I thought Stapleton no fit man for her to converse withal.' Arbella was only permitted to talk to Stapleton through the closed doors of the gatehouse and eventually Henry and Stapleton had to withdraw, leaving Arbella within the four walls of Hardwick and still a captive of her grandmother. At the end of round three the formidable old countess had defeated them all.

Bess wrote to Bronker that very night giving a true report of the day's events before any rumours could reach London. She played down Stapleton's part since she had no wish to have her son Henry accused of treason. It had been a particularly exhausting day for the seventy-six-year-old countess and she was writing her letter 'very late this Thursday night', wearied by her determined granddaughter.[4] And so closed round three in the battle of wills and wits between the two unyielding women. Arbella had lost every round so far, but it was obvious that her grandmother could not forestall Arbella for much longer. That day's events, dominated by Bess, had taken its toll of her strength; Arbella had youth on her side.

14

DESIROUS TO FREE OUR COUSIN

Bronker passed Bess's letter, outlining Arbella's latest escapade, to Cecil, who must have found Arbella's dramatics at Hardwick unnecessary to a degree. The Secretary of State had a lot on his mind as the queen was much worse. The end was approaching gradually. From her position on the floor, supported by cushions, she would allow no doctors near her, nor would she take the medicines offered, preferring her own remedy of broth which had proved itself so efficacious in past disorders. The French ambassador de Beaumont saw her about the time that Cecil would have received Bess's latest report and she was then in no state to concern herself about Arbella, 'so full of chagrin and weary of life'. It is unlikely that they bothered the dying queen with the problem of Arbella. Some nine days later, on 21 March, they finally persuaded the queen to undress and go to bed. There she felt better and sent for more broth.

The council, in the absence of any royal directive, replied cautiously to Bess's letter: 'We are very sorry to find by the strange style of the Lady Arbella's letters that she hath her thoughts no better quieted', and, since it was unlikely that the queen's wishes would be known in the matter, they were unable to authorize Arbella's removal from Hardwick as Bess and Arbella were repeatedly requesting. Temporizing, they suggested that Bess should 'deal with her as mildly with words as you can' and that William Cavendish should take charge of his niece. This was as far as they dared go until the queen's death provided a successor prepared to make a decision. Once more Bronker was sent on the long and familiar journey from London, arriving at Hardwick on 17 March. The council, unaware exactly what the commissioner might find in Derbyshire, had taken a wise precaution of issuing a warrant on 15

Arbella in 1577 at the age of twenty-three
months. The portrait may have been painted
to forward her claim to the Earldom of
Lennox; it is not thought to be a good
likeness.

Margaret, Countess of Lennox, Arbella's paternal grandmother. A detail from her tomb in Westminster Abbey.

COUNTESS OF SHROESBURY

Bess of Hardwick, Countess of Shrewsbury, Arbella's maternal grandmother.

Mary Queen of Scots and
Henry Stuart, Lord Darnley,
her second husband.

Charles Stuart, Henry
Stuart's younger brother and
Arbella's father.

Hardwick Hall where Arbella lived with her
grandmother, Bess of Hardwick.

Sheffield Manor at the end of the eighteenth
century. This was one of the Talbot properties
where Mary Queen of Scots was kept a prisoner
and where Arbella is known to have stayed.

Arbella (styled as the
Countess of Lennox
in 1589 at the age of
thirteen and a half.

ARBELLA STVARTA
COMITISS[...]
[...]TATIS SVÆ 13 ET
ANNO DNI 589

My good Lord. I humbly thanck your Lo:p that it will please you amongst your great affaires to remember my suites to his Ma:ty. For the alteration of my pension I hope I shall shortly haue the meanes to aquaint your Lo:p with it my selfe. If I should name two thousand poundes for my present occasions it would not exceede my necessity, but I dare not presume to craue any certein sume, but referre my selfe wholly to his Ma:ts consideration, and assure my selfe I shall finde your Lo:p my honorable good frend, both in procuring it as soone, and makeing the sume as great as may be. So with humble thanckes to your Lo:p for your continuall fauours, I recomend your Lo:p to the protection of the Almighty. From Sheene the 23. of June. 1603

Your Lo:ps poore frend

Arbella Stuart /

A drawing of a river nymph by Inigo Jones for the masque *Tethys' Festival* in which Arbella took the part of the Nymph of Trent.

The plaster overmantel in the 'Lawn Room' at Hardwick Hall, which is most likely to have been Arbella's chamber. Arbella's arms are at the top right.

One of Arbella's many letters to Cecil asking for a better pension. This one, in her best writing, was written from Sheen, the home of the Marchioness of Northampton, before Arbella was allowed by James to return to Court.

ABOVE LEFT King
James I, by John de
Critz the Elder.

ABOVE RIGHT Anne of
Denmark, wife of
James I, attributed to
William Larkin.

William Seymour, who
married Arbella in
1610, from an original
portrait at Badminton
House.

March instructing all 'deputy lieutenants, sheriffs, mayors, bailiffs, constables and headboroughs, and all others of her Majesty's officers' to assist Bronker if called upon; while their instructions to Bronker included a warrant to bring Henry Cavendish in for questioning. These were measures which might have been necessary in the event of the queen's death bringing about riots and rebellion of disputed succession.

Rather than sending for Henry by the intimidating warrant, Bronker first wrote him a friendly letter asking him over to Hardwick for questioning and afterwards ordering him to attend the council in London for further questioning, giving a generous seven days to pack his bags and settle his business before leaving. Bronker was under no illusions about Henry. Having given the week's grace he reported, 'I have an eye upon Mr Cavendishe, that if he may exceed his appointed time, he may know the force of your Lordship's commands.'[1] With Henry safely out of the way, Arbella's only helper was removed from the stage. Stapleton had already run for it and vanished into London. On this occasion Bronker kept his distance with Arbella, since his previous attempts to get her co-operation had been useless.

He reported back to the council that her wilfulness was much greater than on his previous visits and supposed that this arose out of Arbella's hope for the queen's death. He suspected that she had planned to take ship from Hull to Scotland after her escape. Sensibly Bronker preferred to obtain more reliable information than Arbella was prepared to give him and spent most of his time interviewing other witnesses, refusing Arbella's suggestion that she should be present at the examinations. His conclusion was, as before, that there had been no great political matter involved and that it was just another attempt on Arbella's part to escape from Hardwick. Her grandmother was worn out with Arbella's dramas and he considered it inadvisable that they should continue together under the same roof. The state of Bess's health precluded William Cavendish from taking charge of Arbella, as Bronker suggested, 'Mr William Cavendish being but a weak man for such a purpose, and of little love and respect here'. Although he thought it inadvisable to leave Arbella at Hardwick for longer than two or three days more, he was at a loss to know where she could be sent. There was no one in the area responsible enough to supervise her.

Bronker continued his investigations and was still at Hardwick on 25 March. He was concerned that his warrant to hold Arbella at Hardwick would expire should the queen die, and asked Cecil if he had the authority to detain Arbella in that event. Obviously Cecil had kept Bronker informed of the queen's health. Since he had left the Court at Richmond more than ten days before, the queen had gone from bad to worse and an atmosphere of frantic nightmare had fallen over the Court. Two of the ladies had found a card, the Queen of Hearts, fastened to the bottom of a chair with an iron nail through the forehead. Another, after leaving the queen's chamber, had met a shadowy form in the familiar royal guise three or four chambers off. The air at Court was thick with fear and portent.

But when Bronker was writing his letter to Cecil the queen was already dead. She had died in the early morning of the previous day. There were no riots or rebellions in Derbyshire nor anywhere else in England; Cecil had made sure of a peaceful succession. For some time he had been exchanging secret letters with James in Scotland and the understanding was there. Perhaps Elizabeth knew of these secrets and typically had said nothing, but there was really no alternative successor worth consideration. The council spread a report that Elizabeth had indicated James should inherit her throne – she had made a special sign before she died. This is unlikely, but it helped a peaceful transition. A few days after her death, the queen's body was taken by barge to Whitehall and then to Westminster to lie in state.[2]

The news of the queen's death would have travelled quickly to Hardwick. Probably Bronker was recalled to London, but there is no evidence that Arbella was taken from Hardwick at this time. What evidence there is points in the other direction – Arbella and her disaffected grandmother may have been left to stew it out together until her future could be decided by the new monarch. But truce there would have had to be for Arbella since Henry Cavendish was in London and her main helpers dispersed. The process of the new reign ground on remorselessly and no doubt Arbella found that time passed with appalling slowness.

On the morning of the queen's death, 24 March, James IV of Scotland was proclaimed James I of England and on 5 April he left Edinburgh to begin the slow triumphal progress to take over his new kingdom. Cecil made a fast journey north to welcome his new master. Arriving at York at midnight on 17 April, he saw James the next morning. Details of the progress were changed to include a visit to Worksop Manor. Three days later James, with all his large retinue, arrived at Worksop and was the guest of Gilbert and Mary Talbot. No expense was spared to divert and impress James, each entertainment seeming to exceed another in magnificence. The Court was at Worksop for one night only, yet time was found for hunting as well as other extravagant diversions. It is very likely that Arbella's aunt Mary took the opportunity to press the matter of her niece's removal from Hardwick Hall.

It would have been very difficult for Henry Grey, sixth Earl of Kent, to have refused the order from James requiring him to receive Arbella at Wrest Park for a short period. The order was dated only April and came perhaps from Worksop. By the tone of the letter, the king had been given some of the facts of Arbella's fate at Hardwick over the previous months and whoever informed him had tended to overpaint the picture to make sure of Arbella's removal. This suggests Mary Talbot as the source. James's letter began: 'Forasmuch as we are desirous to free our cousin the Lady Arbella from that unpleasant life which she hath lead in the home of her grandmother with whose severity and age, being a young lady, [she] could hardly agree ...'. In only eight years James would have cause to regret his words. But as far as Bess and Arbella were concerned, indeed they could hardly agree. On 17 April Bess, who had taken all she could support from Arbella, added a codicil to her will cutting out both her granddaughter and her son Henry.

After leaving Worksop the king travelled on to Newark where he celebrated his arrival by hanging a thief, releasing all the prisoners in the castle and knighting nine local worthies – James was always throwing honours about. On 28 April, two days before James reached London, Queen Elizabeth was buried. Arbella, being the only royal princess, was specially requested to attend. She refused point blank, saying that as her access to the queen had not been permitted during her lifetime, she would not be brought on to the stage for a public spectacle after her death. Elizabeth had never shown her cousin any love or concern, but had treated her badly. Arbella's refusal to attend the funeral, although churlish, is understandable.[3]

By the time of the funeral it is likely that Arbella had gone to Wrest Park and was free of her grandmother for the first time in her life. Henry Grey, sixth Earl of Kent, was a distant relative by marriage, his nephew (later the eighth earl) having married the youngest daughter of Gilbert and Mary Talbot. This sojourn with her distant relative could have been passed off as a family matter instead of it appearing that Arbella was under a kind of house arrest.

James had received a popular welcome from his subjects on his journey down the length of England. Thus his reign had started well. But James was a monarch whose nobility of purpose was infrequently matched by practical results. Unlike Elizabeth he was unable to comprehend the temper of his subjects. Where Elizabeth had been sparing and frugal James was extravagant, particularly where his favourites were concerned. There could have been no greater contrast. Admittedly the country was ready for a change, but not one in this extreme direction. However for the moment his defects were concealed. The new reign had started well and although the credit for this must be laid at Cecil's door, it is doubtful if James would have agreed: he had a blind belief in the divine right of kings which led to the conviction that he could do no wrong. There had been no popular clamour for Arbella to succeed Elizabeth. The rumour that she was mad had been skilfully circulated to take any steam out of that proposal. The Catholics abroad and some at home watched the transition for signs of weaknesses to be exploited. Father Rivers, writing inexhaustibly to Father Parsons, reported that the queen had been concerned about Arbella's behaviour and that this concern had contributed to her death. This is unlikely, since she had never shown herself concerned in the past and she was unlikely to have done so when she was dying.

The Venetian secretary in London, Scaramelli, had picked up the rumour of Arbella's proposal to Hertford as early as 20 February. On 20 March he reported that Arbella had been removed from Hardwick but in this he was wrong, for Bronker's letters to Cecil show that she was still there and probably did not leave until late April. The comments of this busy observer, despite the germ of truth in them, are not completely accurate and should be viewed with some circumspection. He was probably correct when he wrote that the King of Scotland's party was spreading rumours prejudicial to Arbella's character in order to destroy any public sympathy for her case. Later in March he reported that Arbella was either mad or pretending to be so.[4]

Another report which received wide circulation and was picked up by Scaramelli was that Lord Beauchamp, Hertford's son and the father of Arbella's proposed husband, had raised an army of foot and horse in the West Country and was proclaiming himself king, but it was all a false alarm. Hertford himself was one of the first to welcome James. Notwithstanding all these portents and rumours, it is very unlikely that when Arbella laid her haphazard plans she had any thoughts of the succession in her head. She was unambitious and the throne was never one of her desires; she said this several times over. All she wished for was her freedom. As for herself the outcome of the events of the past months would have convinced her of her own immunity. She had involved herself in a dangerous plan to escape, one of her helpers had killed himself and the queen had died – but she herself had survived and had been taken from the hated restraint of her grandmother. It is very likely that had Arbella done nothing at all about her own release and left her aunt Mary to ask James for her removal the effect, though far less dramatic, would have been the same in the end. But it is doubtful whether Arbella saw the matter in that light as she rode south to Wrest Park. She would have congratulated herself on her eventual escape, nerve-racking and traumatic as her efforts had been. To Arbella it would have seemed well deserved.

Bess, still indomitable and undefeated, was prepared to concede that she had had more than enough of Arbella. Not only that, but she would also have been upset by the death of the queen with whom she had a special relationship extending back more than fifty years. But now an alien hand was holding the reins of power. Bess who could vividly remember the glories and power of Elizabeth's reign would have felt estranged by all she heard of James's Court. Arbella, who had no reason to mourn the queen's passing, would have welcomed her cousin's new reign. Bess never lived to see how the life of her grandchild turned out; had she done so she would have felt justified in her attitude towards her granddaughter. Arbella, serenely confident that she was invulnerable, was heading for self-destruction.

15

LIVING VERY RETIRED

Arbella's new guardian Henry Grey, Earl of Kent, had been a
widower for twenty years. He was deaf and he was sixty-two, not
as old as her grandmother but nevertheless an old man. Consequently it must have seemed to Arbella that she was existing in
the world of the aged. Neither was Wrest Park exactly the centre
of a whirl of activity, for although Grey's nephew was married to
Elizabeth Talbot, Arbella's cousin, the young couple did not live
at Wrest Park with their aging uncle. No doubt after the tension
and rages of Hardwick the change must have seemed sublime and
moreover it was only an interim accommodation until James made
other arrangements.

The move from Hardwick to Wrest Park would have posed
financial problems. On the death of the queen, Arbella's meagre
pension of £200 from the Crown would have ceased, leaving her
with about £1,400 annually from her own resources. As a royal princess she was expected to keep some sort of state and she had her
court of ladies-in-waiting, an usher and other gentleman servants
as well as her page Richard Owen and the yeoman servants such
as old Freake (her embroiderer) grooms and horsekeepers. This
sort of retinue was costly. At Hardwick her grandmother had sometimes lent money to pay wages or even paid them herself when
Arbella was unable to, and it is likely that the feeding of this
miniature court was lost in the general household expenditure of
Hardwick. Now that Arbella was free of her grandmother and living
at Wrest Park, Henry Grey would expect Arbella to pay her share
of the household expenditure and there is no indication that James
made any arrangements to cover this item. Arbella's freedom,
although welcome and long overdue, was proving costly to her, for

at one stroke she had increased her expenditure at a time when her income was seriously reduced.

Arbella's precise movements in April and May of 1603 are difficult to determine. Her page was still at Hardwick on 6 April and it is likely that Arbella was there as well; that was six days before James arrived at Worksop. By 11 May she was certainly at Wrest Park for James wrote to Grey approving Arbella's request to attend the Court at Greenwich. Scaramelli, whose information has been shown to be often based on unreliable gossip, reported to the Doge and Senate on 1 May that Arbella had gone to meet the king with three hundred horses and to attend the queen afterwards. The account cannot be true for the queen had not by that date left Scotland and there is little likelihood of Arbella finding three hundred horses and riders, let alone paying for the unnecessary extravagance; this report can be dismissed.

However in another report dated 28 May Scaramelli gives an account which has the flavour of truth: 'Lady Arbella, who is a regular termagant, came to visit the King on Sunday last with a suite of ladies and gentlemen.' The Venetian spoils the effect by adding a rumour patently untrue, 'and they say that should the Queen die she [Arbella] would be wedded and crowned at once.' And there is another flaw in the account, for the 'Sunday last' would have been Easter Day and the king, who had previously offered to see Arbella at Greenwich, had left that palace on the Saturday. Scaramelli must have intended to say the Sunday previous to Easter, 17 May, when James was at Greenwich, and this date is confirmed more certainly by a conversation which Gilbert Talbot overheard at Greenwich.

Gilbert in his attendance at Court overheard Cecil and James discussing what should be done with Arbella. This was on 18 May and plainly Arbella was then at Court. James thought that she should be returned to Wrest Park 'from wherein she came'. Cecil's opinion was that she would not go back and suggested Sheen, the home of the Marchioness of Northampton. In dying Elizabeth had bequeathed to James something of a problem in Arbella. She was a princess, and the king's nearest living relative; she had a derisory allowance under Elizabeth, now suspended, an insufficient income and no establishment of her own. Until something could be done about these omissions then obviously Arbella would have to be accommodated with whomsoever would have her.

And so it was to Sheen that Arbella went after her few days with the Court at Greenwich. She was there by 14 June when she addressed letters to Cecil on the pressing question of her pension. By her comments the matter had already been discussed but not resolved. Arbella asked for £2,000: 'it would not exceed my necessity.' Her necessity had to be contained by a stop-gap gift of £666 for which she thanked Cecil from Sheen on the last day of June, but the question of a permanent pension had not been answered. Once more Arbella was in limbo, and she could only be released by James.[1]

When James arrived in England, his stately journey to London was marked by the number of his subjects who drew his attention in the hopes of gaining preferment. James answered 240 of these supplicants by knighting them. In the whole of her reign Elizabeth created only 800 knights and many of these had been made by Leicester and Essex without her approval; if James was going to keep up his opening average then clearly the reign was to be one of profligate creation of titles. In this James lived up to the early high expectations, for in his twenty-three years as King of England, Scotland and Ireland he created nearly 3,000 knights and further debased the system by selling peerages at £2,000 a time; he doubled the number of peers from 59 to 121.

The contrast between James and his predecessor could not have been more extreme. The whole tone and style of the Court was changed and those who lingered on from Elizabeth's reign considered it to be a change for the worse. Yet, although James was offering honours by the armful, curiously he gave little to Gilbert Talbot who had entertained him so well at Worksop and who welcomed his queen there in June on her journey towards London. Gilbert had to wait until December of that first year of James's reign before he was appointed to his father's old honour of Justice in Eyre beyond the Trent. Arbella's allies and firm supporters, Gilbert and her aunt Mary Talbot, were unlikely to be able to gain much for their niece if they could not glean anything substantial for themselves.

Nevertheless Arbella kept up a stream of correspondence with Gilbert and Mary as well as Cecil, asking them to use their influence with James to secure the now essential royal pension. Arbella's energies in this direction are reminiscent of Bess's attempts to get the Lennox inheritance for her granddaughter twenty years earlier. Arbella was in something of a quandary; her real chance of getting something out of James was at Court, and yet until she had a pension she could not afford the extravagant court life which a continuous attendance on her royal cousin would entail, without running into debt. Logically something had to be done, but first there were more important things to attend to.

James's arrival in London coincided unfortunately with an exceptionally severe attack of the plague. It had become endemic in many areas of the country and in 1603 London was not alone in its suffering. The affliction of the City was serious enough to cause James to consider putting off the ceremony of his coronation. It also drove him out of London and for the few days he was there in May he occupied the Tower, relying on its fortifications to keep the infection away. Towards the end of June James went to meet his wife Anne at Easton Neston on the last stage of her journey and carried her home to the clean air of Windsor. Anne, with her blond hair and fair complexion, was dull and indolent with little interest in anything other than her fine clothes and a fondness for masques and court balls. It was remarked that they made an odd couple. She and James already had three children, Prince Henry, aged nine, and Princess Elizabeth, aged seven, who had travelled with their mother, but Prince Charles, a sickly child, had been left behind in Edinburgh. This was wise in view of the plague, for in 1603 over thirty thousand in London alone died of the pestilence – more than one person in five of the City's population.

At last a decision was made on the Coronation: by royal proclamation it was commanded to be held on the day already planned, 25 July, appropriately on the day of St James the Apostle. But all unnecessary ceremony would be omitted and there was a restriction on the numbers of people allowed to gather for the occasion. If a date for Arbella's release from Sheen is looked for then it is most likely that she was freed for the Coronation. As the king's nearest relative and a royal princess it would have been difficult to avoid comment had she not been there, and there was no such comment. It would be an assumption but perhaps a fair one to suggest that Arbella joined the royal party at the great rambling palace of White-hall on 22 July and there met her newly arrived cousin Queen Anne. They were of the same age and apparently got on well together, although it is difficult to understand how, as the only interest they shared was a love of finery. On 25 July the party left Whitehall and processed through the pouring rain to Westminster Abbey for the ceremony which was performed 'in the ancient manner'. The ritual over, James and his queen lost no time in making for the untainted air of Hampton Court. That week there died of plague in London 1,396 persons.

Arbella had certainly left Sheen before 14 August, for she wrote to Gilbert Talbot on that date from the Court at Farnham Castle. The unreliable Scaramelli noted the occasion on 20 August:

Lady Arbella has been summoned to Court and placed near the King and Queen as a princess of the Blood; in her appointments, table and rank she takes precedence of all other ladies at Court. She has already begun to bear her Majesty's train when she goes to Chapel. For the rest she is living very retired, nor is there wanting a certain mystery in the situation.

Arbella had to resort to living 'very retired'; she had no funds to do otherwise.

She followed her letter to Gilbert Talbot of 14 August with another on the twenty-third of the same month to her aunt Mary; both letters asked for their support over her claim for a royal allowance or pension which by then must have become very pressing indeed. But James did nothing until early September, when a meagre £800 per annum was awarded to Arbella 'and of it £200 before-hand', which looks as though £200 of the old allowance by Elizabeth had been paid before she died, and James was giving Arbella only £600 for that year; 'she shall also have dishes for her people.' This brought her total annual income to £2,000. Arbella could have managed on this sum, with economies; but the theme of the Court was extravagance and disorder – with this sort of social life it is unlikely that Arbella's resources permitted her anything but 'living very retired' at Court, and she had nowhere else to live apart from with her aunt Mary.[2]

Not only was the tone of the Court changed but politically many of the faces who had been there so long – too long in fact – quickly vanished into oblivion. Cecil had seen to that and his political opponents were picked off one by one. There had been some concern in the Privy Council that James might not take kindly to councillors who had authorized the death of his mother. They need not have worried; James showed more resentment about the death of Essex than Mary's execution. Cecil was rewarded by James with a peerage, and was created Baron Cecil of Essendon on 20 May 1603, the first of the new peers. It was a just reward and well earned – and James gave the honour without charge.

Cecil had been able to remove his most difficult critics in the rebellion of 1601: Essex had been beheaded and Southampton was in the Tower. Those who were left should have taken the warning. Cecil had been sending to James secret and damning reports on Raleigh, and James therefore arrived with a preconceived hatred of Elizabeth's old privateer. One of the king's first moves was to remove Raleigh from his courtier's position of Captain of the Royal Guard and to call in all monopolies. Raleigh had the monopolies of wine, woollen broadcloth and the tin of the Cornish stannaries. The recall of these privileges of position at Court and of monopoly was logically inevitable, although regrettable to those who had held them under Elizabeth and many of whom were drawing substantial revenues from their offices.

These privileges and monopolies belonged to James to award to whom he wished for services or for loyal friendship. Raleigh however was ambitious and took the reductions of his status in bad humour. His mood was not helped when he was given three weeks to move out of Durham House in the Strand. Raleigh had been given a grace-and-favour lease by Elizabeth, and James was returning the property to the bishops of Durham from whom it had been taken at the time of the dissolution of the monasteries. Raleigh, who had been such a brilliant star in the firmament of Elizabeth's Court, was in eclipse and he felt the humiliation of his position.

Raleigh was at Windsor in mid-July for a royal hunting party when he was singled out by Cecil with the request to see the Privy Council. The council wanted an answer to the question of what he knew about the conspiracy against the king, formed by his friend Lord Cobham. Raleigh gave the foolish reply that he knew nothing and was immediately put under house arrest. The reply was foolish, for the council had evidence that Raleigh did know that his friend was up to something (he was possibly not involved himself), but by his silence he became an accessory.

There were two named plots against James at this time, though it will never be known how much was engineered by Cecil to trap Raleigh. The official account of the trial has deletions and like all treason trials of the time the prosecution was unfairly weighted against the accused. Once a charge of treason was laid, the guilt was assumed and the trial became a stage for state propaganda. The first-named plot was called the Bye or Surprise Plot and the prosecution wove this into the second Main Plot which was the more serious. The Bye Plot was claimed to have been devised by two Catholic priests disappointed in the promises of religious tolerance made by James. They united with an odd ally, Lord Grey of Wilton, who was a strong Puritan – he too was aiming for greater toleration – and for the moment the two extremes were joined in the same endeavour. James and Prince Henry were to be kidnapped and held until they agreed to a general pardon for the conspirators and greater religious freedom. Cecil was to be murdered.

The Main Plot shared the same ambition to murder Cecil but it went further. Count Aremberg, the ambassador from the Spanish Netherlands, had arrived in England with a mission to bring about peace between England and Spain; he saw James and Cecil as the impediments. Lord Cobham knew Aremberg and earlier in 1603 he had tried to interest James in peace but without success. Cobham, with his brother George Brooke and another malcontent, Sir Griffen Markham, also saw James and Cecil as obstacles whose removal would make their own lives more successful. Lured on by Aremberg with promises of arms and money, they planned to assassinate both James and Cecil, marrying Arbella to Lord Grey and putting her on the throne to bring a universal feeling of goodwill all round. Raleigh knew about this plan and it would have suited him had it come off. However Cobham was incapable of planning anything successfully. He had been called 'a most silly Lord, but one degree from a fool'. It was a singular piece of bad planning not to have secured the agreement of Arbella before anything else.

When Cobham eventually got around to discussing the plot with Arbella it had gone too far and involved too many people to be ignored. Furthermore he made the colossal error of writing to her about it in a letter asking her to get in touch with the King of Spain, the Infante and the Duke of Savoy to ask for their assistance in putting her on the throne of England. Arbella's part in the plot was essential to the plotters, but it was not a part she would have had anything to do with; this was appreciated by Cecil and the episode of the letter was not even mentioned in the official report of the trial. Arbella attended the trial of the conspirators as a spectator. It was conveniently held at Winchester where the Court had taken refuge from the plague in London. In his defence Raleigh absolved Arbella with a backhanded piece of observation saying that she was a 'woman with whom he had no acquaintance and one of whom all that he ever saw he never liked'.

Had Cecil felt that Arbella was of any danger to James and consequently to himself, he would have had no hesitation in lining her up with the other accused. In this event Arbella's dramas earlier in the year, hysterical though they were, had served to convince Cecil of her innocence of any desire to supplant James. Cecil even spoke in her defence at the trial: 'Here hath been a touch of the Lady Arbella Stuart, the King's near kinswoman, let us not scandal the innocent by confusion of speech. She is innocent of all these things as I, or any man here: only she received a letter from my Lord Cobham to prepare her, which she laughed at and immediately sent to the King.' Here the Lord High Admiral, the Earl of Nottingham, who was with Arbella, stood up and said, 'The lady doth here protest upon her salvation that she never dealt in any of these things, and so she willed me to tell the Court.' An indication that the State had no intention of involving Arbella is that James awarded the new pension six weeks before the trial opened; there would have been no point in this gesture if Arbella had been destined for the Tower.[3]

The trial received maximum publicity as the State intended; what had not been foreseen was that Raleigh would conduct a brilliant defence which made the prosecution look foolish more than once. Nevertheless the outcome was a foregone conclusion. The two priests of the Bye Plot were found guilty and suffered the agony and indignity of being hanged, drawn and quartered. Grey was also found guilty with Cobham, Brooke, Markham and Raleigh for their part in the Main Plot. All were sentenced to death, but only Brooke was beheaded. The others were reprieved on the scaffold and returned to the Tower.

Cecil's prosecution had done its work: the trial had served as a grand object lesson, the first of the reign. Cecil's main enemies were safely in the Tower and removed from all interference with his policies. Cecil could afford to be magnanimous, having reinforced and consolidated his position. Fortunately for Arbella, he had formed a correct opinion of her character, and on her side she had found in the new Lord Cecil a useful ally. But above all she seemed at last to be free from restraint.

16

WHY SHOULD I
BE ASHAMED?

By the time Arbella arrived at the Court of King James she was
twenty-eight. She had led an isolated life and although familiar with
the Court of Queen Elizabeth twelve years before, she was hardly
equipped to deal with the case-hardened courtiers who surrounded
James and his queen. Now that she was receiving a more liberal
allowance her attendance at Court was unavoidable and she must
have found the experience, although novel at times, distasteful for
the Court was filled with some extremely unpleasant sycophants
of both sexes following policies utterly alien to someone with her
lack of ambition. Although she started with the considerable advantage of being a royal princess in a senior position of attendance on
Queen Anne, in order to survive Arbella would have been forced
to compete to some extent and to conform with the new regime.
In one outlook she found herself in agreement with the harpies
of the Court: 'Our great and gracious ladies leave no ... fault
of the late Queen unremembered,' she wrote to Gilbert Talbot,
although the separate reasons for this conclusion were utterly
different.[1]

William Fowler, secretary to Queen Anne, was one whom Arbella
would have remembered with misgivings. He was the son of
Thomas Fowler, secretary and executor of the will of her late grandmother, old Margaret Lennox. It was Thomas Fowler, William's
father, who had vanished into Scotland with the Lennox jewels left
to Arbella and which she never saw again. William had come to England in 1582 after being expelled from France. He was arrested and,
typically, suborned by Walsingham into acting as a spy on the Scots
queen in return for his freedom. William Fowler affected to be

a poet and in the best tradition of James's Court set out to flatter
Arbella and to let as many others as possible know of his interest.
That summer of Arbella's first year at Court he sent her two sonnets,
one dedicated to her, extremely fulsome in its praise of her. To be
certain of the effect he sent copies to Gilbert Talbot, enclosing with
them a letter announcing his good fortune in making the acquaintance of Arbella and, again exaggerating, he called her 'the eighth
wonder of the world' and later 'the phoenix of her sex'. William
Fowler may have been trying to make up for his father's treatment
of Arbella, or he may have been echoing the empty self-seeking
manner of the Court.[2]

Arbella, used to isolation, must have found herself an alien at
Court. The sort of company which she was forced to keep was sum-
marized in a letter to Gilbert Talbot from the Earl of Worcester:
'First you must know we have ladies of divers degrees of favour:
some for the private chamber, some for the drawing chamber and
some for the bedchamber, and some for neither certain, and of this
number is only my Lady Arbella and my Wife.' He ended his letter:
'the plotting and malice amongst them is such that I think envy
hath tied an invisible snake about most of their necks to sting one
another to death.' Edward Somerset, fourth Earl of Worcester, had
been reappointed Master of the Horse by James, and was third in
the rank of the great court officers under the Lord Chamberlain
and the Lord Steward, occasionally serving as Earl Marshall. His
wife Elizabeth was the daughter of Francis Hastings, second Earl
of Huntingdon, a neighbour of Arbella's grandmother. She, like her
husband, was elderly and the least likely of those surrounding the
queen to make trouble for Arbella.

With the other women of the queen's court Arbella had little in
common: Lucy Russell, the beautiful Countess of Bedford and the
queen's closest confidant; Lady Derby; Lady Walsingham who was
reputed to be Cecil's mistress; Lady Suffolk and Lady Penelope
Rich. For thirteen years Lady Rich had carried on an open liaison
with the Earl of Devon, bearing him five children before her
elderly husband Lord Rich, having stood enough ridicule, divorced
her in 1605, when she quickly married Devon. Arbella might
have found a kindred spirit in the Countess of Nottingham, the new

and young wife of the lively sixty-eight-year-old Lord High Admiral of the Fleet. Lady Mary Stuart, forty years his junior and a distant relative of the king, had married the admiral after a night of dancing with the queen's court at Basing. The Earl of Worcester wrote to Gilbert Talbot this titbit of gossip, adding that during the night of the marriage the bride had been heard singing, but whether to keep her old husband awake or to lull him to sleep, none could say. The old fellow boasted of his stamina on that first night, but the next day went sick of the ague.[3]

Arbella made no friends out of this motley collection of hangers-on. She had none save her aunt Mary and Gilbert Talbot, and her frequent letters to either one or the other and often both on the same day are lively and sometimes witty. They show the Court through her cynical eyes, giving no doubt a true picture, emphasized by classical references which she could never resist. These letters, although deferential to the rank of an earl and his countess, show an affection and familiarity which must have come from Arbella's early years in the Talbots' household after her mother Elizabeth Lennox had died in 1582. Arbella was suffering some trouble with her eyes that autumn and mentioned this more than once in letters to Mary Talbot, carried up by the earl's servant John Hercy.

Some attempt was made by the Talbots to repair the relationship between Arbella and her grandmother, the initiative coming possibly from Mary. One of Gilbert's occasional personnel, Sir William Stewart, saw Arbella at Court and shortly afterwards made a visit to Hardwick and the formidable old dowager countess. To Gilbert he reported that he found her in 'good disposition' and hoped, as a result, for a better feeling in the family. Arbella on her side supported her uncle's petition for the lieutenancies of Derbyshire and Nottinghamshire, which he never got. Possibly his enemy, Sir John Stanhope, Vice-Chamberlain and Privy Councillor, was blocking his attempts, for Gilbert received little help from James. Arbella's influence would have been exerted through Cecil and Queen Anne who, although living her own life at Court, had views which were respected by her husband.

But the small-time occupations of the queen and her ladies

Arbella found tiresome. Writing to Gilbert in December 1603 she said,

'... will you know how we spend our time at the Queen's side? Whilst I was at Winchester, there were certain childish plays remembered by the fair ladies, viz 'I pray, my lord give me a course in your park;' 'Rise pig and go;' 'One penny follow me,' etc. And when I came to Court they were as highly in request as ever cracking of nuts was. So I was by the mistress of the revels, not only compelled to play at I knew not what (for until that day I had never heard of a game called 'Fier'), but even persuaded by the princely example I saw to play the child again. This exercise is most used from ten of the clock at night until two or three in the morning, but that day I made one it began at twilight and ended at supper time.

Arbella in her lonely childhood was uninstructed in the usual childish games.

Plague was still raging in London. Even as late as December the deaths were a weekly average of a hundred. Well clear of contagion from the capital, the Court continued its seemingly pointless progress from palace to palace. Hunting, a favourite court pastime, was an obsession with James, an obsession which made him unpopular with ambassadors whom he kept waiting interminably, and unpopular with his subjects when they found their fences broken and crops trampled. Deer and hare were the quarry. The ladies joined in when the deer were driven past 'standings' and shot at them with crossbows, but they were left behind when the sportsmen rode after the escaping prey until it was finally cornered, exhausted, brought down by hounds and killed.

Somehow, between the frivolous entertainments of the Court, James unwillingly found time for diplomacy. The war with Spain, which had been enduring since 1585, was an enormous drain on the nation's wealth and quite correctly James reasoned that it must be brought to an end. Spain had reached the same conclusion. The summer of 1603 brought the ambassadors of Spain, the Spanish Netherlands and France to the Court to discuss terms which might bring peace to the two exhausted sides. Aremberg from the Spanish Netherlands was there notwithstanding his involvement with the

business over Raleigh and Cobham, but his ambition was peace as
much as was James's. From Woodstock with the Court Arbella
wrote to her uncle Gilbert:

Count Arimberg was here within these four days and presented to the
Queen the Archduke and the Infanta's pictures most excellently drawn.
Yesterday the King and Queen dined in a lodge of Sir Henry Lee's three
miles hence, and were accompanied by the French Ambassador and a
Dutch Duke. I will not say we were merry at the Dutchkin, least you
complain of me for telling tales out of the Queen's coach.[4]

Here plainly they were discussing how peace could be negotiated,
although Arbella makes no mention of the subject to Gilbert. Her
letters almost never mention matters of politics; it was something
she deliberately avoided and which was allied with her lack of ambition. Sir Henry Lee, with whom the royal party dined, was the late
queen's Master of Ceremonies and had been responsible for the
revival under Elizabeth of the medieval jousts. Chivalry and the
gallantry of knighthood were the order of the day at these entertainments when armoured courtiers rode against each other often
with dangerous results. It was a fashion which James continued
throughout his reign and simply transferred the Queen's Accession
Day tilts held in November to his own accession day, 24 March,
calling it King's Day. Thus the popular court entertainment was
not interrupted. In June of that first year of James's reign the Earl
of Cumberland, who had taken the title of King's Knight for these
occasions, nearly killed one of the Alexander brothers who were
among the best jousters of the Court; later Lord North in a similar
escapade had his armour pierced by the lance of the galloping Earl
of Montgomery and the flesh and muscles of his arm were badly
torn.

There was a primitive fascination in the possibility of the entertainment being improved by the sight of blood. A cockpit in Whitehall further indulged the blood lust and these spectacles had zest
added by betting which all courtiers enjoyed; high stakes were
placed on almost any contest. In March of the year following his
succession James, hearing of the lions kept in the Tower, ordered
Edward Alleyn, Master of the Bear Garden, to put on a fight

between three mastiffs and a lion. One lion retired hurt and was replaced; two of the dogs were killed but the third, although badly bitten, survived. Masques and plays were other court enjoyments. Shakespeare wrote plays to order for the King's Men to perform in the great halls of the royal palaces. Ben Jonson likewise produced elaborate diversions and, in uneasy collaboration with Inigo Jones, for the first time in 1605, he brought the art of the masque to perfection with multiple stages and ingenious machinery to provide effects such as clouds substantial enough to carry masquers. The Jacobean Court was one continuous masque itself, costly to provide and free for the onlooker.

It was indeed costly. During that first year of the new reign the charges of the royal household were nearly £100,000, over twice what it had cost to run Elizabeth's Court. James was so prodigal with his pensions and gifts that he gave away in fees and annuities £27,270 in 1603, while the following year it rose to £34,593. The £800 which James had given to Arbella begins to look mean beside the £2,000 awarded to Jane Drummond, the queen's first lady of the bedchamber and cousin to Arbella, and the £3,000 to John Gib, one of James's trusted servants, his groom of the bedchamber. It was Gib who had brought the order to the scaffold to stay the execution of conspirators in the Main Plot. Although Arbella's £800 was more than welcome to her, it was not generous in comparison with the other sums James was throwing about.

Unlike today New Year and not Christmas was the time for gifts. The Lord Treasurer alone reputedly received about £17,000 each New Year from the officers serving under him. With this scale of giving it was important that Arbella should find presents which would not be over-costly and yet not appear too mean to those whom she wished to favour. In December 1603 this was one of her chief concerns; what was she to give the queen? Arbella took her problem to one of the queen's other women, perhaps her cousin Jane Drummond, and, as she described in a letter to Gilbert, asked what would be acceptable from

myself, who am altogether unprovided, and a great Lady, a friend of mine, [Mary Talbot] ... and her answer was, the Queen regarded not the value, but the device. The gentlewoman neither liked gown nor petti-

coat so well as some little bunch of rubies to hang in her ear, or some
such daft toy. I mean to give her Majesty two pair of stockings lined
with plush, and two pair of gloves lined, if London afford me not some
daft toy I like better. ... I am making the King a purse and for all the
world else I am unprovided. This time will manifest my poverty more
than all the rest of the year. But why should I be ashamed of it when
it is other's fault, and not mine? My quarter's allowance will not defray
this one charge, I believe.'

But, notwithstanding the expense, the disorder and the disagree-
able courtiers, Arbella drew some enjoyment out of her existence;
and well she might, for she had known twelve years of the boredom
of Hardwick and the domination of her grandmother. To Gilbert
she wrote of the Christmas preparations at Hampton Court where
he had sent some venison.

Your venison shall be right welcome to Hampton Court, and merrily
eaten. ... I dare not write unto you how I do for if I should say well,
I were greatly to blame; if ill I trust you would not believe me, I am
so merry. It is enough to change Heraclitus [a melancholy philosopher]
into Democritus [a cheerful philosopher] to live in this most ridiculous
world and enough to change Democritus into Heraclitus to live in this
most wicked world.[5]

At Christmas and New Year of 1603/4 Arbella could forget her
troublesome eyes and her redoubtable grandmother, to enjoy the
delights of the court entertainments. Plays and masques were not
a favourite with James; an observer noted at that time

The first holy days we had every night a public play in the great hall,
at which the King was ever present and liked or disliked as he saw cause,
but he seems to take no extraordinary pleasure in them. ... On New
Year's night we had a play of Robin Goodfellow, and a masque brought
in by a magician out of China. There was a heaven built at the lower
end of the hall out of which our magician came down, and ... made a
long sleepy speech to the King. ... he said he had brought in clouds certain Indian and China knights to see the magnificency of this court; and
thereupon a traverse [curtain] was drawn and the masquers seen sitting
in their vaulty place with their torch bearers and other lights.

The masquers then sang a song and presented the king with a sonnet and a jewel said to be worth £40,000 which James was buying from a dealer. The extravagance of the jewel was the sensation of the festival and, with this piece of lavish prodigality setting the conversation buzzing, the Court danced with the masquers until the magician dissolved their enchantment.

The enjoyment of that first English Christmas for James and Anne continued even after Twelfth Night; on the Sunday following the end of the holiday, the queen's masque was performed before the Court and the ambassadors of France, Spain and Poland, with all their retinues. The evening began badly with disputes between the ambassadors about precedence, but the entertainment was a success. *The Vision of the Twelve Goddesses* by Samuel Daniel, was produced, and the writer's achievement was acknowledged when he was made Overseer of the Queen's Plays. Arbella had already told Gilbert Talbot of the intention to put on *The Vision* when she wrote before Christmas, 'The Queen intendeth to make a masque this Christmas, to which end my Lady Suffolk and my Lady Walsingham have warrants to take of the late Queen's best apparel out of the Tower at their discretion'; and, as the earlier observer noted, the goddesses were dressed 'alike, loose mantles and petticoats, but of different colours, the stuffs embroidered satins and cloth of gold and silver, for which they were beholden to Queen Elizabeth's wardrobe. ... Only Pallas had a trick to herself; for her clothes were not so much below the knee but that we might see a woman had both feet and legs, which I never knew before!'

Arbella had started the New Year badly with a raging toothache which put her in a black mood of resentment and must have spoilt her enjoyment of the court pastimes. In writing to Mary Talbot she told her that the queen was extending more and more favour towards her and that, although 'unprovided for' as she claimed, she had given a gift to Cecil. Her offering had prompted Cecil to give her, as an afterthought, 'a fair pair of bracelets. ... I find him my very honourable friend both in word and deed.' Cecil was her most powerful ally. He knew her mind and it can only have been through Cecil that she had been able to get her allowance increased. And so for Arbella, notwithstanding her toothache and the trouble with

her eyes, when that first year of the new reign ended, she had a
great deal on which to congratulate herself. She had escaped from
Hardwick, her finances had been improved, and had been welcomed
to Court by the queen with whom she was in increasing favour.
But her future was in the hands of her cousin James.[6]

17

SUMPTUOUS AND PROFUSE

James I had passed a particularly disturbed childhood and had survived to a distinctly peculiar manhood. The fact of the matter was
that James, deprived of his mother when he was barely one year
old, had grown up without the loving care of any woman, against
a background of killing and violence. His father was murdered and
his mother beheaded; the former disturbed him, but the latter not
at all. Nevertheless he had a lifelong dread of the sight of cold steel.
When James had married Anne in 1589, he had made it clear to
his assembled council that he was marrying only to provide an heir,
'as to my own nature, God is my witness, I could have abstained
longer'. God could also have witnessed that James frankly preferred
men and only tolerated women. At Court the outward signs of this
preference were his fumblings among the codpieces of his
favourites. James was one of the most complicated neurotics who
ever sat on the English throne. He was lazy, thriftless, stubborn
and suspicious, but with it all intelligent. His appearance was unattractive and his comportment far from regal. But to most of the
English he was their king by right and James acknowledged the right
as divine.

Arbella therefore started with the disadvantage in James's eyes
of being a woman. Furthermore, to James who had waited sixteen
years for the throne of England, Arbella represented a threat to his
right, no matter how divine. It suited James to keep Arbella at Court
where he could keep an eye on his cousin and prevent any recurrence
of the nonsense experienced when she was at Hardwick. Barred by
her sex from becoming a favourite of the monarch, all Arbella could
expect was the minimum unless Cecil or Anne could prevail on
James to give more. For the moment Arbella was content, but it

was unlikely that the emptiness of court life would have satisfied her for long and it would have occurred to her that once more the only way out of her predicament would be by marriage, which depended on the whim of her neurotic cousin. Arbella was not really much further forward than she had been under Elizabeth; her freedom was an illusion.

In an attempt to develop a less expensive lifestyle and to give herself a refuge from the vacuity of court life, Arbella suggested to Gilbert Talbot, through Thomas Cook, his London man of business, that she might have rooms in Gilbert's house in Broad Street, London. This would have given Arbella some respite from the royal demands of constant attendance and would have provided somewhere further to keep her belongings during the almost continual peregrinations imposed on the royal Court. The suggestion came to nothing and Arbella was forced to remain where circumstances had placed her – in attendance on Queen Anne.

Arbella had been recently appointed carver to Anne in the New Year of 1604. This was an honour, but one which required the actual use of a carving knife, not a difficult task when all she was required to do was cut off the few slices of meat necessary for the queen's appetite. It is unlikely that Arbella had ever had the need to carve meat before and she wrote to Gilbert Talbot telling him of her experience: 'After I had once carved, the queen never dined out of her bed-chamber, nor was attended by any but her chamberers till my Lady of Bedford's return. I doubted my unhandsome carving has been the cause thereof, but her Majesty took my endeavour in good part, and with better words than that beginning deserved put me out of error.' She ended her letter mentioning a rumour that Mary Talbot was to be the queen's cup-bearer; earlier Mary had been suggested as a lady of the bedchamber.

But Mary and Gilbert were coming up to London in March, as were a great many others. The coronation pageantry, postponed the previous year because of plague was now planned as a progress of triumph through the City. Plague was still active but claiming fewer victims. It was felt safe to name the date for the great diversion of the year and 15 March was decided on. Arbella wrote to Gilbert suggesting that it would be a good idea to persuade her uncle Henry and Grace Cavendish to come with him. Henry was in disrepute for his behaviour in helping Arbella in her attempted escape from Hardwick. In the autumn of the year before, Cecil had requested his attendance in London when his name was mentioned by the conspirators in the Main Plot. Henry did not have a good record in Cecil's eyes and no doubt Arbella was keen to make up for this. She pointed out that Henry and Grace Cavendish could not afford to make the trip unless they came with Gilbert, neither could they afford London unless he put them up at Broad Street.

Gilbert in fact was in financial trouble himself. 'The earl is in debt, his plate and jewels are pawned and set on by suitors for payment,' wrote his brother Edward Talbot to Bess. He was probably not stretching a point for Gilbert had been borrowing money for years. In 1593 he owed the Earl of Huntingdon £5,000, which he repaid by borrowing from Sir Horatio Palavicino, then taking a further sum from Fulke Greville, the Secretary of the Navy, by mortgaging Talbot lands settled on Bess. Greville himself was in financial trouble by 1604 and pressing for his money back. But by then Gilbert owed considerable sums to Sir Robert Dudley; a neighbour, Sir Francis Leake; Michael Hicks, secretary to the late Lord Burghley; and an astonishing £1,000 to his servant Alexander Ratcliffe. With all the debts incurred and to service with interest, it is even more astonishing that Gilbert should have spent £12,000 in 1604 buying Hartington Manor, Derbyshire from the Crown. Originally Hartington had been offered to Gilbert's father in compensation for keeping the Scots queen. At £12,000 it was a bargain, even though £1,000 more than Gilbert was prepared to pay, and in the circumstances difficult to resist, no matter what the price. It is unlikely that he would have been able or willing to finance Henry and his wife for a visit to London for the state procession – even to please Arbella. Her other uncle, William, made the journey to London for the occasion, staying at his house at the top of Holborn, 'nere to Mr Bacon's howse there', and it is also likely that Charles Cavendish witnessed the great ceremonial procession as he is recorded as having returned from London in the late autumn.[1]

Unlike the subdued Coronation the year before, the day of the 15 March dawned without rain and the triumphal progress of the king and queen with the young prince Henry left the Tower of London between ten and eleven o'clock to make a stately passage to Whitehall Palace. It was a slow progress, for the route was marked by seven triumphal arches specially erected under the supervision of Ben Jonson, and each arch reflecting an elaborate compliment to the king or queen. With every arch went a loyal address or speech of welcome, sometimes both, and often music with a song. From Mark Lane to Fleet Street the road had been gravelled and the crowds railed off. The way was lined by the members of the city guilds in their colourful liveries with 'their ensigns and banners distinguishing each company spread before them'. The sixth arch, in Fleet Street, was ninety feet high with a globe of the world turning round, where, extravagantly, the conduit which usually ran with water was that day called the Fountain of Virtue and ran with claret. Beneath all these seven arches passed the king and his Court followed by the queen and her ladies including her carver Arbella and Mary Talbot. Over six hours after the start the procession ended at Whitehall, no doubt to the exhausted relief of the principals taking part.

But there was yet another spectacle of splendour to be acted out that summer, and the players could not disperse until the peace treaty with Spain was signed. This occasion offered greater displays of magnificence for the onlooker to marvel at since the embassies of Spain and the Spanish Netherlands were determined not to be eclipsed by their host. Arbella had already noted the arrival of the Spanish ambassador de Taxis in September 1603, when she commented that he 'has been ingratiating himself with the ladies of the Court' by giving away quantities of costly presents.[2] From that point the negotiations prospered, both sides desired peace and the whole performance was brought to a climax by the arrival of the Constable of Castile Don John de Velasco, with an impressive assortment of earls, marquises, barons and knights together with attendants totalling 234 persons. This enormous party, the commission for peace, arrived at Dover early in August. The day before there had been a frightful storm over London with memorable hail and unprecedented thunder. The commissioners had caught the end of this in the Channel. It had made them sea-sick and they

rested a day at Dover to recover. With them came vast quantities
of supplies including two loads of ice to cool the constable's wine.
On the tenth of the month they processed up the Thames from
Gravesend in twenty-four covered barges. From a distance, in a disguised barge and wearing a mask, watched the queen. Perhaps
Arbella was with her and certainly Cecil was not too proud to satisfy
his curiosity on the same barge.

During the days that followed there were royal entertainments
in which bears fought greyhounds, and mastiffs a tethered bull;
delights which were followed by displays of horsemanship and
dancing on tightropes. Arbella must have witnessed many of these
performances as her attendance on the queen meant that she was
with her mistress a lot of the time. The most splendid occasion
of all was held in the banqueting hall at Whitehall after peace had
been sworn in the chapel on 19 August. It was a feast which even
the Spaniards found 'sumptuous and profuse'. The Constable of
Castile surprised and gratified James with the gift of two cups of
extraordinary beauty set with precious stones. Neither side could
really afford the extravagances of the visit but for James the peace
brought the release of war funds to spend on his own excesses; for
the Spaniards it brought the lightening of a burden they had no
money to sustain. But it was not entirely the end of hostilities for
Spain: the treaty only ended the war with England; it left the Dutch
to continue the fight alone.

Prominent among the guests at every banquet and entertainment
was Count Aremberg, whose original peace attempts had been
cynically used by Cecil to snare his enemy Raleigh. It had been
claimed at the trial that Raleigh had been offered a Spanish pension
of £1,500 for his support. After the official peace was signed and
the potentates had departed, Cecil was made Viscount Cranborne,
and Spain paid him a secret pension of exactly the same sum until
his death in 1612.

After the pageantry and spectacles were over, Gilbert and Mary
Talbot stayed on in London. There were no letters from Arbella
to her aunt Mary until the beginning of October when the Talbots
had returned to Sheffield. Arbella may well have had the company
of her relations all that summer. William Cavendish was around

the Court in late July and Charles was in London for part of the time. Only Henry and Grace Cavendish were missing. Once Gilbert and Mary were back at Sheffield the letters began to flow again. William Fowler, Arbella's self-appointed admirer, had picked up a rumour and wrote in early October, 'The Lady Arbella spends her time in lecturing and reading etc, and she will not hear of marriage. Indirectly speeches were used in recommendation of Count Maurice.'

Fowler was passing on old rumours and Gilbert must have heard this when he had been at Court. Count Maurice of Nassau was commander of the Dutch armies fighting against Spain, a loyal soldier, strongly anti-Catholic and, like his murdered father William the Silent, a quiet man. This proposal had been known in Flushing the year before when Arbella was being astonished by the queen's childish games at Woodstock in September. For the Dutch it would have made a good alliance, but for Arbella it would have been rather a dull union with no community of interest. It would also have prevented James from making peace with Spain.

Also in October Gilbert received a letter from William Herbert, third Earl of Pembroke, then about to marry Gilbert's daughter Mary Talbot. 'A great embassador is coming from the King of Poland whose chief errand is to demand the Lady Arbella in marriage for his master. So may your princess of the blood grow into a great Queen and then we shall be safe from the danger of missuperscribing.' Exactly what he meant by his last word was something possibly even he could not have explained. The thought of his own marriage had gone to his head as his postscript revealed: 'You must pardon my short note, for I am half drunk to-night.' The 'great embassador' returned to Poland with his master's suit unaccomplished.

Pembroke's own engagement had been an on-and-off affair. Earlier in the year Arbella had remarked to Gilbert, 'I hear the marriage betwixt my Lord of Pembroke and my cousin Mary is broken, whereat sometimes I laugh, otherwiles I am angry.' In 1600 William Herbert had distinguished himself and the unfortunate Mary Fitton, one of the queen's maids, by making her pregnant and refusing marriage; this was the reason for Arbella's amusement

and anger. But there was more to the delay than his reputation as
a seducer, which probably did not matter anyway. The negotiations
for the marriage settlement had not gone smoothly. Like most marriages of the wealthy it was not a question of the young people's
emotions nor of their suitability, but of land. Either the Herberts
were being sticky over the settlement or more likely Gilbert in his
financial straits was unable to offer enough. The couple were in fact
cousins: Pembroke's mother Catherine was Gilbert Talbot's sister,
who had married Henry Herbert, second Earl of Pembroke. The
wedding was finally fixed for 4 November, when the ceremony took
place. As it turned out Mary was particularly happy with her experienced husband, notwithstanding the haggling beforehand. It is
likely enough that Arbella was at the wedding, after all it was a
family affair. Mary was five years younger than Arbella and the two
must have known each other well as children.

Within the family attempts had been made to patch up the quarrel
between Arbella and her grandmother. Bess still had her differences
with Gilbert and therefore the two members of her family who could
bring their influence to bear at Court were unwilling to co-operate
with her. It was of little advantage to Arbella whether the schism
was made up with her grandmother or not. Enormous wealth had
given the old lady great power, but since the death of Queen Elizabeth Bess had lost her favour at Court and her power was restricted
to the immediate area in the Midlands where her estates lay. At
Court Arbella was well clear of her formidable old grandmother and
the loser was in this instance Bess; the initiative for peace may well
have come from her.

However the differences between them did not prevent Arbella
from supporting her uncles at Court. The responsibility of a position at Court carried with it the duty of promoting the petitions
of one's family and also those whom one wished to favour. Earlier
in the year Arbella had done something in this way for her uncle
Charles: she had supported the Earl of Kent in a successful applica-
tion for the profitable stewardship of Ruthin; and William, writing
to Bess in early July, told her, 'His Majesty, four days since hath
been moved by my Lady Arbell for me: who promiseth as afore,
at the next call which is thought will be Michaelmas terme, at the

next session of Parliament.' It was not Michaelmas when Parliament
next met. James was having trouble with the Commons and by the
time Parliament was recalled it was the fateful 5 November 1605;
but by then Arbella and William had carried out their business
transaction to the satisfaction of both, and Bess had been forced
to make up her differences with her granddaughter.[3]

18

EARNESTLY
TO COME AWAY

Arbella's second Christmas at the Court of King James brought 1604 to a successful conclusion, marred only by catching measles early in December. She had missed the infection when her cousins went down with the contagion at Sheffield in the 1580s. The queen took the unusual step of isolating her Court, causing Gilbert to comment on her courage, when she was already five months pregnant; he was really criticizing her wisdom. Arbella's discomfort was eased on 8 December by having her pension increased by £1,000, giving her a total income of about £3,000, sufficient to allow her to live at Court with her own retinue of servants – as long as she did not catch the other court infection, extravagance. Unlike the previous Christmas when she had been hard put to find money for New Year gifts, there could be no complaints this year; the increase came just in time. The improvement in her finances may have come about through her own influence with the king, supported by her ally Cecil, but Arbella's claims on the king himself should not at this point be underestimated. She had by this time built up an empathy with her royal cousin which was paying off and would be demonstrated once the Christmas and New Year celebrations were over.

That season the end of the year was remembered for the royal extravagance of the court wedding on 27 December of Cecil's niece Susan Vere to Philip Herbert. Herbert was shortly to be Earl of Montgomery and was the cause of the king's generosity. Susan Vere's husband had little to recommend him apart from his good looks which in so far as James was concerned was enough. He showered gifts upon this fortunate young boor, who treated his royal patron in a singularly off-hand manner, but this did not deter James.

On the occasion of the marriage in the privileged surroundings of the palace at Whitehall, James gave him lands worth £500 a year as well as paying for the whole wedding feast in the royal great chamber and a masque performed in the great hall. The royal honours did not stop there. The next morning before they were up James burst into the bedchamber of the newly married couple wearing only his night-shirt and spent a good hour with them either in the bed or upon it, 'choose which you will' wrote one observer.[1]

By the time of the wedding the queen's self-imposed quarantine was over and, although Arbella's name is not mentioned in any comment, she must have witnessed and even attended the wedding and the queen's masque in the old banqueting hall which followed on Twelfth Night. Certainly Arbella was at Whitehall on 24 December, for she wrote to Gilbert on that date and it would have been unthinkable for her to have avoided the marriage of Philip Herbert three days later when she was related through her cousin Mary Talbot, newly married to Philip's brother William. The masque for Twelfth Night, which was put on by the queen's own players with herself taking part, scored a double first. It was the first time that Ben Jonson and Inigo Jones had collaborated, and the first time that perspective scenery was used in England. This was so revolutionary that some spectators had trouble coping with the novelty.

Jonson wrote the masque entitled *The Masque of Blackness* specially for the queen to perform in, and led on eleven of her court ladies disguised as black Ethiopians (Arbella was not among them). Although it was unthinkable for the Court to take part in plays, it was perfectly in order for the queen and her ladies to make-believe in a masque, but, if there were any speaking parts, then unseen actors spoke the words. A masque was an elaborate mirror, glorifying and reflecting the Court as it wished to imagine itself, and it chose to see courtiers playing the parts of heroes and gods. *The Masque of Blackness* was particularly remembered, if not completely understood, for the impressive sea with monsters and mermaids. It had a mixed reception in the hall at Whitehall as some did not approve of the innovations. Nevertheless the collaboration of Jonson and Jones was there to stay and the duo – an uneasy partnership of divergent personalities – continued to put on masques with increasing appreciation until 1636.

With the end of these delights the Court followed James to his favourite hunting lodge at Royston where he remained until the end of January, then back to London, followed by an exhausting circuit in February and March through Royston, Newmarket, Thetford and Windsor. The constant movement and the hunting which James found necessary was not to the universal taste of the Court. His Master of Horse, the Earl of Worcester, complained to Gilbert Talbot rather bitterly of the pace of life, hunting from eight in the morning till four in the afternoon, by which time they might be as much as four miles from home. All this together with answering letters at night without a secretary left the exhausted earl with only Sundays off. But Arbella for once was not taking part in this strenuous tour of duty.

Exactly what Arbella had been promoting at Court the previous summer with her uncle William cannot be certain. What is certain is that in the spring of 1605, following William's visit to Court eight months earlier, Arbella obtained from James a patent for a peerage with the name left blank; this was a valuable concession to Arbella for she could sell the honour to whom she wished. This royal plum cannot have fallen to Arbella through any other agency but her own influence with the king. Furthermore James obliged Arbella with a letter addressed to Bess, which was in effect a royal command ordering Bess to see her granddaughter. James and Arbella were conspiring together against Bess. The old lady was rather taken aback by the letter from James which allowed her no way out. In writing to her court correspondent Dr Edward Montague, dean of the royal chapel, to whom she had paid a retainer of £300 to induce him to use his position to promote her own petitions, she told him that she found it very strange that Arbella should wish to return to Hardwick when previously she 'had desired so earnestly to come away'. The comment was meant for the king's eyes. But Bess had no choice but to receive her returning granddaughter.[2]

One of Bess's near neighbours, Sir Francis Leake, looking across the valley towards Hardwick, noted in a letter to Gilbert that Arbella had come to see her grandmother. This was 13 March. Bess had previously been reported unwell and it made sufficient excuse for Arbella to want to see Bess. Arbella knew very well of her grandmother's dynastic ambitions and if William became Lord Cavendish it would set the seal on her life's ambition: her dynasty would be part of the ruling aristocracy. William was a notoriously mean man and, even though he was Bess's right hand in all things, she still kept a tight control of her money-bags. Therefore it is unlikely that William himself could have raised the £2,000 which was the going price for a barony and which Bess would be obliged to pay, through William. Some very hard bargaining must have gone on during that visit, but materially it was successful for Arbella who returned to Court with a gift of £300 and a gold cup worth another £100. Furthermore Arbella, who had been removed from Bess's will in 1603, was reinstated, for when her grandmother died she received the £1,000 originally intended.

On 11 April Edward Montague wrote to Bess suggesting that she petition the king for a peerage for William, but by then it had all been decided between Arbella and Bess. William arrived in London on 22 April when the Court was at Greenwich. A letter to his mother told briefly of court gossip and that Arbella was to be godmother to the queen's new daughter Mary, born four weeks earlier. On 4 May William went down to the palace of Greenwich for his enoblement. In the great hall of Greenwich richly hung with arras, James, sitting beneath his cloth of estate and accompanied by his two young sons, created three earls, one viscount and four barons. Among them Cecil was made Earl of Salisbury; his elder brother Thomas Cecil, Lord Burghley was created Earl of Exeter; and Philip Herbert, Earl of Montgomery. It is likely that James gave those honours for no charge, but of the remainder some would have paid the standard fee. This included William Cavendish, and on 8 May he paid £2,000 to Sir William Bowyer of the Exchequer.[3]

Next day in the royal chapel at Greenwich followed the christening. Under a canopy carried by eight barons, including William Cavendish, walked the Countess of Derby carrying the child. She was supported by the Duke of Lennox and the queen's brother Ulric, Duke of Holstein, a godfather, whose name had been rumoured as a possible candidate for marriage with Arbella during his extended stay in England. The party processed into the chapel followed by Arbella and the Countess of Northumberland, both godmothers. After the ceremony, which was led by the Archbishop of Canterbury assisted by Bess's correspondent Edward Montague, in his capacity as dean of the royal chapel, trumpets sounded and the small procession returned as it had come.

And so the Court, in whose thoughtless social whirl Arbella was a principal participant, witnessed a colourful pageantry. Within days of the christening the court gossips had something else to turn their attention to. Sir Robert Dudley, the by-blow of the Earl of Leicester and Lady Sheffield, had his legitimacy tried in the Court of the Star Chamber. Dudley was attempting to prove that his parents had married. Although his mother gave evidence of the marriage with date and place, Dudley lost and was fined £100. He left England with his nineteen-year-old mistress Elizabeth Southwell, one of the maids of honour to the late queen, she in the disguise of his page. They became Catholics and later in the year, with papal dispensation, they married, even though Dudley's first wife was still living. They settled in Florence, and in compensation Dudley was made Duke of Northumberland and Earl of Warwick in the Holy Roman Empire. The case was reported to Gilbert by one of his correspondents, along with other court gossip including: 'The Earl and Countess of Pembroke are at Court, but the Countess is not yet the most tactful of Courtiers.' What kind of *faux pas* can Arbella's cousin Mary have committed?

But the Dudley case was merely a side-show for Arbella; she was not related to any of the parties involved. The pointless carousel of court life carried Arbella through the year. James made a royal progress through the home counties in July and the Court went with him. None of Arbella's letters has survived from that summer. It is fair to assume that she would have kept up her frequent correspondence with Gilbert and Mary Talbot since they were not at Court. If she did then the letters have vanished. In October Arbella wrote to Prince Henry, then aged eleven years and the heir to James's Crown. Arbella was to attend Henry on the day following her letter and she was asking some unspecified favour of him, mentioning Mr Newton and Sir David Murray ('the only intersessors

I have in my suit, or will in any I shall present to your Highness'). If any clue is given as to what she was after, it is a slight one. Newton and Murray were Henry's tutors; but what she was wanting of the prince, which only he could give, might have been a court position for one of her Cavendish or Talbot relatives.

The Earl of Nottingham and his new bride went to Spain with an embassy to return the compliment of the Spanish commissioners and came back that summer richer by £20,000 worth of silver and plate. William Herrick, a goldsmith of Cheapside, drilled a hole clean through the centre of a great diamond for James and to his surprise and that of everyone else he was knighted, which caused a few raised eyebrows. But suddenly James and his fatuous Court were brought up with a severe shock – for a moment the carousel faltered.

One of James' less endearing characteristics was that it did not matter to him what anyone else might think of him; he was there by God's own right and he was perfectly satisfied with himself. It was something of a jolt to discover that there were among his subjects those who were so dissatisfied as to wish to blow him up with gunpowder. It was a very near thing and had the conspirators not been so inefficient they would have succeeded. The Gunpowder Plot was unravelled – or, as some have thought, concocted – by Cecil but James took all the credit and so the monarch was able to salve something from the fright he had been given. Cecil, always quick to use these occasions to his own advantage, if he had not already been leading the conspirators on, used the event to involve the Jesuits and crush their power. The Jesuits were completely innocent of any involvement, except that their leader in England, Father Garnet, knew of the plot through the church rite of confession, but was unable to reveal his knowledge. Garnet was in an agonizing position and his agony was prolonged through his trial until the mortal torment was ended by the executioner. As one observer commented: 'It was looked yesterday [1 May 1606] that Garnet should have come a-maying to the gallows which was set up for him in Paul's churchyard.' His execution being delayed by two days, he met his end on 3 May.

For once Arbella's uncle Henry Cavendish was not involved,

although Gilbert's name was mentioned; and within days of the plot being discovered an order was sent out to the high sheriff, lord lieutenant and justices of the area to watch over the safety of Bess at Hardwick. This may have concealed a desire to watch for Henry and Gilbert (for Henry's sister Mary, married to Gilbert, was known to have Catholic leanings) rather than a kindly care on James's part towards the old lady, a kindness he showed neither before nor ever again.

While Father Garnet was being executed in May 1606, Arbella was writing to Cecil asking him to support her petition to the king for further funds for her maintenance. Obviously she was finding the extravagances of the Court beyond her means. Arbella's allowance was paid quarterly and by the time she was making her petition she should already have received her second payment of £400 for that year on 1 April; perhaps she had found the expense of New Year gifts too much after all. Arbella had made her request to the king herself and had the support of Sir Walter Cope, Chamberlain of the Exchequer. Clearly, in obtaining the support of Cope and Cecil, Arbella was using the services of the two most important men in the government, so her position at Court although ambiguous was consequential enough for them to be involved. But the extent of their involvement is perhaps demonstrated by the fact that she got nothing from her petition. She had to wait until the following year, 1607, before she got anything more, and until 1608 before anything substantial came her way.

Little is heard of Arbella that summer of 1606. She politely turned down an invitation in August from Sir John Holles to the christening of his sister. She replied to Holles from Hampton Court, where she must have been staying during an interlude in the great festivities which attended the visit of the queen's brother the King of Denmark. For, on the day she wrote to Holles, the Danish king was at Windsor with the Court being made a Knight of the Garter. Her refusal may have been caused by a genuine inability to be in two places at the same time, for the festivities lasted many weeks.[4]

The visit by the Danish Court introduced a new dimension to the dissolute Jacobean Court, that of drunkenness, in which the Danes at first excelled, only to be outdone by James's courtiers by the end of the visit. In late July Cecil expensively entertained both kings at Theobalds with a great feast and of course liberal drink, followed by an entertainment involving the Queen of Sheba and King Solomon. The cast was as drunk as the spectators and the Queen of Sheba, unable to stand, attempted to present the Danish king with a rich offering of wine, creams and jellies. Inevitably she fell flat on her face and the casket of goodies fell all over the king. After the Dane was cleaned up, he stood unsteadily and tried to dance with the Queen of Sheba but he too fell down and was carried away to sleep off his excesses. Whatever Arbella may have thought of the Danish Court cannot be known. She may have kept these things to herself for she struck up an acquaintance with the Queen of Denmark and kept contact with the Chamberlain of the Danish Court Sir Andrew Sinclair.

Once again, as when the Spanish commissioners arrived in England, there was an exchange of gifts. It was said that James gave away money and gifts worth £25,000. At the time it looked as though James was giving away more than he was receiving, for the Danish king was observed to be mean. This caused disgruntlement among some members of the English Court until the Danish king, in either a fit of drunkenness or contrition, gave to Prince Henry what every boy might dream of and one of the finest gifts ever received by any teenager – a warship, fully armed, furnished and equipped, said to be worth £25,000. In addition all the queen's ladies were given jewels and that included Arbella, who replied with a gift for the Danish queen. Neither king could afford this scale of benificence but, as long as James received more than he gave, then the country was in credit. The Danes left on 11 August, but the day before had been marked by a splendid display at Chatham when the fleet was reviewed and 2,300 shots were fired off. A vignette of that day was given by Dudley Carleton, writing to his friend John Chamberlain:

Sir Frances Vere of all the company had the honour to be the soundest drunk; and your good friend Sir Hugh Beeston, who came in his company, was as well wet both without and within but of another liquor: for standing on the edge of a small boat with Sir John Lucien to get up into a ship, they toppled it over and went down together to the bottom. ... Sir John was the first ketched up and being pulled up by the breeches, which were but taffetta and old linings, had them clean torn off, and the first things which appeared ... was his cue and cullions, which as the Danes confessed could be no discredit to Kent or Christendom.

With the Danes off their hands the Court including Arbella may well have sighed with relief, but in Arbella's case the relief was short-lived. The Danish King had taken a fancy to Arbella's own lutanist, Thomas Cutting. It was an occasion when Arbella's usual role of supplicant at Court was reversed. Queen Anne wrote to Arbella in March 1607 pleading the cause of her brother, the Danish king. Arbella was then staying at Sheffield with Gilbert and Mary. The queen also got Prince Henry to write to Arbella as well. Whatever Arbella wished in the matter was not of consequence and the desires of Thomas Cutting were not important; he had to go to the wild court of the Danes. And so the poor Cutting sailed for Denmark with a letter from Arbella to the king written in Latin – their common language – giving an outstanding reference for her lost lutanist. It might have been some consolation that John Owen, a schoolmaster at Warwick, and said to be best composer of Latin epigrams since Martial, that same year dedicated his work *Epigrammata* to Arbella.[5]

19

ARBELLA GOES
BEYOND HER

The nearest relative the King has is Madame Arbella, descended from
Margaret, daughter of Henry VII, which makes her cousin to the King.
She is twenty-eight; not very beautiful, but highly accomplished, for
besides being of most refined manners she speaks fluently Latin, Italian,
French, Spanish, reads Greek and Hebrew, and is always studying. She is
not very rich, for the late Queen was jealous of everyone, and especially
of those who had a claim on the throne, and so she took from her the
larger part of her income, and the poor lady cannot live as magnificently
nor reward her attendants as liberally as she would. The King professes
to love her and hold her in high esteem. She is allowed to come to Court,
and the King promised when he ascended the throne, that he would restore her property, but he has not done so yet, saying that she shall have
it all and more on her marriage, but so far the husband has not been
found, and she remains without mate and without estate.

So reported the Venetian ambassador Nicholo Molin in London
to his government in Venice in 1607.

This was probably a very fair comment; Arbella was still sufficiently important in the succession to be worth a long paragraph
in a very long report on the state of England. Otherwise factually
correct, it contained a curious error in giving her age as twenty-
eight when she was almost thirty-two. As he was not out to flatter,
he either made a mistake or else she looked four years younger
than her age. The ambassador had put his finger on the problem
of her finances and, notwithstanding the apparently substantial total
income of around £3,000 and the fact that she and her servants were
fed by the Court, she was finding it very difficult to make ends meet.
The cost of gifts and of her own appearance in costly jewellery and
gowns were not extravagances she could avoid.

No doubt Arbella was borrowing to survive – a common court remedy. Possibly her loans came from Gilbert and Mary Talbot. Earlier in May 1605 she had borrowed £100 from her uncle William Cavendish but no more came from that source. A windfall which cannot have amounted to much came her way in the income from the lands of Lord Ormond in March 1607. This must have been no more than a stop-gap for although the Irish estates of Lord Ormonde were extensive they were occupied by the aged Earl of Ormonde, Thomas Butler. Part of the family's lands has been sequestered by the State on the attainder of Ormonde's three brothers in an Irish rebellion of 1570, lands which eventually went to one of Ormonde's nephews when the attainder was lifted in 1613. This grant to Arbella by the king was possibly a one-off affair and not repeated.

Arbella was now restored to her grandmother's good opinion after the affair of the peerage bought by her uncle William Cavendish. But Bess must have given up any hope of influencing her grandchild. In July that year, 1607, Arbella was proxy for Bess at the christening of the baby son of Gilbert Talbot's daughter Alathea, who had married Thomas Howard, Earl of Arundel in September the previous year. The baby, James, died in 1624 and it was left to his brother Henry to receive the honour of being restored to the dukedom of Norfolk, lost by attainder in 1572. The marriage had been quite a catch for Bess's granddaughter Alathea and must have restored her to favour – she too had been in some unknown trouble – as her grandmother must have been well aware of the possibility of the dukedom. No doubt the whole thing was expensive for Gilbert Talbot who would have been called upon to find yet another settlement and a costly one at that.

It was apparent to all Bess's relatives that she was getting to the end of her remarkable life: those who were out of favour and in need of Bess's money made efforts to achieve forgiveness for real or imagined slights – even Henry Cavendish, who never managed a return to favour. Granddaughters wrote dutiful letters and Bess's immediate family sent their gifts at New Year; Mary Talbot sent her mother a cushion to pray on. The turbulence had gone out of Bess's life and the family were waiting for her end. Gilbert and Mary

Talbot had been forgiven by Bess, as far as possible – the lawsuits over Shrewbury's will had been settled – and Bess gave Mary some 'well wrough ermine'. Mary had thanked her for it at the time of James's christening, adding that it would be worn by her daughter Alathea at the christening 'but not longer'. The peace of forgiveness had fallen over Bess's family.

The Christmas of 1607 saw the completion of a permanent theatre in Whitehall: the old wooden banqueting house had been pulled down and rebuilt in stone by James. Even the Venetians were forced into exclamations of favour over the sumptuousness of the interior. The stage possibly had a proscenium arch and James himself had a chair directly in front beneath an ample canopy, which must have obstructed the viewing of those behind. Ambassadors, such as Molin, had their honour contented, but not their comfort, by being placed near the king but sitting on stools. Around the walls were six hundred boxes in two tiers carried on wooden pillars in the correct classical order of Doric below and Ionic above, all carved and gilded, while from the roof hung festoons and angels. That Twelfth Night the masque, by 1607 traditionally the queen's production, was postponed by quarrels among the ambassadors jealous of their countries' precedence.

It took place on 14 January and was *The Masque of Beauty* devised by Ben Jonson. The queen, immediately followed by Arbella, led on fourteen other masquers, including Arbella's cousin Alathea, the new Countess of Arundel. The principal scene was the Throne of Beauty, flanked by pairs of masquers set in eight squares. Six steps to the throne were covered by cupids played 'by the best and most ingenious youth of the Kingdom'. The production received general admiration, particularly from the Venetians, who were the most experienced of theatre critics. What excited the most wonder was the display of jewellery; one witness commented, 'yet you would have been sure to have seen great riches in jewels, when one lady, and that under a baroness, is said to have been furnished far better than a thousand pounds. And the Lady Arbella goes beyond her; and the Queen must not come behind.'[1]

The winter of 1607/8 was also remembered for the great frost which began on Christmas Eve, and by the time the thaw came on

30 January highways had been made across the frozen Thames, and huge blocks of ice released from further upstream had brought down the bridge at Kingston. Up in Derbyshire the cold was also bringing down Arbella's grandmother Bess. Now about eighty years old and usually of robust health, by the middle of January Bess knew that she was dying. In her small bedchamber at Hardwick with its two hangings of 'forrest work', she lay in her great four-poster, being dosed with treacle – the standard remedy for coughs and chest complaints – by her good Dr Hunton who had moved in to Hardwick to nurse his most celebrated patient. The old countess had an extremely tough constitution, and although she wished to die, for her ambitions were achieved, she lingered on, rallying and sinking, until on 13 February her struggle was at last over and she lay at peace.

On 17 February Cecil wrote to Gilbert Talbot telling him that Arbella was on her way north to meet him. His curiosity drove him to ask for a rough draft or drawing of Hardwick, and in compassion he added a postscript, hoping that Mary was not too upset by her mother's death. But Mary was upset by Bess's death and the only thing Gilbert could think of to distract his wife was to give her more building to get on with. On the day following Cecil's letter Gilbert took physical possession of South Wingfield by expelling Bess's servants, and no doubt he took the same measure with all the other Talbot property involved in the marriage settlement. Bess had seen this coming and before she died had warned William to remove the livestock before it was seized by Gilbert's bailiffs. Arbella was at Hardwick through most of March while her illustrious grandmother lay in state, embalmed, in one of the great rooms. The hushed and silent house was draped in many hundreds of yards of black cloth, making the place into one huge, dark sarcophagus.

What was Arbella doing at Hardwick in those short March days? Was she perhaps helping with the settling of Bess's affairs? It would certainly have been necessary for some close female relative to have taken charge of Bess's personal business, leaving William to deal with the financial and estate matters. Perhaps too Arbella was collecting some odds and ends which she remembered with affection from earlier years. Her hurried departure in 1603 would not have been the time to take with her some of the things she later possessed.

In 1613 she sold some momentoes of the Scots queen to Mary Talbot for £800; and also she had pictures. These were bulky items
and it may have been during this stay that Arbella collected her
possessions. Mary Talbot had been so far forgiven by her mother
for her part in Gilbert's quarrel that she was left the 'Pearl Bed',
but without the hangings, only a partial forgiveness. Mary would
have been pleased to get the bed for it was one which Bess had shared
with Mary's father in the early days at Chatsworth. Bess lay in state
at Hardwick for three months – overlong even for those times –
but the family had important business in London and it seems likely
that one of Bess's dying requests to William was that her funeral
must not interrupt plans already made.

Leaving her dead grandmother, Arbella returned to London;
Gilbert reported to Cecil that she had gone by 23 March. Arbella
took with her, not a draft of Hardwick as Cecil had requested, but
a drawing of Chatsworth for him. On 10 April at eight in the morning William Cavendish, Bess's grandson and the eighteen-year-old
heir to Lord Cavendish, married Christian Bruce, aged nearly thirteen and daughter of the Master of the Rolls Lord Kinloss. Henry
Cavendish called her 'meetly handsome, as they say, of red hair'.
Perhaps in deference to Bess's lying-in-state, the engagement had
been kept secret – it had certainly taken a complicated and protracted bargaining to arrange – and it took many, who expected to
know these things, by surprise. The queen was reported to be dis-
pleased but was soon brought round to the marriage.

Arbella was said to have been responsible for the match. She may
have been, but she denied it, and the arrangement has all the hall-
marks of Bess's doing. Arbella was not at the ceremony, but afterwards Lord Cavendish went to Whitehall himself to ask Arbella to
the wedding dinner; she accepted, stayed to supper and danced till
late. Henry Cavendish observed of the groom, 'Alas! Poor Wylkyn,
he desired ... a woman already grown. ... They were bedded
together, to his great punishment, some two hours.' Lord Cavendish also sent to Henry to join the party; he declined and was surprised and hurt that same night when, as he was harmlessly reading
a book in his chamber, one of Lord Cavendish's servants appeared
and served him with a subpoena – the start of a long series of court

wrangles over Bess's will which estranged Henry from his brother. But with the wedding out of the way the family returned to Derbyshire for Bess's funeral in early May.[2]

Jacobean funerals of the wealthy were macabre affairs and, notwithstanding Bess's expressed wish for no 'vain and idle charges', there were standards due to the rank of a countess which the College of Heralds would see were maintained. The rules insisted that the chief mourner should be a countess, in this case Mary Talbot, supported by two barons or knights, possibly Sir Charles Cavendish and the newly married William Cavendish who had been knighted in March that year. Behind them would have followed a great cortège of mourners all according to their rank; a cortège in which there was no place for a princess as the rank would have been senior to a countess. If Arbella was at the funeral, then she took no part; it is perhaps unthinkable that she would not have been there. She had been given half a piece (about twenty-four yards) of black lawn for mourning by William, but that was only a small part of the yards and yards needed. Over nine hundred yards of black cloth were used to drape the interiors of Hardwick and All Saints Church in Derby where the funeral was held. Vain and idle charges or not, by the time William, who was a mean man, had finished paying for his mother's funeral, it had cost more than the £2,000 which Bess had allowed. The service in the church would have been followed by a funeral feast. Where this was held was never recorded; there were no eyewitness accounts of that day. But Hardwick was too far away and it is likely that the main inn of Derby town was commandeered. Again it is very likely that Arbella would have been there, but once the whole affair was ended she would have returned to London and her duties at Court.[3]

By Bess's death Arbella had been made richer by £1,000, a useful sum to get out of immediate and pressing financial problems, but of little long-term use. She had that spring made a complaint to the Lord Treasurer Dorset that her pension of £1,600 was paid slowly and in arrears; to her inadequate means was added the problem of slow payment of what was due to her. In July her petitions to the king and Cecil for an increase in her pension brought some results; Arbella was awarded the right to license innkeepers for the

sale of oats to travellers. Out of the 2s 6d cost of the licence or recog-
nizance, Arbella was to be allowed to keep 6d to herself, but then
she had the heavy cost of collecting these small sums. It is very likely
that she farmed out this monopoly to an operator who paid Arbella
an annual rent; this would have been no more than a few hundred
pounds, but from Arbella's point of view it would have been a useful
contribution, no matter how small. With these additions to her capital and her income, Arbella bought herself a house in Blackfriars
sometime during that summer. By this time the tensions of court
life would have become almost unbearable – Blackfriars would
become a refuge where she could indulge her own simple preference
for study. This was something that she could afford for the first
time in her life.[4]

20

MAKE GOOD MUSIC

Although in principle Arbella's purchase of a house in Blackfriars provided her with a *pied-à-terre*, it does not seem to have been a refuge which she used frequently. Only one letter survives written from her new address, and it is the only letter in which she mentions her new establishment. On 8 November 1608 she wrote to Gilbert Talbot in her typically lively style, 'For want of a nunnery, I have for a while retired myself to the Friars.' In any event it was not a property which Arbella would have much opportunity to use in the short time of freedom she had left to her. Apart from the fact that she bought the Blackfriars property from the successors of Sir Thomas Cheney, a former Warden of the Cinque Ports, at Michaelmas for £200, nothing more is heard of her new refuge. Later in November for no stated reason, Arbella sent her pictures to Mary Talbot in Derbyshire, which would have left her new walls astonishingly bare.

Arbella was not at Court that Christmas. Sir John Harington reported her indisposition on 21 December: 'I hear now that my Lady Arbella is fallen sick of the small-pox, and that my Lady Skinner attendeth her and taketh great pains with her.' By the first day of February Arbella was well enough and reported to have returned to her lodgings at Court. She had returned in time for the queen's masque at Candlemas on the day following. Although Arbella's cousin Alathea was in the cast she was not in it herself, but was however a spectator of this, the most memorable of all Jonson's masques, *The Masque of the Queens*.

The art of the masque had become stereotyped in its performance. The 'entry' or presentation of the masque opened the spectacle; this was followed by the 'main' in which the masquers

performed their dance, turning into the 'revel' when the masquers
danced with the spectators before the final 'going-out'. In *The
Masque of the Queens* Jonson successfully broke the rules by preced-
ing the 'main' by an 'anti-masque' to provide a dramatic contrast
to what followed. The piece opened with a grotesque scene of
witches in 'an ugley hell' and smoke drifting up to the top of the
roof of Whitehall banqueting house. Full of preposterous gesticula-
tion, the witches acted in the reverse of everyday custom, even to
dancing back to back. Suddenly at the height of their dance came
a great blast of many instruments and the whole scene vanished.
In its place appeared the House of Fame: 'a great piller with diverse
wheeles and devices for moving rounde thereof', a fantastic piece
of revolving scenery with Bell-Anna and eleven virtuous queens
aboard it; they were of course the queen and her ladies. *The Masque
of the Queens* was a spectacular and diverting production by Jonson
and his patron the queen; it was also his most polished example of
the art of the masque. And although Arbella has left no comment
on the spectacle, it must have been a performance which she
appreciated and enjoyed.[1]

Arbella was still at Court at the end of March when she wrote
a letter from Whitehall addressed to Charles Gosling or Gesling,
who had been one of Bess's servants at South Wingfield. Arbella
certainly knew him well enough to write on familiar terms asking
him to find out if there was anything in a rumour of the engagement
of one of Sir Charles Cavendish's sons. Her postscript nostalgically
recalled the past, which could not have been all dark days: 'Remember the old buck of Shirland, and the roasted tench I and other good
company ate so savourly at your house, and if thou be still a good
fellow and an honest man, show it now or be hanged.' But the bulk
of Arbella's correspondence was with Mary and Gilbert Talbot. In
June she wrote not from her own house in Blackfriars but from Gilbert's Broad Street address. Obviously fully recovered from her
earlier indisposition, she was in one of her best of moods and willing
enough to be taken in by conjuring tricks. 'I assure you within these
few days I saw a pair of virginals make good music without the help
of any hand.' But Arbella was planning a grand progress through
the Midlands and would soon be seeing old friends and places she

had known before she came to Court. In effect it was to be her grandmother's great London visit of 1591/2 in reverse.

Arbella had more than one reason for making this semi-royal and
uncomfortable tour in her heavy unsprung coach, a tour which by
the time she returned had cost her over £300 of money she did not
possess. Earlier in that year Arbella had petitioned the king for the
licence to import forty thousand hides from Ireland annually. This
had not gone to Arbella but another petition for the licensing of
brewing, the selling of wines and *aqua-vitae* in Ireland was given
to her. It was later reported to have been worth £1,500, but this
was wild rumour and it was probably only worth half that sum. In
August, before Arbella started her tour, she wrote a brief note to
Cecil thanking him for his support of her successful petition; but
there were others who had also contributed to this happy outcome
and it was partly to visit these distant friends that Arbella made
her long excursion into the Midlands of her childhood. Also she
wished to restore her health in St Ann's Well at Buxton, as she was
no doubt run down after her recent attack of smallpox. Perhaps too
she had a wish to return to scenes and people she had known from
the past when during the early years she had lived in harmony with
her grandmother. The plague had returned to London and was
worse than ever, which may have added to her wish to be out in
the clean country air of her childhood.

On this expensive excursion Arbella was partly financed by a gift
of £100 from Gilbert Talbot and by the repayment of a loan of £80
made to Andrew Clayton, one of her mother's old servants; and
now that her allowance was being paid more promptly there would
have been £400 for the quarterly payment from the Exchequer.
Arbella left Whitehall in her coach on 22 August, taking with her
a retinue which included Freake, her embroiderer, and John Dodderidge, who had last been heard of in the Gatehouse Jail for his
part in Arbella's attempted marriage to young Seymour; the whole
party was mounted on twenty horses. The riders in their liveries
would have made an impressive sight escorting the royal princess
in her trundling coach.

The first night was spent at St Albans at an inn. Lady Arundel
had sent her coachman to guide them thus far. Alathea was then

expecting another baby and the loan of a coachman was a friendly and helpful gesture. The following night was spent at Toddington with Lady Cheney, who was the daughter-in-law of Sir Thomas Cheney, whose house in Blackfriars Arbella had bought. The night of 26 August was spent with Sir James Croft at Northampton; his father had been on the embassy to the Duke of Parma in 1588 and he would have known of Arbella's proposed marriage to Rainutio Farnese. And from Northampton the progress took the party to Prestwold near Loughborough in Leicestershire and to the house of Sir William Skipworth where the queen had stayed on her journey to London in 1603.

None of Arbella's hosts on her progress up to now had been closely involved in her life before, so far as evidence goes. They were people she could have met at Court but they were in no sense professional courtiers, and any ties of friendship she may have had with them would have been slight. Arbella appears in this case to have been acting with all the imperious behaviour of top royalty. By wishing herself and her large retinue on her hosts she was conferring an honour. The only reason she could have had for staying at these houses on the route was that they were well placed for overnight stops. From Arbella's point of view there was a saving in expense between the cost of an inn and the gratuities she was expected to give in private households. It cost Arbella a total of £10 15s od for the night at St Albans, but for one night with Lady Cheney her gratuities came to only £7 15s od, and of course it was far more comfortable.

From Loughborough onwards Arbella was back in her own familiar country. Stopping for ale and cakes at an alehouse beyond Nottingham, they reached Mansfield where Lady Bowes, her next host, had sent not only her coachman but coach horses as well to pull Arbella's heavy conveyance. And so by evening on the longest haul of the progress – Arbella covered fifty miles that day – they reached Waltham Hall near Chesterfield and were welcomed by Lady Bowes. It had not been a lucky day, the coach had broken a spring-tree at Glapwell, within sight of Hardwick Hall. While waiting for the repair, Arbella bought three and a half yards of crimson baize for a petticoat. Hardwick Hall was not one of her stopping places, not because she disliked her uncle William, but simply because he was then at Derby Assizes.

At Waltham Hall Arbella rested four days. Here she was among friends, and indeed Lady Bowes had been a friend of her grandmother; they had occasionally exchanged gifts. The Waltham Hall estate had belonged to the Foljambe family and Lady Bowes had, as Isobel Wray, married Godfrey Foljambe, and when widowed, Sir William Bowes. The Foljambes were related to Bess on her mother's side and any blood relationship counted as cousinship – Bess had addressed them as 'cousin'. Furthermore Sir William Bowes had been a witness to one of the codicils of Bess's will. Here were all the ties of family relationship, old association and friendship, for Arbella. But not only were there ties of sentiment; later that year Arbella wrote to Isobel Bowes saying that she seriously thought of buying a house near Waltham Hall and commissioned her friend to find one for her as a refuge more distant from Court. Where Arbella thought she was going to find the money from she did not say; but obviously she felt that she had roots in this remote area of England.

During this interlude with the Bowes, the mayor and brethren of Chesterfield sent a deputation with a gift to their royal visitor. In fact 'royal' was also the adjective for the gratuities which Arbella was expected to award in her turn. The officers of Chesterfield each returned richer by £1; the household at Waltham were given £6 13s 4d; a preacher at Sheffield on the Sunday was presented with £2; Lord Rutland's musicians at Waltham were given £1 for their performance; and the poor of Chesterfield were given £2 as Arbella passed through the town. These were the gratuities expected of a royal princess and which it would have been unpardonable for Arbella not to have given. The greater part of Arbella's expenses on this progress were sums simply given away as rewards for service or charity.

On 2 September, a Saturday, Arbella arrived at Sheffield to stay with the Talbots. Only four days earlier Gilbert had written from Tankersley, one of his other Yorkshire estates, warning his steward to prepare the castle for Arbella's visit. She arrived with the gift of a freshly killed stag, presented to her by Sir Peter Frecheville as she passed through Chesterfield. The party remained with the Talbots for six days. There was stag-hunting in the park at Handsworth, the house built by Gilbert's father on the edge of Sheffield, and Charles Cavendish sent over his own musicians, probably accompanying them himself. At Sheffield it was time for reunion with Arbella's favourite relations far away from the formality of the Court and a time for recalling old and shared memories. Not only that, but old friends made contact with Arbella and sent gifts either in appreciation of her status or from affection. From Sheffield Arbella made a deliberate excursion to stay at Melwood Park (just south of Epworth in Lincolnshire), where Mary, Queen of Scots had stayed in 1569. It was not on her route, but she had a definite point in making the detour, for Melwood was the home of Sir George St Paul, who had supported her successful petition for the newly won licence for ales and wines in Ireland; it is also likely that he had been recruited by Gilbert. After four days at Melwood Arbella's business and pleasure was done and she returned part of the way by boat on the Trent to Stockwith, no doubt more comfortable than travelling over the abominable roads in her unsprung coach. The following two days were spent with the Talbots at Worksop Manor in Nottinghamshire, where they had entertained James in 1603, and then she moved on to Chatsworth via Aston.

Chatsworth had been entailed on Henry Cavendish, therefore on Bess's death it had gone to Henry outright. Bess however had willed the contents to William; she had altered her will to this effect after Henry's attempt to help Arbella escape from Hardwick. Henry was in financial trouble and the house without its contents was useless. On 31 August, nearly three weeks before Arbella's visit, Henry had sold Chatsworth and all its lands to William for £8,000. Negotiations had been going on for some time, made difficult by the quarrel between the brothers following the subpoena served on Henry the previous year and the lawsuits which followed. Perhaps too he felt William had influenced their mother against him. While Arbella was staying at Chatsworth, she was the guest of her uncle William. The servants in the house were certainly his and he visited Chatsworth some time that month. Chatsworth was convenient for the spas of Buxton and her uncle Henry sent a guide over from Tutbury to escort Arbella to Buxton where she spent three days either bathing or drinking the water from St Ann's Well before she left for Sheffield to stay with the Talbots again. This time they were probably at Sheffield Lodge, for Gilbert wrote to Cecil from the lodge to thank him for his help in Arbella's successful petition for the Irish licence, hinting that he had been one of his niece's sponsors. Arbella in fact had two firm allies in her aunt and uncle, and Mary later proved to be an incredibly staunch friend, suffering years in the Tower for her support of Arbella. But at this moment Gilbert was still in financial trouble; he had now got back the income previously settled on Bess, his mother-in-law, totalling more than £3,000 a year, but his expenses were still outstripping his income, possibly because of court extravagances. Gilbert's gift of £100 to Arbella at the start of her progress is doubly generous in the light of a letter written that summer from Mary and Gilbert to Sir Michael Hicks asking for a loan of a 'good sum of money'.

Arbella's next visit was perhaps motivated purely by sentiment. She crossed Nottinghamshire to Rufford Abbey to stay with Gilbert's sister Mary, married to Sir George Saville – Rufford Abbey, where her mother had fallen in love with her father, where Bess had sealed the lightning wooing with a speedy marriage. She stayed only two nights at Rufford before she was on her way to another appointment with the nostalgic past at South Wingfield, where she had spent some days of freedom from Bess's authority so long ago, when the steward had reported her to be out of hand, or refusing to go to bed or do her school work. Wingfield, which was seldom used by the Talbots, was an unusual house in that the great chamber was placed between the hall and the kitchens. And it was in this great chamber, with its splendid fifteenth-century window overlooking the inner court, that Arbella would have dined in state as befitted her royal status. The two grooms of the great chamber were given £1 between them. Other gratuities brought the total of largesse for the one night to £9 6s 8d, an unusually large sum, but at least two of the servants, John Mercer and 'Oul Sutton', had been at Wingfield when Arbella had lived there as a girl.

The main purpose of Arbella's progress was now over and she began her return to London and the Court, her travelling made easier by the loan of a horse-litter from Gilbert Talbot. The coach had not been a success on the difficult Derbyshire roads. The way had been so bad in places that the holes had to be filled in before they could pass; the heavy vehicle had suffered almost continuous breakdowns in these remote by-ways; and finally her coachman broke his leg. Arbella would have been far more comfortable travelling in Gilbert's litter and in the past this had been her grandmother's preferred method of journeying. The return to Court was made in the same regal manner as the journey north. Leaving Wingfield they spent the night of 28 September at Quarndon House near Loughborough with the Farnhams, who had been at Court in the old days of Elizabeth.

From Loughborough, by way of Market Harborough, where they put up at an inn, they went first to Easton Manduit to stay with Sir Christopher Yelverton, an old man who in a legal capacity as Sergeant Yelverton had helped Bess and later became speaker in the Commons in Elizabeth's reign. One of the other sponsors of Arbella's petition for the Irish licence had been Henry Yelverton, a relative of Sir Christopher. The next night was spent at Wrest Park, where Arbella had gone to Henry Grey after her dramatic exit from Hardwick. Here Arbella rested five days and Gilbert's litter was returned to Derbyshire. The delay at Wrest Park may have been due to the necessity of having the coachman's leg properly set. And finally on the last lap of the progress Arbella was met at Toddington in Bedfordshire by a messenger, with the news that Alathea had given birth to a son only days before. Their last night was spent at an inn in St Albans and Arbella at last returned to London on 9 October, to Broad Street, after having been away from the gossip and ennuis of the Court for a period of forty-eight days. No doubt the change had done her good, but her days of freedom to make this type of royal progress were now numbered. It was the first Arbella had made and it was also to be her last.[2]

21

MELANCHOLY HUMOUR

Once back in London, Arbella pressed Cecil and the king for help with her finances. Writing to Cecil she suggested that, instead of the free diet for herself and her retinue at Court, James should pay her an extra allowance of £1,000 annually. The arrangement would have permitted Arbella to spend long periods away from Court but it was unlikely to receive James's approval as he preferred to have his cousin where he could see what she was up to. Another suggestion put to Cecil was that the king should pay off her debts and she would return the Irish licence. There had possibly been problems in farming out the licence; on paper it looked so generous but it was turning out a disappointment. When Gilbert had written to Cecil from Sheffield Lodge in the late summer, during Arbella's visit, he had hinted at the problems of collecting dues from the wild and undisciplined Irish. Arbella was attempting to put her affairs in some sort of order. Her royal cousin was probably unwilling to recognize that he had placed Arbella in a cleft stick: by insisting that she attend Court he was committing her to expenses which could not be met from the allowances he gave her. Arbella was trapped again by her royal blood. And as before, when she was trapped, Arbella's behaviour became unpredictable.

Almost as soon as Arbella returned to Court her friend Isobel Bowes wrote telling her that Sir George St Paul at Melwood had found a property which would suit her. Obviously this was something which had been discussed during that Midlands progress. But Arbella's plans to escape from Court were far more than just a wish to move into the country.

By the end of the year Arbella was in trouble again. One of her

Blackfriars neighbours, James Beaulieu, writing to a friend on 29 December gave the first surviving report:

... my Lady Arbella is committed to her chamber, to occasion having grown by the acquaintance and familiarity of a certain Lady Skinner, a great papist, who being visited by one Douglas, a Scotsman, was the cause that he was going to travel abroad, the Lady Arbella was content by this means to entertain correspondence for a marriage with some prince of Germany, and namely the Duke of Moldavia. The Lady Arbella lived for some time before retired from Court which men ascribe to her studious and melancholy humour.

In using the adjective 'melancholy' the writer was by current belief referring to a medical condition. One of the four body fluids essential to life was labelled melancholic – cold and dry – an excess of any one affected one's outlook and mood; a greater excess affected health. Arbella was judged to be suffering from too much of the cold and dry humour, a common result of undue learning and study. The melancholic had a passion for solitude, and an extreme of the condition led to madness.

Another correspondent at Court gave similar news of Arbella's detention. On 30 December: 'I can learn no more of the Lady Arbella, but that she is committed to Lord Knyvet, and was yesterday before the Lords.' Two of Arbella's servants, Hugh Crompton, her gentleman usher, and one of her ladies-in-waiting, were close prisoners. On 8 January the Venetians were at it again adding their views to the reports and rumours: 'one of the two ladies who, as I reported on the 19 November, had become a Catholic, is the Lady Arbella.' The other lady to whom he referred could well have been Mary Talbot, whose true faith had been recently uplifted by having the luck to acquire a small portion of the Cross and the measurements of the body of Mary Magdalene. All these were rumours but how much they were based on the truth may never be known for certain, for the acts of the Privy Council, recording their proceedings for this period, were burnt in the fire of London in 1666.

Certain it is that Arbella's freedom was restricted and that she was closely examined on some matter. The Venetians continued their report with:

His Majesty had a hint last week that she intended to cross the sea with a Scot named Douglas, and had some idea of marrying him. He accordingly sent his Captain of the Guard [Viscount Fenton], and the Baroness, his wife, to take Lady Arbella from the house of the Seymour family, under pretext of friendship and an invitation to sup with them ... to the Palace, where she was placed under guard for several days. Douglas too was arrested, and some of her servants and waiting maids, seals were put upon her affects. She is now at liberty, however, which is not the case with the others. ... The Lady Arbella was brought before the King and Council and answered well.

From all these rumours it is possible to distinguish the truth. It is very unlikely that Arbella would have become personally involved with the Duke of Moldavia. This man was a notorious mountebank who had taken in James with his plausibility when he came to England in 1607, and when he left in November of that year he had received a royal pension of £300. His name was Stephano Janiculo, sometimes called Bogden, for Bugdania was another name for Moldavia, a princedom in what is now Rumania, for which there were at least two other pretenders to the title walking about Europe. Janiculo claimed that he was going to marry Arbella, even though he was already married to a Venetian. His claim caused Arbella some distress when an allusion to his proposed marriage to her was made in one of Jonson's plays, *Epicoene*, produced at the end of November 1609 – just before Arbella was examined.

Later Arbella managed to have the comedy suppressed. The Moldavian aspect of the rumours can be dismissed as having been inspired by the performance of Jonson's play. There was some basis of truth in the mention of a Douglas, for Arbella's grandmother Lennox had been one before she married; but the Douglas rumour is not mentioned again. And there was no truth at all that Arbella had become a Catholic. If anything Arbella's beliefs now bordered on Puritanism, but this old hope by some, for Arbella's conversion, was always cropping up. From what followed afterwards, the Seymour rumour mentioned by the Venetians is the most likely cause of Arbella's embarrassment. Although many of the ambassador's reports to the Doge and Senate have proved to be wrong, in this instance he may have got his facts right.

By 12 January Arbella was cleared of any conspiracy and had returned to Court. It was given out that Arbella's previous reluctance to appear at Court was due to her lack of means; and that preparations for a voyage by her gentleman usher, Hugh Crompton – for it was he and not Douglas – was a personal matter; while the fact that she had considered buying a house in Lincolnshire was explained by her wish to economize. 'She confesseth that fault of her womanish credulity in the matter of love with the Prince of Moldavia, and in the people's opinion remains somewhat touched with the spot of Popery,' reported a contemporary. Arbella may have been happy to let the Moldavian affair become a cover to her involvement with the Seymours. She was forgiven, the king gave her a cupboard of plate worth £200 for the New Year, and she returned the compliment with a rich pair of slippers. The king also gave Arbella 1,000 marks to pay her debts. It was rumoured that the king was to increase Arbella's allowance by another £500. Certainly Arbella had need of this sudden and late royal generosity; she had a household of twenty-two servants which cost her £156 a year, without taking into account anything else.

But Arbella was not yet completely in the clear. On 2 February she had a visitor to her chamber at Court, and obviously it was not for the first time. It was William Seymour, second son of Lord Beauchamp and grandson of the Earl of Hertford. By 15 February it was reported, 'The Lady Arbella was lately again called before the Lords upon a new marriage which she has in hand to have concluded ... with the second son of Lord Beauchamp for the which fond proceedings of her she is strangely censured but notwithstanding she is left to live in the state as she did.' William Seymour was called before the Privy Council to explain himself on the twentieth of that same month. He made no mention of earlier visits nor of Arbella's social call at 'the house of one of the Seymour family'. In the main he took all the blame on himself and appeared something of a guileless young man. He told their lordships that as a younger brother he had to make his way in the world and so conceived the notion of proposing himself in marriage to Arbella, which he said was the purpose of his visit on 2 February, 'and she a lady of great honour and virtue and', he added in the light of later wisdom, 'as I thought of great means'. To have believed that, William Seymour must have been extraordinarily deaf to court gossip which had been buzzing with the details of Arbella's insufficient means.

Arbella did not dismiss this apparently unexpected proposal. She had been attracted by the Seymour family before when she wished to escape from Hardwick. Now when she wished to escape from Court, this visit from a younger Seymour must have appeared to her as predestined fate – that is, if she had not already made overtures. Twice more they met, once at a house in Fleet Street and a second time only two days before Seymour's examination, at the home of a Mr Baynton. Both times, said Seymour, the matter of marriage was discussed, but he made it clear that nothing would have been done without the king's permission. This of course was easy to say and could not be proved one way or another. He also told the council that he understood that Arbella had been given permission to marry whomsoever she wished. The council accepted this naïve explanation, which was extraordinarily trusting of them, but Cecil may have been lulled into believing too much in Arbella's lack of ambition for the throne. Arbella was once again restored to Court. She should have taken the two episodes as an awful warning but, with her belief in her own ability to survive, this was the last thing she was likely to do.[1]

William Seymour was a pleasant, pudding-faced young man with a long nose and fair hair. He was then aged twenty-two against Arbella's thirty-five. He had left Magdalen College, Oxford in 1605 and when he made his proposal to Arbella had been in and about Court for two years. Young Seymour may have given the impression of ignorance of Arbella's finances, but about his own family's troubles he must have been fully aware. If he was to survive he would have to marry money. His grandfather the old Earl of Hertford, who had led the embassy to Brussels in 1605, which was alleged to have cost him £12,000, was by 1609 in debt to the huge sum of £72,000.

The only explanation which makes sense of the reliable rumours is that before Seymour made his visit on 2 February Arbella had already encouraged him to make the proposal, and had indeed already decided on her course of action when she left on her Midlands progress. The house in Lincolnshire was to be a refuge when the uproar of discovery had died down, and her attempts to get her allowance increased were part of the plan for independence away from the Court.

Seymour's statement that he would not proceed without the king's permission was accepted; what had taken place over the past few weeks was allowed to be forgotten and Arbella was again reinstated at Court. The unreliable Venetians reported her as having attended the barriers (or jousting) for Prince Henry on 4 January, when she was either in the care of Lord Knyvet or confined to her own apartments. A draft of a letter in William's hand, perhaps never sent, may have been written in February breaking off the proposed marriage. Had Arbella received the note then it would have been of little consequence to her, as she would have considered it as being dictated by William's promise to the king. If she did receive it then she was not deterred, she had her grandmother's resolve and like her, once set on a course there was no deflecting her from it.

But, promise to the king or not, Arbella was not going to let young Seymour slip out of her net. About Whitsuntide, which was at the end of May that year, William met Edward Rodney at Lambeth. Rodney was a friend of whom the Earl of Hertford disapproved. He may have had good reason, and his reason was later justified. William told his friend that 'he found himself bound in conscience, by reason of a former pledging of his faith to marry her'. Rodney, who later poured out all this conversation under pressure of an examination, added that William did not reveal 'the means which he had used in reobtaining of her love'. Indeed he did not for Arbella had probably never let him off her hook.[2]

On 22 March the Irish licence at last was passed and granted but she shared the proceeds with Sir George St Paul and Henry Yelverton. The Venetians, in reporting this ten days later, as usual only got the story partly right in calculating Arbella's share as nearly £2,000; it is more likely that she got only a few hundred pounds a year.

It would be nice to report that Arbella had her portrait painted at this time and the reason would have been her undertaking with William Seymour; if she did, then the painting has been lost among the host of anonymous Jacobean ladies beguiling us from their frames. Of Arbella in later life there is only one original which by tradition has been said to represent Arbella Stuart, and the attribution comes from a copy of the portrait supposed to have been made by Robert Peake the Elder, which now hangs on the staircase at Longleat. The original from which this was taken was bought by the Ministry of Works in 1946 and now hangs in Marlborough House; this has been attributed to Gheeraerts the Younger. There is one other copy, also attributed to Peake, which hangs at Syon House. The original shows a woman in court dress and hairstyling of about 1605, a date at which Arbella had no reason to have her likeness painted. It bears little similarity to the earlier portrait of Arbella in 1589, which admittedly is a bad one, and comparisons between portraits of a girl aged thirteen and a half and a woman of thirty must be unreliable.

If this later painting attributed to Gheeraerts is indeed of Arbella, notwithstanding the inconvenient date, then the opinion of some of her contemporaries is correct – she is not beautiful, by our standards she is not even pretty or attractive. It would be more satisfactory to dismiss this painting as not being of Arbella at all. However the subject is wearing dress and jewellery of great cost, and Arbella was extravagant in these matters; four ropes of large natural pearls are worn over her shoulder in the style of a bandoleer and the dress too, heavily embroidered, apparently has pearls on it. A cross of large black diamonds hangs from her neck.

If the portrait is not of Arbella, at the least it shows someone in a similar walk of life, a lady of the Court wearing a farthingale dress. And it might easily have been something like the heavily embroidered farthingale dress covered with pearls which Arbella wore for the ceremony when Prince Henry was created Prince of Wales in 1610. One whole week had been set aside for the celebrations which lasted from 31 May to 6 June, the climax was the installation of the young prince at Westminster on 4 June. It was a day of great splendour and of course extravagance. Both Houses of Parliament were assembled and every notable of the land decorated with full colourful pomp to match a ceremony necessary to impress all with the importance of the occasion. In an upper room of the Court of Requests at Westminster sat the king's other son, the future Charles I. With him was his sister, later Queen of Bohemia, and Arbella with others of the queen's ladies. Down below in the great room of the Court of Requests the creation of the new Welsh prince was acted out against a background of colourful dignitaries and heralds dressed like cards from a new pack.

With the long ceremony at last brought to a successful conclusion, trumpets rang out a mighty blast supported by the rolling of drums. The deafening fanfare lasted a full fifteen minutes while the king, the prince and the whole Court of Westminster and of Parliament descended into Westminster Hall, and from there to the riverside and a waiting barge which rowed the principal actors of the day to Whitehall stairs with trumpets sounding on board all the way. That evening the prince dined with the new Knights of the Bath, created two days earlier at a ceremony held in Whitehall, after which each new knight had been ceremonially bathed in his own tub. But this night none but the prince was host. The king dined privately in the privy chamber and Arbella would have been at neither feast.

The night of the fifth was marked by Samuel Daniel's *The Masque of Tethys's Festival* played in honour of the new Prince of Wales. Henry's brother, the ten-year-old Charles, acted in the 'anti-masque' attended by two great sea-slaves and ten little girls, all daughters of earls and barons. They danced a complicated number of many changes to the absolute delight of all who watched. But Arbella was not among the spectators of the masque. The 'anti-masque' was followed by the 'main' led by Tethys, queen of all the rivers; this was Queen Anne bringing in Arbella as nymph of Trent, appropriately a river of her native Derbyshire. The other nymphs followed, including Alathea, nymph of Arun, a play on her title of Arundel. The queen and her attendant nymphs danced until within one hour of sunrise of that short summer night, when all retired to sleep off either their excesses or the exercise to be ready for the last day of the festivals. The king and queen had obviously forgiven Arbella for her earlier indiscretions.

But the king, the queen and Cecil were making a mistake. Both Arbella and William had been warned of the severe consequences should they marry. Why then did these two continue with their folly? Was Arbella in love with William by this time? Or, perhaps more likely, had she convinced herself that she was? William on his side had let the older Arbella persuade him that his promise of marriage was binding and she would not release him from it. In effect Arbella was repeating her earlier plan of escape from Hardwick. William, who owing to his improverished state could not expect a wealthy alliance, could look forward to a comfortable life married to Arbella and supported by her royal allowance. The Venetians were surprised that William should have allowed himself to become involved with the mature Arbella, but they were being unrealistic: his family's lack of money was the reason.

22

GRIEF OF MIND

The festivals of Prince Henry's creation as Prince of Wales had been over for only three weeks when, on what appears to have been a sudden decision dictated by circumstances, Arbella and William Seymour married on Wednesday 22 June 1610 at about four in the morning. The sudden departure of the king from Greenwich during the previous day may have caused the two to take the chance offered.

On the Thursday evening William Seymour had gone into London to the lodgings of his friend Edward Rodney to ask him to act as witness to their marriage. The two had returned to Greenwich by boat downriver at about midnight accompanied by Edward Kirton, one of William's gentleman servants. The three went to Arbella's chamber. As William later briefly confessed, they 'did sit up in the Lady Arbella her chamber until they were married'.

The long wait may have been due to difficulty in finding an obliging priest to marry them, but at last one was found in Crayford, seven miles distant, the unordained son of the Dean of Rochester. Arbella did not make the same mistake as Catherine in having only one witness; she had six as well as the minister. The witnesses were divided equally among the two parties. On Arbella's side at the marriage were two of her ladies-in-waiting, Mrs Biron and Mrs Bradshaw, and her gentleman usher Hugh Crompton, who had been with Arbella since before 1591. On William's side was his friend Edward Rodney, his gentleman servant Edward Kirton and a Mr Rawes, or Reeves. With this number to witness the marriage there could be no possible doubt of its fact, particularly as Hugh Crompton carefully noted their names in Arbella's account book with the place and time.

These witnesses and the minister were running a great risk by becoming involved in the clandestine marriage, but they were told by Arbella that she had the king's approval. Perhaps they were all sworn to secrecy; secrecy or not, the fact of the marriage had leaked out by 8 July. It is surprising that it had not been discovered earlier – they had contrived seventeen days of undetected married life.

William was sent for by the council on the 8 July, and from there he was taken to the Tower and the care of William Waad, later dismissed for crooked dealing. Arbella was given one day more of freedom, then a warrant was issued on 9 July ordering Sir Thomas Parry to restrain her liberty and lodge her in his house at Lambeth. As one contemporary commented, 'the great match which was lately stolen betwixt the Lady Arbella and young Beauchamp provides them both of safe lodgings.' Reeves and Crompton too were arrested, and thrown into the Marshalsea Jail. The Venetian ambassador reported the whole story somewhat late on 28 July, although the matter had been known by the Court almost as soon as the two were taken into custody. 'Both were summoned before the Council,' he wrote. 'The young man who was brought in first denied the fact; she, however, freely confessed it and excused the denial of her husband on the score of fear.' The Venetians may have got it wrong again; there is no other witness to William's failure to admit his marriage, and his confession of that day is short, straightforward and truthful. There it was; the matter was done. Arbella would have been sure of her own survival by one means of providence or another and William was the only man ever to have been associated with Arbella in a serious marriage proposal who had lived as far as the altar.[1]

James took a very grave view of Arbella's disobedience. Since the two were undoubtedly married there could be no undoing it, but they could be kept strictly apart so that there was no risk of children from the union of royal blood. There was a lot to be said for James's attitude: contested successions were notorious as a cause of civil war. On the other hand the queen, Prince Henry and Cecil all tended to support a policy of leniency towards the guilty pair. But by now Cecil's policy towards Arbella had been proved to be at fault and his advice was rejected. Although the general opinion at Court was that forgiveness would shortly follow, general opinion was wrong.

However in Arbella the expectancy of release burned bright. As a first step towards reinstatement she wrote to the council asking them to intercede with the king on her behalf. She expressed her sorrow at being the cause of James's displeasure, but offered no apology for her undutiful proceedings in marrying the only man forbidden to her. In another letter to James she defended herself by telling him that in her seven years at Court he had never found a husband for her, and that as a natural outcome of his negligence she had taken matters into her own hands – in other words the fault was not hers but James's. This argument cut no ice with the king. Arbella was overlooking the fact that she had been warned more than once not to marry William Seymour and the most recent caution had been in February. There was no excuse for her frowardness. Arbella had deliberately flouted her royal cousin; for James that was an additional reason for keeping Arbella shut away.

But if Arbella saw no wrong in disobeying the king, William Seymour was not blind to this aspect of their marriage. One petition written by William during this period survives. In it he apologizes for offending the king and in the same letter asks that he should have more freedom in the Tower 'to the recovery of my health, which through my long and close imprisonment is much decayed'. Arbella too was concerned about William and his health. She wrote addressing her husband with strict formality:

Sir – I am exceeding sorry to hear you have not been well. I pray you let me know truely how you do and what was the cause of it, for I am not satisfied with the reason Smith gives for it. But if it be a cold, I will impute it to some sympathy betwixt us, having myself gotten a swoln cheek at the same time with a cold. For God's sake, let not your grief of mind work upon your body.

For the moment, even with her swollen cheek, Arbella was determined not to let grief destroy her own health. But the time was to come when she realized that she had been defeated by the State's authority and then her own health was destroyed and she also.

Although she was shut away, Arbella's accommodation was not unenviable. She had lost her freedom to come and go as she pleased, but the household of Sir Thomas Parry, Chancellor of the Duchy of Lancaster, was a comfortable one. She still had her servants, apart from Crompton, who was kept in the Marshalsea. About her were three ladies-in-waiting and no less than eleven gentleman servants, underlining her royal status. This royal retinue was supported by only sixteen yeomen and others, which is a low number, but then Arbella had no need of cooks and bakers; the needs of her household had been supplied by the Court. However her yeomen servants included the ever-faithful John Dodderidge, Freake the embroiderer, and a laundry maid.

No doubt William was as comfortably waited on at his lodgings in the Tower. Arbella made several attempts to get Hugh Crompton, her usher, out of his unenviable placement. On 16 July she wrote to Gilbert Talbot, who was a privy councillor – his signature had not been on the warrant for Arbella's arrest – asking that he use his influence to release her imprisoned servants: 'I ... know not how to maintain myself.' This appeal must have brought some result, for three days later she wrote again to thank Gilbert for his care 'in disposing of my servants'. But Gilbert had not been completely successful, for Crompton was still inside the Marshalsea in August, as was William's servant Edward Reeves. In appealing to Gilbert for her servants' release she pointed out that there was a dangerous contagion in and around the prison and, should they die, she would be responsible for her servant's debts – a novel argument for the release of prisoners.

The minister who had married them was not forgotten by Arbella. As he was a key figure in the proof of the marriage it was essential that he should not be lost sight of as in the case of Catherine Grey. Her account book for November 1610 noted: 'Paid ... to the horse servant for going down for Mr Blague to Crayford when he was sent for by the Lords.' And in December there was a payment to the same Blague of £11. But what the poor man's thoughts were as he faced his predicament are something we are unlikely to know.

Her finances continued to be a problem to Arbella, although by her confinement her Court extravagances were reduced. The Crown was paying a diet money to Parry which covered the cost of herself and servants, but she still had her old debts to service. On the day she was arrested she had paid out interest of £25 on a loan of £500

secured on jewels held by a goldsmith Gorson, or more likely it was
Gosson of Fetter Lane. For the moment James continued to pay
the allowance of £400 quarterly and she still had the income from
her monopolies and estates. The economies of living which were
to be forced on Arbella would allow her more cash to spare for
clothes for herself, which she eccentrically continued to buy, and
presents for the influential; but for the moment she still retained
the extravagance of her costly retinue which amounted to £156
annually.[2]

From appeals to the king and the council Arbella turned to her
friends. On 22 July she wrote to the queen to thank her for mediating
with James. She also appealed indirectly to Henry Howard, the Earl
of Northampton, said to be of 'venemous and cankered disposition',
but where that got her cannot be said. In October she wrote yet
again to the queen enclosing a petition for the king; these she sent
under a covering letter to Jane Drummond, whom she would have
got to know well at Court, for Jane was the queen's first lady of
the bedchamber and one of only two Scots whom Anne allowed
herself to bring into England. Arbella asked Jane Drummond to
pass her letter and petition to the queen, at the same time enquiring
of Jane what she thought was in store for her – her initial optimism
was beginning to evaporate. Jane's reply could have given no comfort at all to the restricted Arbella: she feared that there would be
no easy end to her troubles and the only comment James had made
to Arbella's petition was 'Ye had eaten of the forbidden tree'.

Although involuntary constraint was no novelty to Arbella, Jane
Drummond's reply must have made her realize that she had placed
herself in a dangerous predicament and that the old and tried recipes
for release were simply not working. In none of the appeals, petitions and requests for help did she admit that she had disobeyed
the king – this was her psychological blind-spot. However, for the
moment undefeated, she tried again and sent, by way of Jane Drummond, a pair of gloves embroidered by herself for the queen. She
also wrote to other unnamed correspondents who might have been
likely to intercede in her troubles, which she now realized might
be more than a temporary inconvenience. Arbella was repeating her
programme of 1603 at Hardwick when she had deluged letters on

anyone who might have helped and many who certainly would not. It had worked then but only because there had been a change of power and policy on the throne. She had been lucky; plainly her methods were not working this time.

Judging by the number of letters written by Arbella during this period of her restricted freedom – and what survives must be only a part of the whole – there could have been no injunction preventing her correspondence. But no doubt copies of all Arbella wrote and received were sent to Cecil, the council and the king. Her letters were often taken by a servant Smith; since his name does not appear on Arbella's wage list, then he may have been one of William's servants.

Arbella's state of mind at this point is curious. Her reactions to restrictions on her freedom always brought out the bizarre in her make-up. In a reply to Jane Drummond she wrote, 'I say that I never heard nor read of anybody's case that might be truely and justly compared to this of mine, which being truely considered will be found so far differing as there can be no true resemblance made thereof to any others.' Arbella had lived with the romantic story of Catherine Grey and could not have forgotten it. Just who did she think she was fooling, herself or Jane Drummond, or the council who would have had a copy of that letter? Likely enough she believed what she had just then written, and likewise she had come to believe that she had never disobeyed the king. That she was repeating all over again the old formulae used at Hardwick indicates that she had not noted the changed temperature and circumstances at Court. Arbella was living again in her own imagination, a comforting refuge in time of calamity. She chose only to believe what suited her purpose and those who did not believe with her could only be wrong. This was her subconscious survival kit and it must have been severely shaken by Jane Drummond's comments.[3]

23

HIGHLY OFFENDED

Christmas of 1610 came and went but during the Twelfth Night celebrations Arbella was sent for by the council. This incident was reported to the Earl of Rutland on 4 January by his London steward, Thomas Scriven: 'That day the Lady Arbella is called before the Lords at Westminster in the Court of Wards Office, and I hear it – as yet a great secret – that she shall be sent to Durham, and there committed and confined to that Bishop's charge, with intent that she and her husband shall not come together.' One of the council members was Gilbert Talbot but he was reported sick of the gout – this may have been a diplomatic absence. The Venetians also got hold of a similar story; in fact they had been sending back to the Doge and Senate frequent references to Arbella's plight, some of it the usual unreliable gossip. In September they had reported that the king had been incensed when Arbella signed a petition in her married name of Seymour. This was probably correct, for it would have been typical of James to react with fury and Arbella did sign most of her letters 'Seymour' or with an ambiguous 'A.S.'. But in reporting the move they added that William Seymour was in the Tower for life and more closely guarded than before. Something had prompted James to wish Arbella at the other end of his kingdom. James was not by nature a spiteful man, but he had the highest regard for the authority of his kingship and Arbella had disobeyed him. There may have been more to it than just that.

During September Arbella had believed herself pregnant. Her stomach had swelled and her clothes had been let out. Rumours confirmed that she was to have a baby, and Dr Moundford was called in. Here was the reason for Arbella not renouncing her marriage, for signing herself with her husband's name. But it was only a false alarm. All Arbella was delivered of was 'an issue, or flux of blood which came from her'. This must have been a severe disappointment to Arbella; nevertheless she could try again for, notwithstanding the Venetians' statement that William was under close guard, he had a considerable amount of freedom to come and go within the Tower. There is from the evidence a strong suggestion that Arbella and William were seeing something of each other, even spending nights in each other's arms in the Tower. If they were, then James' decision to move the lovers as far apart as possible made sense from his point of view. On the other hand, if there was to be any sense in Arbella's marriage to William Seymour, then she just had to become pregnant and have a child.

Arbella was given official notice of her removal to Durham on 28 February. Scriven reported this to his master: 'On Thursday afternoon last, the Viscount of Fenton was sent to Lambeth to the Lady Arbella with direction to will her to prepare for her present journey to Durham, which I think will be before the King's return.' James was as usual hunting at Royston, and he wanted his cousin out of the way before his return to London. Arbella appealed to the Lord Chief Justice and the Lord Chief Justice of Common Pleas for a writ of habeas corpus, but it was all useless. The king had made up his mind and no judge was going to be so stupid as to try to alter his order. On 13 March a warrant was sent to the Bishop of Durham, William James, committing Arbella to his care. The king put his case clearly:

Whereas our cousin, the Lady Arbella hath highly offended us in seeking to marry herself without our knowledge (to whom she had the honour to be near in blood), and in proceeding afterwards to a full conclusion of a marriage with the selfsame person whom (for many just causes) we had expressly forbidden her to marry; after he had in our presence, and before our Council forsworn all interest as concerning her, either past or present, with solemn protestations upon his allegiance, in her hearing, never to renew such motion again. Forasmuch as it is more necessary for us to make some such demonstration now of the just sense and feeling we have, after so great an indignity offered unto us, as may make others know by her example...

James was essentially a truthful man – he had no reason to be otherwise – and this was a plain statement of his side of the story. He put it well, and behind the verbiage it can be seen that he was besotted with his authority and had forgotten that he too was a human being. Two days later, on 15 March, ten members of the council, of whom Gilbert Talbot was one, signed a warrant to Sir Thomas Parry ordering him to deliver his prisoner to the bishop.

This warrant was followed by another on the same day signed by only six, again including Gilbert. The first night stop on the long journey to Durham was to have been at Barnet but there had been some delay in the preparations and the second warrant went to Sir William Bond at Highgate instructing him and his wife to put up the prisoner for that night; the party was so late starting that they would never make Barnet that day. But Highgate was to be more than an overnight stop. Arbella remained there a full five days, having become ill – so ill that the journey could not continue. She had contrived something similar at Hardwick when she had been unable to get her own way, and it had been a ploy used continually by Mary, Queen of Scots. Arbella may have been present when Bess, her grandmother, had dismissed the opinion that her prisoner Mary was ill at all, when all others thought she was dying. Arbella was repeating history and repeating herself.

Arbella had with her Dr Moundford, President of the College of Physicians, now her personal physician. She had recruited his sympathies and he believed that his patient's illness was genuine. They had arrived at Highgate at around nightfall after a distressing journey in the course of which Arbella had fainted more than once. By the time they arrived at their destination she had worked on herself so well that she had to be carried into the house and was not asleep until midnight. Naturally the following morning Arbella told the bishop that she was too ill to go any further. If it was a masterly performance, all were taken in. But it may have been a genuine illness. It is very likely that on leaving London Arbella had discovered that she was not pregnant and that, with the realization that she was being moved far away from William and the possibility of conception, she became overwrought with despair and her grief of mind worked upon her body to make her ill.

Dr Moundford sent to the council for instructions due to this unforeseen set-back. Unrelenting, the king's advisers ordered the prisoner to be taken six miles to Barnet. It was an uncomfortable journey for all. Arbella, carried in a litter, was reluctant to proceed, and the unfortunate bishop had to 'recourse to the methods prescribed'. Again it sounded like one of Mary's forcible removals. Gilbert Talbot, when he heard what had happened, wrote at once to Moundford thanking him for his concern for Arbella: 'For my part I can do her very small service more than by my prayers.' Gilbert wrote the truth, for only that day he had tried to mitigate Arbella's lot by pleading with James, but it had got him nowhere. 'It was enough to make any sound man sick to be carried in a bed in that manner she is' was all he got from James, who felt no sympathy for anyone who defied his God-given authority. James too could remember something of his mother's dramas, although not at first hand; he was suspicious and sent down his own Dr Hammond on 26 March. Hammond was with Arbella for two days; even he was moved to compassion and recommended that she stay at Barnet until she was well enough to make the rest of the journey.

By now Arbella was absolutely determined to go no further on the detestable journey to Durham. A friend, Lady Chandos, sent a note of sympathy and a cordial to Moundford offering the doctor whatever he needed from her own household, all for his patient. Arbella's determination got what she wanted: on the advice of Dr Hammond, the council ordered that she be moved to East Barnet to the house of Mr Conyers. Immediately Arbella felt better. She welcomed the move. On 31 March she dressed herself for the first time for many days, but when they were unable to leave because Mr Conyer's house was not ready for them, Arbella had 'a violent attack in the head'.[1]

The king, through his council, had given Arbella a month to recover before the projected journey to the distant corner of England recommenced. But until the property of the obliging Mr Conyers had been discovered there had been trouble in finding a suitable house and, by the time Arbella had been moved, one week of the precious four had gone by. The party transferred to East Barnet on All Fool's Day and Arbella was extremely sick on the way. Once she had arrived at East Barnet, the good bishop immediately left her in the charge of Sir James Croft and went off to Durham to prepare his palace for Arbella's expected but delayed arrival. He stopped on the way at Royston to interrupt the king's hunting and report Arbella's state of health. Seven months later the bishop confessed to 'half a year's sickness and lameness, the relics of his attendance on Lady Arbella' and went to Bath to recover. The deplorable events of the astonishing journey of a few miles which had endured for two whole weeks had been too much for him.

With her change of keepers, Arbella's restrictions eased and, as the days of her permitted rest drew to an end, it seemed to Croft that his prisoner was in no better state to maintain the long journey to Durham than she had been before. He reported her condition to the council. She was better than she had been, according to his report, but she could not yet walk the length of her bedchamber. That was on 17 April. Arbella put on a convincing demonstration of a declining lover, passing her time in bed or lying on it fully dressed. Croft's kindly report brought a further extension of the truce and his prisoner was allowed to stay on resting in his concerned and relaxed care. Even ten days later Arbella was in no better shape and Croft sent another report to the council. By now it was 28 April and the deadline was extended to 6 May as the final and ultimate day for the delayed journey to begin.

Arbella supported Croft with a petition of her own to the king in a less indignant mood than her previous petitions had shown. She thanked her cousin for 'these halcyon days' and asked to be restored to his favour. She signed herself as his 'almost ruined subject'. But there was still only one way by which Arbella could have been restored to favour and that would have been for her to renounce her marriage and to apologize to James for disobeying his order; this was the last thing Arbella was likely to do. Also Durham was one of the last places she wished to go to. Arbella had told Croft that it was 'clean out of the world'. Finally Croft and Moundford both tackled the king, taking with them yet another petition from Arbella. She wrote her case with infinite care, but avoiding the only gesture which would have saved her. Mary Talbot lobbied the king's current favourite, Robert Carr, who had been made Viscount

Rochester; Prince Henry added his voice to the chorus behind Arbella; while Gilbert did what he could with his prayers.

It was all useless. James could only give way if Arbella saved his honour, and the only relief Arbella received was a further extension to her stay at East Barnet; the deadline was now 5 June. By her tactics Arbella had gained nearly twelve extra precious weeks and the time had not been wasted by her friends. It was a respite which Arbella put to good and immediate use.

Under Sir James Croft there had been an easing of Arbella's restricted freedom at East Barnet. Some visitors were permitted. Prince Henry sent one of his chaplains to attend the royal prisoner, so adding his prayers to those of Gilbert. Mary Talbot was another visitor. The Venetians noted Mary's visits – '. . . she was not allowed to go in the past.' This time their reports were right – they even credited her with obtaining the extra days' grace for Arbella. Somehow Arbella had scraped together £2,800, of which £1,800 was from Mary Talbot, including £850 which Mary had given to Arbella in payment for some needlework of Mary, Queen of Scots (later said to be not worth an eighth of the sum paid). This needlework could be the octagons and panels now at Oxburgh Hall, which may have arrived there through Mary Talbot's daughter Alathea. Arbella's aunt was the prime mover and financial backer in a daring plan to spirit Arbella out of England into the safe care of Mary's Catholic friends on the Continent.

The day appointed for the dreaded journey to distant Durham was Wednesday, 5 June but on Monday began what might have been one of the great romantic escape stories of all time. Between two and three in the afternoon of the Monday Arbella left the house in East Barnet disguised as a man. With her was William Markham, one of her loyal gentleman servants. She had achieved this extraordinary metamorphosis with particular ease by telling her chaplain's wife, Mrs Adams, that she was going out for the night to say goodbye to William Seymour for the last time and would return the next morning. The simplicity with which Arbella convinced Mrs Adams suggests that this was not the first time she had done this. The chaplain's wife helped her to dress the part, putting her into a man's doublet and a man's peruke with long locks covering her own hair

– the peruke had been made by a French clock-maker – completing
the ensemble with a black hat, cloak and rapier. Leaving the care
of her easy jailor for the last time, Arbella trudged off with William
Markham for a mile and a half to 'a sorry inn' where Hugh Crompton, released from prison, waited with horses.

The long walk after the inactivity of recent weeks was clearly telling on Arbella when she reached the inn. The ostler, curious about
Arbella's bizarre appearance, thought that 'the gentleman would
hardly hold out to London'. He noted that Arbella had difficulty
mounting the gelding he held for her, 'yet ... being astride in un-
wonted fashion, the stirring of the horse brought blood enough into
her face' as she rode unsteadily off towards Blackwall. It was fourteen miles across country and the three, Arbella, Markham and
Crompton, made their destination at six o'clock that evening and
found waiting for them at an inn, Edward Reeves, Edward Kirton
and Arbella's lady-in-waiting Ann Bradshaw, with William's luggage stacked around them. So far the escape had gone smoothly
and the six must have met with relief.

The carefully laid plans had arranged for William Seymour to
arrive at Blackwall but this did not happen; William was delayed.
However the hopeful and nervous group on the waterside at Blackwall could not know this and, while they waited, time was passing
and with it the favourable tides. Into one boat went Arbella and
Ann Bradshaw with the baggage, and a second boat took Crompton,
Reeves and Markham, leaving Kirton at the inn to wait for William's
arrival. With him was a maid who was probably left because the
boats were overloaded. Kirton and the maid waited, but William
did not come. An hour and a half passed and still there was no sign
of William; moreover they were being watched by a curious waterman. Suspecting that something had gone wrong, the two left Blackwall by a third boat disappearing downriver into the gathering night.

The destination of the escapers was a French boat, a bark
anchored downriver off Leigh some twenty-one miles from Blackwall. For Arbella and her companions that night must have been
a very fraught experience; they did not know what had happened
to William, neither did they know if their escape had been discovered. As the watermen rowed through the night, Arbella could

not know if the lights they saw from the shore or from passing boats were those of parties called out to search for them. On they went past the lights of Greenwich Palace where James was staying. Arbella may have wondered if the council was meeting at that very moment to discuss how best to recapture the fugitives. They were making good time, swept down by the racing ebb-tides but at Gravesend the oarsmen struck and would go no further. The tide may have turned and the difficult part of the night was ahead, but the offer of a double fare by Crompton bribed the reluctant watermen to continue the extraordinary journey through the night. At Tilbury they pulled for the shore to allow the rowers to refresh themselves with a drink. This must have been a worrying interlude for the figures left huddled in the two boats but it passed off without mishap, and when the watermen returned the party continued on its way. At the best of times those long reaches of the Thames can be eerie: the wide salt flats and mudbanks are made more frightening by the mysterious cries of night birds and the swishing gurgles of the strong tide-waters. It was quite a feat which Arbella and her party had wished on the watermen, since the tide was against them for half the journey and would have added to the difficulty of keeping the two boats together in the dark and of finding their course. The discomfort of the night would have been compounded by the cold night winds which always seem to blow even in high summer. It was expecting a lot of the oarsmen whose only involvement, in what must have appeared to them as an increasingly dangerous business, was financial.

Arbella had inherited some of the stamina of her grandmother to have survived this long night without sleep in a small open boat. Only days before she had been fainting and hysterical, yet here she was enduring the strain of a seemingly endless journey, at the same time knowing nothing of William nor what had become of him. But even more endurance was needed before the adventure was over.

When at daybreak the two boats arrived at Leigh, there was no sign of the French bark. Their disappointment must have been acute – the boat was in fact eight miles further on. But there were plenty of ships at anchor and Crompton in desperation offered the captain of a coaster any price to alter his course from Berwick and take them to Calais. Suspicious of this extraordinary offer and request to go in the opposite direction from that on which he was bound, the captain was made more so by the figure of Arbella in the boat, strangely muffled up in a black cloak and showing 'a marvellous fair white hand' when she pulled off a glove. He made particular note of the other members of the group: Reeves, aged about forty and running to fat; Crompton, younger and wearing a black beard; and Ann Bradshaw, in a black hat, whom he took to be Moll Cutpurse (a notorious thief and heroine in Middleton and Dekker's play *The Roaring Girle*) on the run. The whole thing was irregular and puzzling to the seaman. Wisely he turned down Crompton's offer but civilly pointed out the French ship they were looking for, now flying the French flag. He watched them as they went.[2]

Once on board Arbella was inclined to hold back, waiting for William's chance arrival, but Crompton and the others convinced her that they must think of their own safety and be away as soon as possible. By the time they had boarded the French bark the tide was too low to allow them to sail and they wasted two hours waiting for favourable water before they were at last away making slow progress against adverse winds which would blow them back to England. Meanwhile their escape had been discovered.

24

TRICKS AND GIGS

On the day before Arbella's escape – the Sunday – William Seymour's friend Edward Rodney had taken rooms in the parish of St Mary Overy, near the river and opposite the Tower. In the course of that day his landlady was surprised by the quantity of bulky baggage which her new tenant brought with him. The following day – the day of Arbella's escape – another bag was left in the rooms. There was too a great deal of coming and going of servants, and one, who might have been Ann Bradshaw, came to fetch a black wig made for Arbella by the obliging French clock-maker the evening before.

On the Monday morning William's gentleman servant Reeves who, like Crompton, had been released from prison, arrived, followed soon after by Ann Bradshaw. Again the landlady's curiosity was tested, for she saw all the bulky baggage being loaded into a waterman's wherry from where it was rowed to the inn at Blackwall. This was about two in the afternoon, even as Arbella was disguising herself as a man in East Barnet. As far as Rodney's landlady was concerned curiosity was added to curiosity by the mysterious doings of these gentlefolk and their servants when Reeves and Ann Bradshaw went out of the house in a furtive way and hired a boat at Pickle Herring near the Tower to carry them down to Blackwall where the luggage was waiting. Luckily the landlady suspected no treasonable goings-on, only a romantic elopement, and her gossip went no further than her family and friends.

All this preparation had taken a great deal of organization. The complicated business of finding a French ship willing to carry the escapers had been undertaken by someone experienced and trustworthy. This, and the finding of the French clock-maker prepared to supply the wigs, had been carefully thought out, but the plan involved too many people. Arbella and William were cumbered by servants and helpers who were making the whole more complicated than it need have been. But since the servants were involved with their masters, the punishment for the offence would fall on them as well, and their escape was nearly as essential as that of the two principals. Simple plots are the most foolproof, and the complicated time schedules of this particular escape plan involving no less than nine people was its undoing.

William Seymour as it happened had not been faced with much difficulty in his escape from the Tower; he was only late starting. But the time lag was fatal. He employed a means used many times both before and since. His lodgings were in St Thomas's Tower, close to Traitors' Gate on the river side of the fortress, but the windows of his rooms were narrow and as a way of escape impossible. Telling his barber Thomas Batten that he had toothache and wanted no callers that night William shut himself in his room. That Batten chose to interpret this order as an intention on William's part to slip out of the Tower and spend the night with Arbella, returning the next morning, is another indication that William had been meeting Arbella. William Seymour then disguised himself in a black wig and beard, and clothes of tawny-coloured cloth – the clothes of a carter's lad. It was now eight o'clock in the evening, and by this time Arbella had arrived at Blackwall and was already two hours downriver on her way to Leigh. Having put on his disguise, he slipped out of his door and walked out of the West Gate behind an empty cart which had been unloading billets at his lodgings. Why William should have left his escape so late was something he never explained, but his fatal delay may have been due to the late arrival of the carter. Leaving the shelter of the cart at the West Gate, he went down Tower Wharf past more guards and found his friend Rodney still loyally waiting with a boat at the Iron Gate landing. An hour later they were passing Blackwall.

Because they were late they made no stop at Blackwall but continued with the tide carrying them quickly onwards. As the boat was not so heavily loaded as Arbella's had been, the two reached Leigh without needing to bribe their watermen with double money.

Nevertheless they were too late to catch the Frenchman, which had sailed, and there was a storm coming up. They were lucky, and paying another waterman the huge sum of £1, they had themselves rowed out to a collier, the *Charles*, which was perfectly happy to take them to Calais for £40. The two men had not excited so much attention as the women had in the earlier party, and the captain of the *Charles* apparently saw nothing particularly surprising in the wish of two men to make an unexpected passage to France. The only surprise was his luck in finding passengers willing to pay £40.

Even now the escape might have succeeded had they previously made contingency plans for the two groups to rendezvous in France in the event of them not meeting up as arranged; astonishingly this had not been foreseen. But now there was another factor working against them. By eight o'clock that morning, when Arbella was sailing out of the lower reaches of the Thames and William was about to leave Leigh in the *Charles*, their escape was known to the authorities and the chase was on.

Edward Rodney shared his lodgings with Francis Seymour, the younger brother of his friend William, and before Rodney left on that Wednesday afternoon he had written a letter in vague terms which he hoped would explain his sudden absence; this was to be delivered on the Tuesday. As soon as Francis had the letter the ambiguity which was intended to save him from anxiety had the effect of sending him straight to William's lodgings in the Tower, past the protesting Batten at the door to find that William had gone. It needed little time to take the disturbing news to Sir William Waad, the Lieutenant of the Tower, and only a short time after that a rider was thundering down the road to the king and council at Greenwich Palace, past which Arbella and William had safely rowed the night before.

Consternation out of all proportion was the reaction at the palace. Arbella and William were no serious threat to James. Once landed in France they could become the focus of Catholic intent to replace James, but it was not a movement which would have had any support in England. James's consternation was caused by his attachment to his divine right to rule, to which he attributed all his actions and orders. Arbella and William had once more gone against him and must be brought back to face awful punishment. The only sensible reaction came from the old Earl of Nottingham, Lord High Admiral and Arbella's friend, who advised James to let them go.

Immediately a proclamation was issued ordering the arrest of William and Arbella by anyone who found them; Markham, Crompton and Rodney were included. By then it was known that the fugitives were on the high seas and the proclamation would have been ineffective. But more effective was the order to Admiral Sir William Monson to search them out at sea. On land the route the escapers had followed was easily traced and some had heard that the destination was Calais.

By nightfall of the Tuesday many of those connected with the escape were locked away. Mary Talbot was in the Tower, where she was to remain for many years; poor old Sir James Croft, who had dozed while Arbella walked out of East Barnet, was in the Fleet; and likewise the chaplain's wife Mrs Adams, who had helped Arbella to stuff her petticoats into man's hose for a disguise, was in the Gatehouse Jail at Westminster; Batten, the barber, had been thrust into a dungeon in the Tower by Waad as soon as he found William gone; and Dr Moundford, like Mrs Adams, was a close prisoner in the Gatehouse. Gilbert Talbot had been sent for to be questioned. The rumour spread that Lord Hertford, William's grandfather, had died of shock. In the circumstances he might have done, but in fact he was well and had been sent for by the king. Foreign powers were asked to return the refugees should they land on their shores. All possible steps were taken to retrieve James's honour.

Meanwhile Admiral Monson had calculated that the ships of the escapers would reach Calais about nightfall on the evening of Tuesday. They had the wind against them delaying progress but the same wind would also hold back his own ships sweeping the Channel between England and Calais. Arbella could have reached Calais and safety but she lingered, hoping that William would catch them up, and in delaying she was sighted by a fast pinnace, the *Adventure* under Captain Crocket who gave chase. The Frenchman did not give up easily, no doubt urged on by Arbella and Crompton, but it was no match for the faster and smaller vessel which shortly over-hauled the escapers. It took thirteen shots before the Frenchman heaved-to wallowing in the choppy swell of the Channel, and the *Adventure* sent over a boarding party armed with shot and pikes. There the naval boarding party arrested Arbella and Ann Bradshaw along with Crompton, Reeves and Markham.

This was the end of Arbella's escapade; it was also the end of Arbella, though she did not at that moment realize it. With some spirit she said that she hoped William had sailed free. As the *Adventure* was too small to hold all the prisoners, the French vessel was turned round and used to take the party back to England. They sailed into Sheppey, from where the unhappy five were taken by boat back up the Thames to London. With them went an extra prisoner, Tassin Corvé, the French captain. And so Arbella's last adventure was over and she had to prepare herself for the con-sequences. She had some consolation when told that Monson had called off the chase for William now that the principal offender had been captured, but she would have been happier still had she known that William had landed at Ostend. The adverse winds had forced them clear of Calais and, had Arbella known it, she could have landed in France and eventually met up with William. By hanging back in the Channel she had brought about her own capture and her final disaster.[1]

As Arbella entered the Tower she must have realized that she had no hope of release nor of pardon from James. Although in the past she had been blind as to his real nature, there could be no doubting the outcome now that she had defied him a second time. This was a serious blow to her pathetic belief in her own survival.

By the end of that week of doom, captains and watermen, gentle-folk and servants, anyone remotely connected with Arbella's escape was shut away until questioning should establish their innocence or guilt. But guilt of what? Arbella had never been charged with any offence and her restricted liberty was an illegal act, as she real-ized when she had asked the Lord Chief Justice for a writ of habeas corpus. Since her offence was never charged how then could anyone be guilty of aiding her escape? That was not quite the point, for had James wished he could have charged Arbella under the act of

1535 forbidding her marriage without his approval, but he had not done that. Arbella had disobeyed him and that was cause enough. All her contemporaries recognized this and if Arbella had come down to earth before it was too late she would have recognized the same. Had she taken after her grandmother Bess, who supported the authority of the Crown, then Arbella would have been assured of a safe and comfortable future, but she chose instead to rebel as her other grandmother, old Margaret Lennox, had done throughout her life. Arbella had brought about her own destruction.

Those who aided Arbella had mixed reasons for doing so. Mary Talbot was genuinely fond of her niece, but she was masterful like her mother Bess, and like Arbella she rebelled against established authority. It has never been explained why or how Mary Talbot become mixed up with the Catholics. In aiding Arbella so dangerously she was intending to embarrass James by shipping her niece overseas into the arms of foreign Catholics. Mary must have known what the consequences to herself would be. She may have trusted in Gilbert as a privy councillor to get her out of the inevitable trouble, but the exact reason for Mary to have chosen this suicidal course is all but inexplicable. Gilbert, it is true, was a disappointed man; the honours which had been his father's did not all come his way, and some even went to his greatest enemy Sir John Stanhope, created Lord Stanhope, so making Gilbert more bitter. Under James Gilbert never prospered and this may have had something to do with Mary's rebellion; on account of her trouble Gilbert resigned his place as a privy councillor.

As for Arbella's other active helpers, they were her servants whose future was tied to hers and as far as possible they did her bidding. Hugh Crompton, her usher, and Ann Bradshaw both suffered for their loyalty, as John Dodderidge had suffered in 1603. The queen, Prince Henry and Jane Drummond all supported Arbella because they knew her well and liked her enough, but their support went no further than petitioning the king; while Cecil, sick and prematurely aged, had been alienated by Arbella's foolishness.

The formal examination of the prisoners was held on 15 June. Arbella answered with descretion and sense; there was little else she could do. Mary Talbot on the other hand did her case no good at all 'crying out that all is but tricks and gigs'. After this interlude they were led back to their lodgings in the Tower and some of the other accused remained locked away until they had learned their lesson. Just before the examination Sir James Croft petitioned to be allowed free from his prison in the Fleet, pointing to his thirty-six years of faithful service. Hugh Crompton was not freed until July 1615, but one by one the prisoners were eventually released, all except Arbella and Mary Talbot.

On the Continent William was safe. The Archduke Albert, Governor of the Netherlands, ignored James's request to return William as a prisoner and allowed him to stay unmolested. In fact he was no longer a threat to James. From his landing at Ostend he went to Bruges and sent a messenger to find Arbella. Learning of the capture he petitioned Cecil, asking to be allowed to live quietly abroad with Arbella. He was told this was no deal but that as long as he continued to live in Holland he would be left alone. Later that year he was rumoured to have become a Catholic. On 3 September he left Brussels for Paris. Edward Reeves had joined him by the New Year. William had become a pathetic exile of no consequence and no regular income other than a small annuity from his grandfather, and smaller gifts from Arbella.[2]

Was Arbella in love with William Seymour? When the plan of marriage was first discussed and agreed upon she was certainly not in love with William; this was just another means of escape. After they were married Arbella's attitude changed. Possibly clandestine nights with William in the Tower and before were the reason for the change for, by the time they made their escape, Arbella's concern for William went beyond thoughts of her own safety, and if this is a measure of love then Arbella loved William.

25

NO OTHER WAY

Once again Arbella was illegally deprived of her liberty. Furthermore what money and jewels she had on her at the time of capture were taken from her – to pay the expenses incurred in the chase. Of the original sum of £2,800 which she had raised for the escape, all that was found was £868, a parcel of gold and her jewels, which were handed over for safe keeping to Sir William Bowyer, a teller of the king's receipts and responsible for paying Arbella's pension out of the Exchequer. It is not known which part of the Tower was allotted to Arbella. It has been speculated that she was put in the Bell Tower, but this is a small chamber and it is unlikely. Mary Talbot was put into the queen's lodgings with three or four rooms and allowed six servants, and it is unlikely that Arbella as a princess was given less. Certainly she petitioned to be allowed Mrs Chaworth, Ann Bradshaw and at least three other servants, including an embroiderer, to attend her. But once inside the Tower Arbella was forgotten by James. She had caused him inconvenience enough and now that she was shut away he could return to the pleasures of his court favourites and his everlasting hunting. Arbella's future was bleak.

At about Christmas time Arbella drafted a petition to the queen and as before enclosed another for the king. It brought no response from James, who did not wish to be reminded that his cousin was still alive – but only just alive. Arbella had become very sick after her arrest and in a pathetic letter to Viscount Fenton she asked not for anything so remarkable as her release but simply an easing of her circumstances: 'I can neither get clothes nor any posset ale for example, nor anything but ordinary diet, nor any complement fit for a sick body in my case when I call for it, not so much as a glister.'

Arbella was facing a problem common to all prisoners in the Tower lacking money for diet: for an easier life they had to bribe their jailor. Also she was concerned about nine items of jewellery, unaccounted for by Bowyer's list.

It must have been some consolation to Arbella to have her aunt Mary with her in the Tower, and no doubt the two were able to meet. Mary too was embarrassed for money; as late as August one of her servants was writing to Sheffield for funds saying that his mistress had no money with which to pay for her diet. But Gilbert's opinion was that his wife would not be long in the Tower, and Mary had handed over to Gilbert what money she had before she went. Gilbert, writing from Whitehall, instructed his Sheffield steward to use his discretion as to whom he told of Mary's imprisonment. If Gilbert imagined that the inconvenience was temporary, then he was sadly off course: Mary's plight was only slightly better than that of her niece. She had at least the semblance of a trial which was denied to Arbella.

On 30 June 1612 Mary Talbot's case was heard in the Star Chamber; this was not to decide her guilt but rather the sum of the punishment. She did not help her case by refusing to answer, pleading only that she had the privilege to answer to her peers and that anyway she had previously made a binding vow which prevented her answering. This inconvenient response together with the prosecution case put by the formidable Sir Frances Bacon ensured that her sentence should be the heaviest; and so it was – she was fined £20,000 and confined during the king's pleasure, which meant indefinite imprisonment. It was after all only to be expected in view of her Catholic beliefs. Gilbert's earlier optimism had been unjustified.

On 24 May 1612 Cecil died in great pain and even greater wretchedness from cancer; he was forty-nine. So James lost his best councillor and the one most likely to keep the king from political excesses. His death made no difference to Arbella, as both James and Cecil were in agreement that she should remain shut away in the Tower. It may be coincidence that immediately after Cecil died Arbella's allowance from the Exchequer was cut by half; the entry in the receipt book of the Exchequer shows her pension as being

£1,600 during her life, but this is crossed through and noted '*obit*', thereafter. From July she was only paid £800 annually in half-yearly instalments.[1]

The following year Arbella suffered a further loss when Sir William Waad, the Lieutenant of the Tower, was sacked in early May charged with having embezzled jewels from Arbella. This may have been a trumped-up charge for, a short time before this, a new prisoner had entered his care, Sir Thomas Overbury, who had fallen foul of the intrigues and politics of James's rotten Court. Overbury had opposed the ambitions of the Howard family in their attempt to get Frances Howard divorced from the young Earl of Essex and married off to Rochester, then James's favourite. The Howards had successfully contrived to get Overbury into the Tower, where hopefully they could remove by poison the obstacle impeding their progress. Waad by his strict interpretation of the regulations prevented any interference with his prisoner; within days Waad had gone and his place had been taken by a completely pliable successor, Sir Gervas Elwas. Then Frances Howard was able to send her poisoned tarts and cakes to Overbury without interruption; thus the Howards got their way. Overbury died in mysterious circumstances and Frances married Rochester. For two years they lived with their guilty secret until it all came out and they were tried. Arbella may have consoled herself with the thought that she was lucky to be missing the notorious corruption of the Court.

The months passed with hope fading for Arbella. She tried again to win some sort of response from James when Prince Henry died in November 1612. It was a brief letter telling him of her sadness and it was a genuine emotion, but it brought neither answer nor acknowledgement. As far as James was concerned his cousin was dead also. But although Arbella was effectively removed from the active world, she was not freed from its worries. Lord Grey of Wilton, who had been put into the Tower for his part in the Bye Plot, was still there in 1613. In May of that year he was in trouble over one of Arbella's women. Examined, the lady confessed that it was no more than 'a matter of love and dalliance'. John Chamberlain, writing of this to Sir Ralph Winwood, the Secretary of State added, 'The Lady Arbella is . . . restrained of late, though they say her brain continues cracked.' This same restraint was mentioned by another correspondent to Winwood on 20 July – Thomas Bull, who conceitedly attributed this to his own doing. He had been courting one of the Pierrepont ladies, cousin to Arbella (her name is in Arbella's accounts later that year). Bull told Winwood that 'some speech of my Lady Arbella's in some of her distempers ... speaking somewhat of my Lady Shrewsbury and me' had resulted in himself being committed to the Tower and in Arbella and Mary Talbot being kept more closely confined, while his lady love was put in the charge of one of the clerks of the council, and 'thus remained for full 12 weeks without ever stepping out of our lodgings'. Bull was overestimating his influence. The truth was more likely to be that the restraint of the prisoners was thought necessary during the period of the murder of Overbury, but neither correspondent was able to know of this; it was all kept secret.

Arbella had not yet lost all her optimism. Her former acquaintance or even friendship with Princess Elizabeth, the king's daughter, gave her hope that she might be released for the marriage of the princess to the Elector Palatine of Bohemia in February 1613. It was just a possibility that the king in a humane moment would relent. But James had become less and less humane and Arbella was forgotten. She had even gone so far as to buy four new gowns, including one reputed to have cost her £1,500 – an extravagance – but then she had little else to spend money on and she had always been fond of finery. Two years later, after Arbella was dead, one of her gowns, heavily embroidered with pearls, was taken from her effects to pay a debt of £400 – for pearls supplied to her and never paid for. Even in the Tower Arbella was living beyond her means.

On the Continent in his exile William Seymour had to support himself on an annual £400 from his grandfather, supplemented by payments of small sums from Arbella – £62 in January 1614 and £40 in March of the same year – and perhaps she sent William the *Book of Hours* which had been left to her by Mary, Queen of Scots. She dedicated it with the words 'Your most unfortunate Arbella Stuart'. During the French Revolution this book was taken to Russia and was last seen in the Hermitage Museum at Leningrad.

From Arbella's lodgings in the Tower the prospect of release was becoming more and more remote. All those who might have helped her were either overseas or still locked away. Gilbert had already admitted that he could do nothing and anyway he was seriously unwell. Arbella's uncles, William, Lord Cavendish and his brother Sir Charles, both followed their mother's later course; they had nothing to do with their troublesome niece. And Henry Cavendish, who had previously been so active in helping his niece and hindering his mother, had faded from the scene. However on 25 July 1613, with just over two years of imprisonment behind him, Hugh Crompton was released from the Fleet. Crompton may have had something to do with what looks like an attempt to get Arbella out of the Tower, but the report is so vague and ambiguous that it is impossible to know what, if anything, happened. One would like to know if William Seymour was behind the plan. On 23 November Gilbert Talbot was authorized to have Mary home, perhaps to nurse him in his sickness, but two days later she was ordered back to her prison lodgings. The reason given was as enigmatic as it was cryptic, but suggests an attempt to help Arbella escape: 'The place intended for the escape was under the study of Mr Ruthven. It had been carried out in great mystery and secrecy.' No more was said about it. No one was arrested at that time, unless the process took longer than usual, and Chamberlain, writing eight months later provides the clue, 'Dr Palmer a divine, and Crompton a gentleman usher, were committed to the Tower last week for some business concerning the Lady Arbella who is far out of frame this mid-summer moon.' Later that same month Edward Reeves was charged with being involved in a plan for Arbella's escape. For certain some attempt had been made and it had failed, but more than that cannot be added. One is left with tantalizing glimpses of the past – Arbella's accounts show a payment of £20 to Dr Palmer; was he the same Palmer who was charged with Crompton?

With the failure of this latest plan for escape all hope must have gone for Arbella. She lost the will to live, refused the useless physic and allowed no doctors to see her. In September 1614 the council sent Dr Felton to see Arbella. He was not a doctor of physic but of divinity, which indicates that there was concern about her spiritual welfare. Slowly Arbella withdrew from life, while around her life went on and would not leave her alone. Her devoted and loyal lady-in-waiting Ann Bradshaw left, perhaps through ill health. She returned to her native Derbyshire, to her husband at Duffield, another old servant of Bess's household. Samuel Smith, the loyal servant who joined Arbella about the time she married William, had been allowed back to her in the spring of 1614 after Ann Bradshaw had gone, and it was Smith who dealt with callers and kept creditors away. Nicholas Hooker, a goldsmith of Friday Street in the City, obtained permission from the council to see Smith about a debt owing to him – perhaps Arbella knew nothing of his visit. Finally it was Smith who had the agony of watching his mistress starve herself to death, refusing all food and sustenance. Arbella died on 25 September 1615.[2]

Samuel Smith was not the only one who was distressed by Arbella's death. Mary Talbot had been told two days before her niece died that she was much better, when it must have been plain to all that she was only a short step from death. Mary said that her own heart was so full of her loss that she could think of nothing else.

The day after Arbella died, Sir Ralph Winwood, directed Dr Moundford, as president of the College of Physicians, and five members of the college to examine her body – the Overbury murder had recently come to light and James was nervous – 'and thereupon certificate to be made of what disease she died as to their judgement shall appear'. The following day the six physicians went to the Tower at eight in the morning and did the post-mortem. They found that the cause of her death was:

a chronic and long sickness; the species of the disease was 'illam jamdiu producem in cachemiam' which increasing as well by her negligence as by refusal of remedies (for a year she would not allow doctors to feel her pulse or inspect her urine) by long lying in bed she got bed-sores and a confirmed unhealthiness of liver, and extreme leanness, and so died.'

Briefly they found that Arbella had starved herself to death and there was no other reason for her dying. Her body was embalmed, as had been her grandmother's, and with only a small ceremony at Westminster Abbey on 27 September she was placed in the vault of Mary, Queen of Scots, near the coffin of Prince Henry. At least Arbella was finally among friends.[3]

It has often been claimed that Arbella died mad. On balance this is unlikely to be true and the official evidence makes no suggestion that her mind was unbalanced. Chamberlain, the indefatigable correspondent of Winwood and Carleton, was partly responsible for the rumour; Chamberlain did not know her at first hand and he enjoyed making a good story for his friends. 'Far out of frame this midsummer moon' was an irresistible phrase. His rumour was helped by the fact that in starving herself to death Arbella in effect committed suicide, a current indication that her mind was temporarily disturbed. Again at Court Arbella was a misfit and out of tune; she plainly hated the corruption and aimlessness of James's Court. Consequently her behaviour was looked on as eccentric and bizarre. It all added up to the conclusion that she could not have been normal to have done as she did. That was not necessarily so, for even if her extraordinary philosophy, resulting from her peculiar upbringing, was singular, it did not make her mad. Furthermore it is very unlikely that anyone would have attempted to rescue a mad woman from the Tower in 1613. And when at last, imprisoned, Arbella realized that her philosophy was based on a faulty premise, it was too late; she must then have become fully aware of what was happening to her and with the awareness she knew that fate had nothing more for her, nothing to look forward to. She quite simply gave up hope of happiness in this world and departed, looking forward to something better in the next.

William Seymour, lurking in exile in Europe, was no threat to James after Arbella's death. Early in January 1616 when he petitioned the king to be allowed to return, his request was granted. He landed and saw James personally at Newmarket in February. William was forgiven. In James's eyes William had never been the culprit and later in the year, in November, he was restored to favour and created a Knight of the Bath. Notwithstanding his unfavourable beginning, William, through unexpected circumstances, brought his family name back into full favour and influence in affairs of state. William's father Lord Beauchamp, the son of Catherine Grey, died in 1612; his elder brother Edward in 1618; and when his grand-father, the eighty-two-year-old Earl of Hertford died in 1621, William inherited the Seymour estates, heavily in debt. He did not inherit the title, for his grandfather's marriage to Catherine had been made illegal by Elizabeth. William married a second time, this time the daughter of Queen Elizabeth's favourite the Earl of Essex, and they called one of their daughters Arbella. It took the oppor-tunity of the Civil War to fully restore the Seymours. William served the king with distinction and at the Restoration Charles II rewarded him by making the marriage of his grandparents valid. He was then made Duke of Somerset, a title dormant since the execution of his great-grandfather, the Lord Protector of Edward VI. The old Earl of Hertford would have been satisfied had he known of this future for his grandson. William too was presumably satisfied, though he died in 1660 only weeks after the title of Somerset was restored to him.

Mary Talbot's future was not so satisfactory. She petitioned the council for her release from the Tower and was given her free-dom on Christmas Day 1615, it is said to nurse her husband Gilbert, who died the following year. However the enquiry into the rumour of Arbella having had a child was held in June 1618 and once more Mary Talbot refused to answer questions on the same grounds as before, that she had made a vow which was unbreakable, though she relented far enough to say she disbelieved the rumour. The council was so angered by Mary's attitude that she was immediately put back into the Tower; the issue was not her intransigence but her religion. The old fine of £20,000 was resurrected – it had never been enforced – and Worksop Manor was seized by the Crown in lieu of payment. Mary remained in the Tower, occupying the best lodgings, until November 1623; she died in 1632. Hugh Crompton was transferred to the Fleet Jail and nine weeks before Arbella's death was released on bond of good behaviour. He and Edward Kir-ton joined the household of William Seymour and were members of Parliament for Great Bedwyn in the 1620s. Crompton died in 1645 and Kirton in 1654.

After Arbella's imprisonment in the Tower, her Cavendish uncles had no more to do with her. William chose to spend his vast wealth on another title and in 1618 he paid the enormous sum of £10,000 for the vacant earldom of Devonshire. Another investment William dabbled in was 'adventuring', the financing of colonizing expeditions to Russia, the East and West Indies and America. In the year Arbella died he was spending on average £2,500 on such speculation. He died in 1626. Her two other uncles did not live long after Arbella's sad death. Henry Cavendish sired a great many illegitimate children in both Staffordshire and Derbyshire, dying in 1616 in debt. Through his illegitimate son Henry came the Lords Waterpark who continued to live on the old Cavendish lands at Doveridge near Chatsworth until this century. Charles Cavendish died in 1617, almost as wealthy as his mean brother William, and from Charles came indirectly the dukes of Portland who until 1977 occupied the Welbeck lands which Charles had bought from Gilbert Talbot in 1607. From Arbella's aunt Frances who married Henry Pierrepont came the dukes of Kingston and eventually the earls Manvers. Except for Arbella all Bess's grandchildren succeeded in lives which would have brought approval from their grandmother; only Arbella, who might have enjoyed the greatest and most glorious success as a queen, failed. It was a failure which did not trouble Arbella.

In writing her draft letter to Viscount Fenton pleading for better circumstances in the Tower, Arbella crossed out lines and altered words she thought better of sending. One line crossed through ran: 'And if you remember of old I dare to die so I be not guilty of my own death, and oppress others with my ruin too, if there be no other way.' Indeed there was no other way as Arbella realized.[4]

ABBREVIATIONS

The following abbreviations have been used in the note reference:

Manuscript collections calendared by the Historical Manuscript Commission

HMC(Bath): Longleat MSS at Longleat House, Wilts.

HMC(Downshire): The manuscripts of the Marquess of Downshire

HMC(Hastings): The manuscripts of the Hastings family

HMC(Portland): The manuscripts of the Duke of Portland

HMC(Rut.): The manuscripts of the Duke of Rutland at Belvoir Castle, Leics.

HMC(Sals.): The manuscripts of the Marquess of Salisbury at Hatfield House, Herts.

Col. of Arms: joint HMC publication with the Derbyshire Archaeological Society of *A Calendar of Shrewsbury and Talbot Papers in the College of Arms*, ed. G. R. Batho

Lambeth Palace: another joint publication by the HMC and DAS is *A Calendar of the Shrewsbury Papers in the Lambeth Palace Library*, ed. E. G. W. Bill

APC: Acts of the Privy Council. Published by the Public Record Office

PUBLIC RECORD OFFICE

SP(Dom.) State Papers Domestic
SP(Hol.) State Papers Holland
SP(Ven.) State Papers Venetian
SP(Spain) State Papers Spanish

Folger: refers to the Folger Shakespeare Library at Washington, Mass., USA.

NOTES

1 SO FAR IN LOVE
1 Cooper, *The Life and Letters of Lady Arabella Stuart* (1866), vol. I, p. 33.
2 *Ibid.*, p. 31.
3 SP(Dom.), 12/99, no. 13.
4 Col. of Arms, vol. G, f170.
5 Cal. of Scots Papers, vol. V, no. 202.

2 ARABELLA COMITESSA LEVINOX
1 For the names of the godparents I have relied on E. T. Bradley, *Arabella Stuart* (1889), vol. I, p. 34, which does not give a reference. Both Cooper, in her *Life of Arabella Stuart*, and Bradley – copied by P. M. Handover in *Arbella Stuart* (1957) – give the place of baptism as Chatsworth on the evidence of a Stuart pedigree (Harlèian 588, ff1 and 23); however the place name of Chatsworth on the pedigree was added later in another hand. In view of the evidence of the correspondence addressed from Hackney I am inclined to believe that Arbella was baptized from her paternal household at Hackney.
2 The detail of Margaret's debt to Bess is in SP(Dom.), 64/30, no. 333. Bess's obtaining of a dowry for Elizabeth is described in Landsdowne 40/41. Shrewsbury's comment on the Stuart marriage is in Col. of Arms, vol. F, f103.

3 SHE ENDURED VERY WELL
1 The references to the allowances are found in SP(Dom.), Eliz. I, vol. CLII, pp. 42, 43 and 53, also Cal. of Scots Papers, vol. VI, nos 95 and 96. Bess's letter mentioning that Arbella has been left at Chatsworth is addressed to Walsingham and dated, from Sheffield, 29 December 1578, HMC(Sals.), vol. II, no. 675.

2 Jane Grey's comment on her parents is taken from Roger Ascham, *The Scholemaster* (1570), p. 47.

3 For the full details of Shrewsbury's quarrel with Bess, and the 1572 deed of gift see David N. Durant, *Bess of Hardwick* (1977), ch. 8.

4 OF VERY GREAT TOWARDNESS

1 The will of Elizabeth Stuart, dated 16 January 1581/2, is in Hardwick Drawer 279 (4). Bess's letter to Burghley of 6 May 1582 is in Lansdown 34, p. 143, and that to Walsingham, SP(Dom.), vol. CLIII, p. 53.

2 The reference to the interview between the queen and Esmé Stuart is from SP(Span.), 1580–6, pp. 241–3, 244.

3 For details of the quarrel between Shrewsbury and Bess, see Durant, *Bess of Hardwick*, ch. 8.

4 Lord Paget's letter dated 4 March 1584, SP(Dom.), vol. CLIX, p. 8; and Leicester's letter dated 26 June 1584 is from Miss Lloyd's MS. at Althorp House, pp. 6–7; Beale's letter dated 23 May 1584, HMC(Rut.), vol. I, p. 166.

5 Mary's letter to Mauvissière dated 21 March 1584 is printed in J. D. Leader, *Mary Queen of Scots in Captivity* (1880), p. 551. For full details of the episode of the rumours and the 'scandal letter' see Durant, *Bess of Hardwick*, pp. 129–31.

5 IT WOULD BE A HAPPY THING

1 For the details of Walsingham's involvement in the Babington Plot see P. Johnson, *Elizabeth I* (1974), pp. 283–6.

2 The Armada was reported to Burghley and Walsingham on 10 December 1585, SP(Dom.), vol. CLXXV, no. 16.

3 Mendoza's suggestion of the marriage is in a letter dated 24 December 1586, SP(Span.), 1580–6, p. 688; Walsingham's offer to Parma, SP(Hol.), vol. XVIII.

4 The reference to court procedure is from Paul Hentzner, *A journey into England in the year 1598* (printed at Strawberry Hill in 1757), pp. 51–2.

5 The letter from Charles Cavendish to Bess, undated, is in Hardwick Drawer 143 (10). The report from Chateauneuf, the French ambassador to Henri III, dated 27 August 1587, is in Agnes Strickland, *The Tudor and Stuart Princesses* (1888), p. 215.

6 The details of Harington's visit to Arbella are in J. Harington, *Tract*

on the Succession to the Crown (1602?), p. 44. The inventory of Arbella's plate is in Hardwick Drawer 143 (8).

6   GOOD LADY GRANDMOTHER

1   Arbella's letter addressed from Fines is printed in HMC, 3rd Report, p. 420.

2   Arbella's behaviour at Court in 1588 is described in a report to the Doge and Senate in 1603, SP(Ven.), vol. IX, p. 541. Her own remarks on the same incident, also made in 1603, are given in Bradley, *Arabella Stuart*, vol. 2, p. 152.

3   The part which Crofts played in the negotiations is set out in Conyers Read, *Mr. Francis Walsingham and the Policy of Queen Elizabeth* (1925), vol. 3, pp. 272–3. The comment by the Venetians is in SP(Ven.), vol. X, p. 41. The queen's enquiry after Arbella is in Folger Xd 428 (115).

4   For the previous history of the *Talbot* see Durant, *Bess of Hardwick*, pp. 105–6; J. K. Laughton, *The Defeat of the Spanish Armada* (1894), vol. 1, p. 31, vol. 2, pp. 287, 326, 337.

5   Kinnersley's letter to Bess, dated 5 November 1588, is in Folger Xd 428 (44).

7   I PRAY YOU SEND ME HER PICTURE

1   Shrewsbury's prophesy is found in SP(Dom), vol. CCXXXIII, no. 73.

2   Phelippes's letter of 31 October 1591, SP(Dom.), vol CCXL, no. 53; the letter referring to Mr Hildyard, SP(Dom.), vol. CCXXXIX, no. 164; the letter from Moody of October 1591, HMC(Sals.), vol. IV, p. 144.

8   THEY ARE VANISHED INTO SMOKE

1   For more details of this visit to London, see Durant, *Bess of Hardwick*, ch. 11. The reference to the blue and white starches is in Hardwick MS.7, f11v. The pair of bracelets is accounted for in Hardwick MS.7, f10v.

2   Arbella's cynical comment is from a long undated letter printed in Bradley, *Arabella Stuart*, vol. 2, p. 166; for Hilliard's payment see Hardwick MS.7, f30. The reference to communion at Easter is in Hardwick MS.7, f19; likewise Arbella's gift to Mrs Digby for her new baby.

3   For the despatch of Burghley's agent to Flushing see HMC(Sals.), vol. XIII, p. 465. For the reference to Spanish shoes see Hardwick MS.7, f23.

4 The adventures of Dingley the priest are found in his confession SP(Dom.), vol. CCXLII, no. 121.

5 Bess's letter to Burghley dated 21 September 1592 is printed in Cooper, *Life … of Arabella Stuart*, vol. 1, pp. 119–23.

6 Burghley's diary note is in HMS(Sals.), vol. XIII, p. 467.

9   MY JEWEL ARBELLA

1 Durant, *Bess of Hardwick*, p. 229.

2 The main details of the loan to Willoughby are *ibid.*, p. 177; for the valuation of the lands see SP(Dom.), vol. CCLXV, no. 82. The purchase of Skegby is accounted for in Hardwick MS.9, f33.

3 The payments of the sums of £100 are in Hardwick MS.7, ff35, 36v. There are other references to similar sums in William Cavendish's account book MS.23, in which the folio pages are not numbered. The payment of the legacy is recorded in Hardwick MS.7, f83v.

4 The gifts to Arbella are accounted for as follows: £350, Hardwick MS.7, f92; £20 for 'vials', *ibid*, f140v; the bone lace, Sheffield Public Libraries, ex Philippes, f17; £100 for the pearl, Hardwick MS.8, f60v.; and 'certain household stuff', Hardwick MS.7, f84.

5 Payment to Thomas Hood is recorded in Hardwick MS.7, f194, and Bess's letter to Burghley dated 21 September 1592, is in Lansdowne, vol. 7, f2.

10   YE DRAWING-ROOM DOOR

1 The queen's players visited Chatsworth in 1593, Hardwick MS.7, f63v; Hardwick in 1596, *ibid.*, f161v; and again in 1600, Hardwick MS.8, f104. Lord Howard's players were at Hardwick in 1600, *ibid*, f.108v; Lord Ogle's in 1593, Hardwick MS.7, f78; in 1594, *ibid.*, f110v and in 1595, *ibid.*, f139; Lord Pembroke's in 1600, Hardwick MS.8, f82v. The group at the drawing-room door at Christmas 1596 are mentioned in Hardwick MS.7, f172; and the Singing of Starkey, Good and Parker in 1601 in Hardwick MS.8, f150.

2 Thomas Wilson, *The State of England Anno Dom 1600* (1936), Camden Miscellany, vol. XVI.

11   SHE WOULD BREAK FORTH INTO TEARS

1 The details of the New Year gifts are taken from J. Nichols, *The Progresses, Processions and Magnificent Festivities of King James I*, (1788–1821), vol. 3, p. 460. The rumour of Cecil's marriage to Arbella is mentioned in SP(Dom.), vol. 289, no. 72. The argument

on the succession is printed in Handover, *Arbella Stuart*, pp. 309–
13.

2 Arbella's comment on Essex is contained in a long letter to Bronker,
printed in Bradley, *Arabella Stuart*, vol. 2, p. 158.

3 For Starkey's confession see *ibid.*, pp. 92–7.

4 For Dodderidge's confession see HMC(Sals.), vol. XII, pp. 583–6,
and Bradley, *op. cit.*, vol. 2, pp. 98–9.

5 'The report of the Earl of Hertford's man', from which this account
is taken, is in HMC(Sals.), vol. XII, pp. 627–30, and Dodderidge's
letter to Arbella is in *ibid.*, p. 536–7.

12 SOMEWHAT TROUBLED

1 For a more detailed account of Catherine Grey's marriage see Durant, *Bess of Hardwick*, pp. 40–4.

2 Bronker's report to the queen is in HMC(Sals.), vol. XII, pp. 593–
6.

3 Bronker gives his account of the return journey in HMC(Sals.), vol.
XII, pp. 596–7. The statement from David Owen appears in *ibid.*,
p. 605.

4 The letters intercepted by Pusey are in HMC(Sals.), vol. XII, p. 606,
608–9; Bradley, *Arabella Stuart*, vol. 1, pp. 118–19. The letter from
Cecil and Stanhope, dated only 1602–3, is in *ibid.*, pp. 626–7.

13 VAPOURS ON HER BRAIN

1 Arbella's submissive letter to the queen, Bradley, *Arabella Stuart*,
vol. 2, pp. 100–3. She also wrote another short letter of apology to
the queen, *ibid.*, pp. 99–100. Her letter revealing her secret lover,
but not his name, *ibid.*, pp. 103–13, was sent on 2 February 1603
by Bess to Stanhope and Cecil with a covering letter, HMC(Sals.),
vol. XII, pp. 682–3. Arbella's letter of 6 February 1603 to Cecil and
Stanhope, asking for Bronker, Bradley, *op. cit.*, vol. 2, pp. 113–18.

2 For Starkey's confession see Bradley, *op. cit.*, vol. 2, pp. 92–7. For
Arbella's letter to Edward Talbot see *ibid.*, pp. 119–20. Bess's letter
to Cecil telling him that Arbella was refusing to eat, *ibid.*, pp. 120–
1. The date for Arbella's return from Owlcotes is taken from William
Cavendish's account book, Hardwick MS.23 (unnumbered folios).
For Bronker's list of questions with Arbella's ridiculous answers on
2 March see Bradley, *op. cit.*, vol. 2, pp. 124–9.

3 Arbella's long and often hysterical letters to Bronker are printed in
ibid., vol. 2, pp. 137–60. Her comment on men on 4 March, *ibid.*,

p. 143; on 7 March, *ibid.*, p. 146; and the remark 'they are dead whom I loved' on 9 March, *ibid.*, p. 148.

4 Bess's weary letter written late at night on 10 March, describing the events of the day to Bronker, HMC(Sals.), vol. XII, pp. 689–90. Stapleton's earlier visit to Hardwick is recorded in Hardwick MS. 7, f106.

14 DESIROUS TO FREE OUR COUSIN

1 The cautious reply by the council to Bess on 14 March 1603 is printed in Bradley, *Arabella Stuart*, vol. 2, pp. 690–2. The warrant from the council to assist Bronker, HMC(Rut), vol. I, p. 388, and in a letter dated 16 March, addressed to the council, Bronker mentions his warrant for Henry Cavendish's arrest, HMC(Sals.), vol. XV, p. 4.

2 The report of the visions seen at Court before Elizabeth's death is taken from J. Chamberlain, *The Letters of John Chamberlain*, ed. N. E. McClire (1939), vol. 2, pp. 188–90. The fact that the queen never named James as her heir is dealt with in Johnson, *Elizabeth I*, p. 436.

3 The visit made by James to Worksop and Newark is described in Nichols, *Progresses etc.*, *of Jas. I*, vol. I, pp. 85–93. The king's order or request to Henry Grey is printed in HMC(Sals.), vol. XV, p. 65. Arbella's refusal to attend Elizabeth's funeral is given in Sloane 718, ff37–9.

4 Scaramelli's report is published in SP(Ven.), vol. IX, p. 541. Bronker states that Arbella is at Hardwick on 25 March 1603, HMC(Sals.), vol. XV, p. 4.

15 LIVING VERY RETIRED

1 Evidence that Arbella's page Richard Owen was still at Hardwick on 6 April is in HMC(Sals.), vol. XV, pp. 40–1. James gave his approval that Arbella should attend Court, *ibid.*, p. 82. Scaramelli's report of Arbella's 300-horse-power visit, SP(Ven.), vol. X, p. 42. Gilbert Talbot's report of the conversation between James and Cecil, dated 18 May 1603, is in Lambeth MSS, vol. 709, f86. Arbella's letter addressed to Cecil from Sheen, about her pension, Bradley, *Arabella Stuart*, vol. 2, p. 176. Her thanks to Cecil for the increase, *ibid.*, p. 179. The sum of £666 is given in Nichols, *Progresses etc.*, *of Jas. I*, vol. I, p. 426.

2 Arbella's letter to Gilbert Talbot from Farnham Castle, dated 14 August 1603, is in Bradley, *op. cit.*, vol. 2, p. 180, and the report from the unreliable Scaramelli is in SP(Ven.), vol. X, p. 82. Arbella's

increased pension is given in Nichols, *Progresses etc.*, *of Jas. I*, vol. 1, p. 272, and also in Col. of Arms, vol. M, f120.

3   The details of Raleigh's trial are mainly taken from Harleian 39; the account begins on p. 275 and thereafter is scattered as a page filler. The same source and others are used in D. Jardine, *Criminal Trials* (1832), vol. 1, pp. 389–520, published in 1832 by The Library of Entertaining Knowledge! The comment on Lord Cobham is from A. Weldon, *Secret History of the Court of James I* (1811), vol. 1, p. 342, while Arbella's reaction on receiving Cobham's letter is given in Nichols, *op. cit.*, vol. 1, p. 296–7.

16   WHY SHOULD I BE ASHAMED

1   Arbella's comment on the ladies of the Court is given in a letter to Mary Talbot, dated 23 August 1603, Longleat MSS, Talbot letters, vol. II, f190.

2   Fowler's overblown admiration of Arbella is contained in two letters, one of 11 September 1603, printed in E. Lodge, *Illustrations of British History* (1791 and 1833), vol. 3, p. 169, and the other, dated 8 December, but unpublished, is in Col. of Arms, vol. K, f163.

3   Gilbert's letter to Worcester is published in Lodge, *op. cit.*, vol. 2, p. 227, and Worcester's letter to Gilbert about Nottingham's marriage night, dated 24 September 1603, Col. of Arms, vol. K, f129.

4   Arbella's letter to Gilbert commenting on how the Court passed their time, written from Fulston on 8 December 1603, is in Longleat MSS, Talbot letters, vol. II, f208, while her letter from Woodstock addressed to Gilbert and dated only 16 September is in Col. of Arms, vol. K, f124, but published in Nichols, *Progresses etc.*, *of Jas I*, vol. 1, p. 263.

5   Arbella's letter of 8 December 1603 addressed to Gilbert, concerning the New Year gifts, Longleat MSS, Talbot letters, vol. II, f206. And her letter written to Gilbert from Hampton Court dated 18 December 1603 is in Add. MSS 22, 563, f47.

6   The description of the play, *Robin Goodfellow*, is from Dudley Carleton's letter to his friend Chamberlain dated 15 January 1603–44, in *Dudley Carleton to John Chamberlain, Jacobean Letters* (1971), ed. Maurice Lee, p. 53. The masque *The Vision* is forecast in Arbella's letter to Gilbert of 8 December 1603, Longleat MSS, Talbot letters, vol. II, f206. She confessed to toothache in a letter to Mary Talbot, Sloane MSS, vol. 4164, f195. The gift from Cecil is mentioned in her letter dated 11 January 1603–4 written to Gilbert, *ibid.*, f187.

17 SUMPTUOUS AND PROFUSE

1   Arbella's comment on her carving is given in her letter, dated only 1603–4 (but probably March), to Gilbert, Longleat MSS, Talbot letters, vol. II, f232. Her letter dated 3 February 1603–4, also to Gilbert, suggesting that he might pay for Henry and Grace Cavendish to visit London, *ibid.*, f222. Henry Cavendish is mentioned in connection with the Main Plot in Col. of Arms, vol. M, f124.

Gilbert's debts are covered by Folger Xd 428 (81); L. Stone, *An Elizabethan, Sir Horatio Palavicino* (1956), pp. 193–9; his debts to Greville, Col. of Arms, vol. M, ff266 and 7; to Robert Dudley, *ibid.*, ff173, 278; to Francis Leake, *ibid.*; to Michael Hicks, A. Smith, *Servant of the Cecils. Life of Sir Michael Hicks* (1977), pp. 150, 156–7, 172, 205; to Alexander Ratcliffe, Col. of Arms, ff226, 296, 591. It has sometimes been suggested that Fulke Greville was involved in some way with Arbella. I have found no evidence of that whatsoever.

Gilbert's purchase of Hartington, Derbyshire is in Col. of Arms, vol. M, ff181, 187. The evidence for William Cavendish's visit to London is Hardwick Drawer 143 (14).

2   Arbella's letter from Woodstock, dated 16 September 1604, addressed to Gilbert, mentions de Taxis, Col. of Arms, vol. K, f124.

3   Pembroke's letter from Woodstock, dated 3 October 1604, addressed to Gilbert is printed in Nichols, *Progresses etc.*, *of Jas. I*, p. 458 n. Arbella's remark to Gilbert about Pembroke's marriage in a letter dated only 1604 (but probably March) is in Sloane MSS 4161, ff118–19. William's letter to Bess on 4 July 1604, about Arbella's promotion of his peerage, Folger Xd 428 (23).

18 EARNESTLY TO COME AWAY

1   The reference to the queen isolating her Court is given in HMC(Sals.), vol. XVI, p. 382. Arbella's increased pension is granted in SP(Dom.), Jas. I, vol. X, no. 56. And the reference to James having a romp in the marriage bedchamber is given in a letter from Dudley Carleton to Chamberlain, dated 7 January 1604–5, ... *Jacobean Letters*, ed. Lee, p. 66.

2   Worcester's letter to Gilbert, dated 4 December 1604 from Royston, complaining about the late hours, Col. of Arms, vol. K, f233. Bess's letter to Montague is printed in part, in Cooper, *Life ... of Arabella Stuart*, vol. 2, p. 49 without giving the reference. The letter cannot be traced.

3   Sir Francis Leake noted Arbella's arrival in a letter to Gilbert dated
    13 March 1605, Lambeth MSS, Shrewsbury papers, vol. 704, f82.
    Bess's generosity to Arbella on the occasion of the visit is taken
    from Cooper, *op. cit.*, vol. 2, p. 49 in which a letter (undated) is
    quoted but no reference is given. The letter has not been traced.
    The reinstatement of Arbella's legacy is given in a list of William's
    disbursements after his mother's death, Hardwick Drawer 143.
    Montague's letter of 11 April 1605, addressed to Bess is in Col. of
    Arms, vol. L, f7. William's payment of £2,000 for his peerage is
    accounted for on 8 May 1605, in his account book, Hardwick MS.23
    (unnumbered folio pages).

4   The comment on the Countess of Pembroke is in Col. of Arms, vol.
    L, f15. Arbella's letter to Prince Henry, dated 18 October 1605, Har-
    leian MSS 6986, f71. The news of Father Garnet's hanging is given
    by Dudley Carleton to Chamberlain in a letter dated 2 May 1606,
    ... *Jacobean Letters*, ed. Lee, p. 80. The warrant to watch over the
    safety of Bess is in HMC(Rut.), vol. I, p. 399. Holles's invitation to
    Arbella is in HMC(Portland), vol. IX, pp. 152–3.

5   The report of the drunkenness at Theobalds is given in Harington,
    Nugae Antiguae (1792), vol. I, p. 348. The account of Sir John
    Lucien's ducking is in a letter dated 20 August 1606 from Dudley
    Carleton to Chamberlain, Lee (ed.), *op. cit.*, p. 88. The letters to
    Arbella asking her to let her lutanist go to Denmark are printed in
    Bradley, *Arbella Stuart*, vol. 2, pp. 215–21.

19   ARBELLA GOES BEYOND HER

1   Molin's report to the Doge and Senate, dated only 1607, is in
    SP(Ven.), 1603–7, p. 517. Arbella's loan from William Cavendish is
    accounted for in his account book on 18 May 1605, Hardwick MS.23
    (unnumbered folio pages). The note of the windfall of the income
    from the Ormond lands is in SP(Dom.), vol. XXVI, no. 81. The gift
    of the ermine by Bess to Mary Talbot is in Folger Xd 428 (118).
    The Venetian report on the new theatre is in SP(Ven.), vol. XV, p.
    111. The comment on the jewellery at the Twelfth Night masque
    in 1607 is taken from SP(Dom.), vol. XXVI, p. 394.

2   Cecil's letters to Gilbert Talbot of 17 February and 7 March 1608
    are in Col. of Arms, vol. L, ff141 and 149. Gilbert reports Arbella
    leaving Hardwick in a letter to Cecil dated 23 March 1608, SP(Dom.),
    vol. XXXI, no. 86. The comments and reports on the Cavendish mar-

riage are in Col. of Arms, vol. L, f155, vol. M, f519, and Add. MSS
4161, ff70–2.

3   For an account of the funeral of Bess see Durant, *Bess of Hardwick*,
pp. 224–5. The details of the enormous yardage of mourning cloth
are from the account book of William Cavendish, Hardwick MS.29,
ff28, 43 and 90.

4   Arbella's complaint to Dorset about slow payment of her allowance
or pension, April/May 1608, is from Lansdowne 165, f96. The award
for the licence of oats is in Col. of Arms, vol. L, f158.

20   MAKE GOOD MUSIC

1   Arbella's letter dated 8 November 1608 from Blackfriars addressed
to Gilbert is printed in Bradley, *Arabella Stuart*, vol. 2, p. 254. The
reference to the purchase of the house at Blackfriars is taken from
Handover, *Arbella Stuart*, p. 250 (no reference given). Arbella's
pictures are referred to in a letter addressed to Mary Talbot dated
28 November 1608, Lambeth, Shrewsbury papers, vol. 702, f133.
Harington reported Arbella as being down with smallpox in a letter
dated 21 December 1608, quoted in Bradley, *op. cit.*, vol. 2, p. 281.
A letter to Gilbert, dated 4 February 1609, reports Arbella attending
the masque, Lambeth MSS, Shrewsbury papers, vol. 702, f153. The
description of the revolving scenery or device is taken from Harris,
J., with Orgel, S., and Strong, R., eds, *The King's Arcadia* (1973),
p. 40.

2   Arbella's letter to Gesling dated 28 March 1609 is printed in Bradley,
op. cit., vol. 2, p. 224. Her assurance to Gilbert that she had seen
a pair of virginals play by themselves is in a letter dated 17 June
1609, published in Lodge, *Illustrations of British History*, vol. 3, p.
372. The reported value of the Irish liquor licence is given in
HMC(Hastings), vol. IV, p. 9. The details of Arbella's finances and
journey are from Hugh Crompton's accounts, Longleat, Seymour
papers, vol. XXII; partly published by Canon Jackson in *Wiltshire
Archaeological Magazine*, vol. IXX, pp. 217–26.

    Something of Henry Cavendish's resentment towards his brother
William is shown in Col. of Arms, vol. M, f553, when in November
1608 a legal reconciliation was attempted, to which William
responded and Henry did not. William's visit to Chatsworth is
recorded in Hardwick MS.29, f76. Gilbert's request to Hicks for a
loan is quoted in Smith, *Servant of the Cecils* ..., p. 130.

21   MELANCHOLY HUMOUR

1 Arbella's request, in December 1609, to Cecil to trade her Irish liquor licence in return for a higher allowance or pension is printed in full in Cooper, *Life... of Arabella Stuart*, vol. 2, pp. 96–7. Gilbert's letter to Cecil dated September 1609, *ibid.*, pp. 94–5. Isabel Bowes's letter to Arbella dated 5 December 1609 is in Harleian 7003, f55. Beaulieu's letter dated 29 December 1609 is printed in HMC(Downshire), vol. II, p. 211. His news is confirmed in a letter of one day later printed in SP(Dom.), vol. XXVI, p. 576, while the Venetians added their share in SP(Ven.), vol. XI, no. 427.

   The details of Stephano Janiculo, alias Bogden, are found in C. H. Herford and P. Simpson, *Ben Jonson* (1931), vol. 5, pp. 217–18 and 219. The reports of Arbella's involvement with the Prince of Moldavia, are taken from letters in HMC(Downshire), vol. 11, pp. 6, 17, 211, 216–17 and 219. The king's gift of recompense to Arbella is reported in R. Winwood, *Memorials of the Affairs of State in the Reigns of Queen Elizabeth and King James the First* (1725), vol. 3, p. 117. The cost of Arbella's servants is taken from Longleat, Seymour papers, vol. XXII. Arbella's appearance before the council on 15 February 1610 is reported in HMC(Downshire), vol. II, p. 240. Seymour's signed confession dated 20 February 1610 is in Harleian 7003, f59.

2 The details of the heavy debts of the Earl of Hertford are in HMC(Bath), vol. IV, pp. 347–8. The draft letter written by William Seymour, breaking off his association with Arbella is published, in *Wiltshire Archaeological Magazine*, vol. XV, p. 210. William's comment to Rodney that he felt bound to marry Arbella is in Harleian 7003, f62.

22   GRIEF OF MIND

1 William's confession of marriage is in Bodleian, Tanner MSS, vol. LXXV, f353. The names of the witnesses with the time and date are noted in Crompton's accounts, Longleat, Seymour papers, vol. XXII. The witty reference to 'safe lodgings' is from Winwood, *Memorials of the Affairs of State ...*, vol. 3, p. 241. The Venetians reported the arrests in SP(Ven.), vol. XII, no. 24.

2 Arbella's first petition to the council, Harleian 7003, ff90–1. Her petition to the king, *ibid.*, f57. William apologizes to the king, *ibid.*, f113. Arbella's letter to William, *ibid.*, f150. Her letter of 16 July 1610 to Gilbert, *ibid.*, f71. Her letter of 19 July 1610 to Gilbert, *ibid.*,

f74. The payments to Blague, the minister, are noted in Longleat, MSS, Seymour papers, vol. XXII, for 24 November and 18 December 1610. The payment to Gosson is from the same account.

3 Arbella's letter to the queen dated 22 July 1610, is printed in Cooper, *Life ... of Arabella Stuart*, vol. 2, p. 127. Her appeal to Henry Howard, a privy councillor, was through a third party, Cotton, Vespasian, vol. F, f35. Arbella's letters to Jane Drummond are in Harleian 7003, ff61 and 66–8. The petition to the queen in Bradley, *Arabella Stuart*, vol. 2, p. 246–7, enclosing one to the king, *ibid.*, p. 246. Jane Drummond's discouraging reply is in Harleian 7003, f64. Arbella's extraordinary letter to Jane Drummond, that she could not recall a similar case is in *ibid.*, f66.

23 HIGHLY OFFENDED

1 Thomas Scriven to Rutland, dated 4 January 1611: HMC(Rut.), vol. I, p. 427. The details of the rumoured pregnancy are in APC 1616–17, pp. 133–5. Thomas Scriven to Rutland, dated 4 March 1611: HMC(Rut.), vol. I, p. 428. The request for a writ of habeas corpus: Harleian 7003, f132.

Warrant to Bishop of Durham, dated 13 March 1611: *ibid.*, ff94, 96 and 97. Warrant to Parry, dated 15 March 1611: *ibid.*, f98. Warrant to Bond, dated 15 March 1611: *ibid.*, f102. Report by Bishop of Durham to council on Arbella's state of health dated 16 March 1611: SP(Dom.), vol. LXII, no. 30: and on 21 March 1611, *ibid.*, nos 39 and 39 (1). Moundford to Gilbert, dated 29 March 1611, Harleian 7003, f116.

The details of Arbella's forcible removal to East Barnet are from: Bishop of Durham to council, 21 March 1611, SP(Dom.), vol. LXIII, no. 17; Croft to council, 31 March 1611, *ibid.*, no. 48, and on 2 April 1611, *ibid.*, no. 49. Gilbert offers his prayers on 22 April 1611, in Harleian 7003, f144.

2 Bishop of Durham to Cecil, dated 23 January 1612, SP(Dom.), vol. LXVII, no. 27. Croft to council, dated 17 April 1611, *ibid.*, vol. LXIII, no. 38; and the expression 'clean out of the world' is taken from the same source. Venetian report, SP(Ven.), vol. XII, no. 235. The comment by the ostler is given in Winwood, *Memorials of the Affairs of State ...*, vol. 3, p. 179. The statement by John Bright, captain of the *Thomas* of Lynn bound for Berwick, who refused the passage to Calais is in SP(Dom.), vol. LXIV, no. 30.

24 TRICKS AND GIGS

1 Francis Seymour to Earl of Hertford, dated 5 June 1611, SP(Dom.), vol. LXIV, no. 8. The proclamation for Arbella's and Seymour's arrest, dated 4 June 1611, Rymer T., *Foedora*, 20 vols (1704–35), vol. XVI, p. 710, and HMC(Rut.), vol. IV, p. 211. List of prisoners, dated 4 and 5 June 1611, Harleian 7003, f140. The account of the capture of Arbella is taken from *ibid.*, ff128 and 130.

2 The formal examination is reported in Winwood, *Memorials of the Affairs of State* ..., vol. 3, p. 281. Crofts's petition dated 13 June 1611, SP(Dom), vol. LXIV, no. 33. Warrant to release Crompton is dated 12 July 1615, APC 1615–16, p. 257. Request to Archduke Albert is printed in Winwood, *op. cit.*, vol. 3, p. 278. William Seymour's group is described in HMC(Downshire), vol. III, p. 213.

25 NO OTHER WAY

1 Arbella's jewels are valued in Harleian 7003, f138 and the warrant, dated 30 June 1611, authorizing the use of her money to pay for the capture, SP(Dom.), vol. LXIV, p. 67. Mary's lodgings are referred to in Col. of Arms, vol. M, f588. Arbella's undated (but about Christmas 1611) draft petition to the queen, Harleian 7003, f78. Her letter to Fenton (undated), *ibid.*, f153.

Mary's appeal to Sheffield for funds, Lambeth MSS, Shrewsbury papers, vol. 702, f170. Gilbert's opinion on Mary's imprisonment, Col. of Arms, vol. M, f588. Mary's trial in the Star Chamber, 30 June 1612, J. Spedding, *The Letters and Life of Sir Francis Bacon* (1857), vol. 4, p. 298. The details of Arbella's allowance or pension, PRO, E403/2367.

2 Arbella's letter to James in November 1612, Nichols, *Progress etc., of Jas. I*, vol. 1, p. 563. Chamberlain's letter is in Winwood, *Memorials of the Affairs of State* ..., vol. 3, p. 454. Bull to Winwood, 20 July 1613, HMC(Buccleuch), vol. 1, p. 139. Arbella's gown is mentioned in APC, 1615–16, pp. 263 and 302, and SP(Dom.), vol. LXXII, no. 28.

Arbella's payments to William Seymour are accounted for in Longleat, Seymour papers, vol. XXII. Mary was allowed home, SP(Dom.), vol. LXX, nos 23 and 27. Chamberlain's letter dated 7 July 1614, *ibid.*, no. 58. Reeves being charged is mentioned in T. Birch, *The Court and Times of James the First* (1848), vol. 1, p. 338. Dr Felton sent to Arbella, APC, 1614–15, pp. 548–9. Smith returns to

Arbella's service by an order dated 29 April 1614, *ibid.*, pp. 422–3. Arbella's debt to Hooker, *ibid.*, p. 606.

3 Mary's reaction to Arbella's death, HMC 2nd Report, Appendix VII, p. 83. The report of the post mortem, HMC 8th Report and Appendix part 1, p. 228b.

4 The rumour of Arbella's child is in APC 1618–19, pp. 183–4. The seizure of Worksop in payment of the £20,000 fine is given in Sheffield Libraries, Arundel Castle MSS, W, f151. Mary's final release in 1623 is given in SP(Dom.), vol. CLIV, no. 17. The purchase by William Cavendish of the earldom of Devon in 1618 is accounted for in Hardwick MS.29, f544. (Although he purchased the dormant title of Devon, formerly in the Courtney family, the earldom was often referred to as Devonshire.) His adventuring investments are accounted for in MSS 23 and 29. Arbella's letter to Fenton is in Harleian 7003, f153.

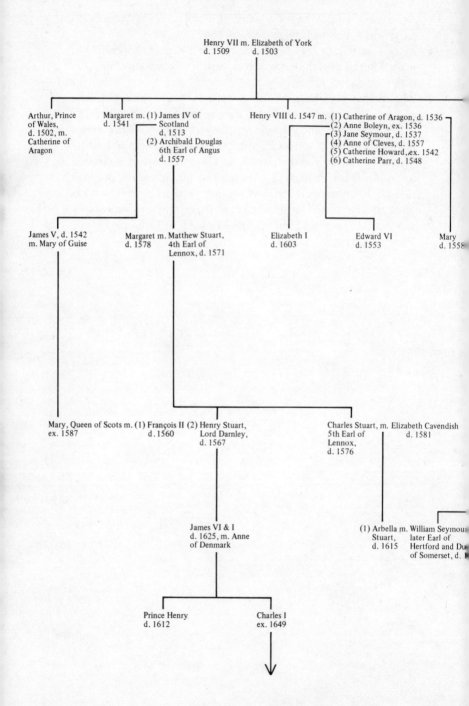

TUDOR/SEYMOUR

Henry VII m. Elizabeth of York
d. 1509   d. 1503

Arthur, Prince
of Wales,
d. 1502, m.
Catherine of
Aragon

Margaret m. (1) James IV of
d. 1541   Scotland
               d. 1513
          (2) Archibald Douglas
              6th Earl of Angus
              d. 1557

Henry VIII d. 1547 m. (1) Catherine of Aragon, d. 1536
                      (2) Anne Boleyn, ex. 1536
                      (3) Jane Seymour, d. 1537
                      (4) Anne of Cleves, d. 1557
                      (5) Catherine Howard, ex. 1542
                      (6) Catherine Parr, d. 1548

James V, d. 1542
m. Mary of Guise

Margaret m. Matthew Stuart,
d. 1578   4th Earl of
             Lennox, d. 1571

Elizabeth I
d. 1603

Edward VI
d. 1553

Mary
d. 1558

Mary, Queen of Scots m. (1) François II (2) Henry Stuart,
ex. 1587   d. 1560   Lord Darnley,
                                         d. 1567

Charles Stuart, m. Elizabeth Cavendish
5th Earl of   d. 1581
Lennox,
d. 1576

James VI & I
d. 1625, m. Anne
of Denmark

(1) Arbella m. William Seymour
    Stuart,   later Earl of
    d. 1615   Hertford and Du
                 of Somerset, d.

Prince Henry
d. 1612

Charles I
ex. 1649

GENEALOGICAL TABLES

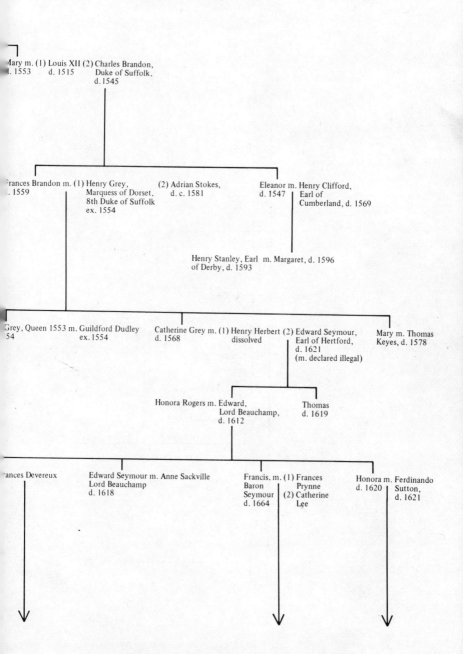

Mary m. (1) Louis XII (2) Charles Brandon,
d. 1553   d. 1515   Duke of Suffolk,
d. 1545

Frances Brandon m. (1) Henry Grey,   (2) Adrian Stokes,   Eleanor m. Henry Clifford,
d. 1559   Marquess of Dorset,   d. c. 1581   d. 1547   Earl of
8th Duke of Suffolk   Cumberland, d. 1569
ex. 1554

Henry Stanley, Earl m. Margaret, d. 1596
of Derby, d. 1593

Grey, Queen 1553 m. Guildford Dudley   Catherine Grey m. (1) Henry Herbert (2) Edward Seymour,   Mary m. Thomas
54   ex. 1554   d. 1568   dissolved   Earl of Hertford,   Keyes, d. 1578
d. 1621
(m. declared illegal)

Honora Rogers m. Edward,   Thomas
Lord Beauchamp,   d. 1619
d. 1612

rances Devereux   Edward Seymour m. Anne Sackville   Francis, m. (1) Frances   Honora m. Ferdinando
Lord Beauchamp   Baron   Prynne   d. 1620   Sutton,
d. 1618   Seymour (2) Catherine   d. 1621
d. 1664   Lee

CAVENDISH

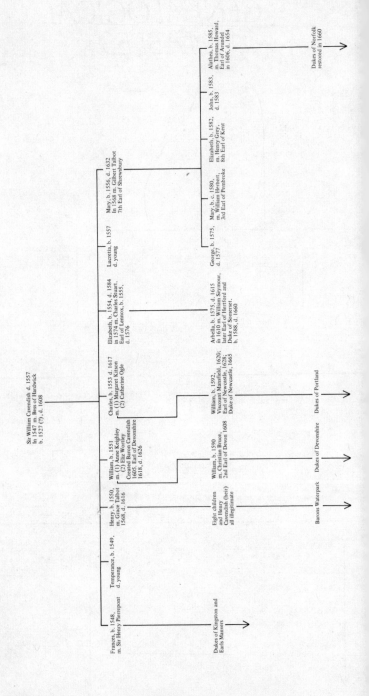

Sir William Cavendish d. 1557
In 1547 m. Bess of Hardwick
b. 1527 (?), d. 1608

Frances, b. 1548, m. Sir Henry Pierrepont

Temperance, b. 1549, d. young

Henry, b. 1550, m. Grace Talbot 1568, d. 1616

William, b. 1551 m. (1) Anne Keighley (2) Eliz. Wortley Created Baron Cavendish 1605, Earl of Devonshire 1618, d. 1626

Charles, b. 1553 d. 1617 m. (1) Margaret Kitson (2) Catherine Ogle

Elizabeth, b. 1554, d. 1584 in 1574 m. Charles Stuart, Earl of Lennox, b. 1555, d. 1576

Lucretia, b. 1557 d. young

Mary, b. 1556, d. 1632 In 1568 m. Gilbert Talbot 7th Earl of Shrewsbury

Eight children and Henry Cavendish (heir) all illegitimate

William, b. 1590 m. Christian Bruce, 2nd Earl of Devon 1608

William, b. 1592, Viscount Mansfield, 1620; Earl of Newcastle, 1628; Duke of Newcastle, 1665

Arbella, b. 1575, d. 1615 in 1610 m. William Seymour, later Earl of Hertford and Duke of Somerset, b. 1588, d. 1660

George, b. 1575, d. 1577

Mary, b. c. 1580, m. William Herbert, 3rd Earl of Pembroke

Elizabeth, b. 1582, m. Henry Grey, 8th Earl of Kent

John, b. 1583, d. 1583

Althea, b. 1585, m. Thomas Howard, Earl of Arundel in 1606, d. 1654

Dukes of Kingston and Earls Manvers →

Barons Waterpark →

Dukes of Devonshire →

Dukes of Portland →

Dukes of Norfolk restored in 1660 →

MANUSCRIPT SOURCES

CHATSWORTH

Hardwick MS.7 23 November 1591–8 January 1598.

Hardwick MS.8 15 April 1598–August 1601.

Hardwick MS.9 30 September 1593–16 April 1598.

Hardwick MS.23 William Cavendish's account book 1599–1607.

Hardwick MS.29 William Cavendish's account book 1608–28.

Hardwick Drawer 143, containing miscellaneous Cavendish papers.

Other Hardwick Drawers numbers 143, 144, 145 and 367 also contain miscellaneous Cavendish papers but with few references to Arbella Stuart.

Sixteenth-century manuscript 'Lives of the Earls of Shrewsbury' by Nathaniel Johnson.

FOLGER SHAKESPEARE LIBRARY, WASHINGTON, USA

Xd 428 Cavendish/Talbot letters. Part of the Phillips collection, nos 20556–20558. Acquired by the library in May 1961. Many of the letters in this collection were used by the Rev. Joseph Hunter in *Hallamshire* (1819), but the majority have never been published.

LONGLEAT

Seymour papers, vol. XXII. Arbella's account book kept by Hugh Crompton partly published by Canon Jackson in *Wiltshire Archaeological Magazine*, vol. IXX, pp. 217–26.

Talbot Letters. Two volumes of holographed letters, the second containing a great many concerning Gilbert and Mary Talbot.

ALTHORP HOUSE, NORTHANTS

Miss Lloyd's MS. 'Memoires of Elizabeth Hardwick Countess of Shrewsbury and her Descendants'. Holographed manuscript by Rachael Lloyd containing letters of which the originals have vanished.

Harleian MSS: vol. 39. A very disconnected account of Raleigh's trial begins on p. 275.

    vol. 6286. Contemporary transcription of the examinations in the Hertford-Grey marriage.

    vol. 6986. Contains two letters from Arbella to Prince Henry.

    vol. 7003. A collection of letters mainly concerning Arbella's time at Court and covering the period of her marriage and its immediate consequences.

Additional MSS 22, 563. Transcripts from the Weymouth papers. The granddaughter of William Seymour married the first Viscount Weymouth.

Sloane: vols 4161 and 4164. Thomas Birch's transcriptions of a great part of Harleian, vol. 7003, plus others.

CALENDARS

Public Record Office
State Papers Domestic
State Papers Holland
State Papers Venetian
State Papers Spanish
Acts of the Privy Council

A Calendar of the Shrewsbury Papers in the Lambeth Palace Library, ed. E. G. W. Bill. Derbyshire Archaeological Society Record Series, joint publication with HMC 1966.

A Calendar of Shrewsbury and Talbot Papers in the College of Arms, ed. G. R. Batho. HMC joint publication with Derbyshire Archaeological Society, 1971.

Catalogue of the Arundel Castle Manuscripts in the Sheffield City Libraries and Talbot Correspondence (part of Bacon Franks MSS), ed. R. Meredith, 1965.

Calendar of Scottish Papers, volume V.

Historical Manuscript Commission Reports
Salisbury (Cecil), 24 vols.
Rutland, 4 vols.
Bath IV, Seymour papers.
Downshire II and III.
Portland II.
Buccleuch I.

PREVIOUS BIOGRAPHIES
ON ARBELLA STUART

Bradley, E. T., *Arabella Stuart*, 2 vols (1889)
Cooper, E., *The Life and Letters of Lady Arabella Stuart*, 2 vols (1866).
Both these biographers did a great deal of research in the British Library
manuscript collections. Mercifully they were not inhibited in any way
from publishing letters and other evidence in full. Good Victorian biographies are valuable sources for modern biographers.

Strickland, Agnes, *The Tudor and Stuart Princesses* (1888)
This biography should be used with caution as she allows her imagination
to run away from facts. She causes Arbella to fall in love with Essex with
no great reason other than to please her readers. Although I think there
was something on Arbella's side, it was not the passion painted by Agnes
Strickland.

Hardy, B. C., *Arbella Stuart* (1913)
Handover, P. M., *Arbella Stuart* (1957)

BIBLIOGRAPHY

Ascham, R., *The Scholemaster* (1570)

Auerback, E., *Nicholas Hilliard* (1961)

Birch, T., *The Court and Times of James the First*, 2 vols (1848)

Boynton, L., and Thornton, P., *The Hardwick Hall Inventories* (1970)

Chamberlain, J., *The Letters of John Chamberlain*, ed. N. E. McClure, 2 vols (1939)

Clifford, A., *The Diary of Lady Anne Clifford*, ed. Vita Sackville-West (1923)

Doleman, R., *A Conference about the next succession to the Throne of England* (1594)

Durant, D. N., *Bess of Hardwick* (1977)

Fraser, A., *Mary Queen of Scots* (1970)

Girouard, M., *Hardwick Hall* (1976)

Harington, J., *Tract on the Succession to the Crown* (1602?)

Harington, J., *Nugae Antique*, 3 vols (1792)

Harington, J., Trans., *Orlondo Furioso* (1591)

Harris, J., with Orgel, S. and Strong, R., eds, *King's Arcadia* (1973)

Harrison, G. B., *The Elizabethan Journals*, 3 vols (1938)

Harrison, G. B., *A Jacobean Journal* (1941)

Harrison, G. B., *A Second Jacobean Journal* (1958)

Herford, C. H., and Simpson, P., *Ben Jonson* (1931)

Hunter, J., *Hallamshire* (1869)

Jardine, D., *Criminal Trials*, 2 vols (1832)

Johnson, P., *Elizabeth I* (1974)

Labanoff, A. I., *Recueil de Lettres de Marie Stuart*, 7 vols (1844)

Lacey, R., *Sir Walter Raleigh* (1973)

Laughton, J. K., *The Defeat of the Spanish Armada*, 2 vols (Navy Record Society 1894)

Leader, J. D., *Mary Queen of Scots in Captivity* (1880)

Lee, M., ed., *Dudley Carleton to John Chamberlain, Jacobean Letters* (1971)

Lodge, E., *Illustrations of British History*, 4 vols (1791 and 1833)

Nichols, J., *The Progresses, Processions and Magnificent Festivities of King James I*, 4 vols (1788–1821)

Orgel, S., and Strong, R., *Inigo Jones – The Theatre of the Stuart Court*, 2 vols (1973)

Read, C., *Mr. Secretary Walsingham and the Policy of Queen Elizabeth*, 3 vols (1925)

Read, C., *Mr. Secretary Cecil and Queen Elizabeth* (1955)

Read, C., *Lord Burghley and Queen Elizabeth* (1960)

Rowse, A. L., *The England of Elizabeth* (1950)

Smith, A., *Servant of the Cecils. Life of Sir Michael Hicks* (1977)

Spedding, J., *The Letters and Life of Sir Francis Bacon*, 4 vols (1857)

Stone, L., *An Elizabethan, Sir Horatio Palavicino* (1956)

Strong, R., *Portraits of Queen Elizabeth* (1961)

Strong, R., *The English Icon* (1969)

Weldon, A., *Secret History of the Court of James I*, 2 vols (1811)

Williams, N., *All the Queens Men* (1972)

Winwood, R., *Memorials of the Affairs of State in the Reigns of Queen Elizabeth and King James the First*, 3 vols (1725)

PORTRAITURE OF ARBELLA STUART

The only certain portraits of Arbella hang at Hardwick Hall. The earliest, dated 1577, has probably always remained in the house. This is a three-quarter length, on a panel $22'' \times 16\frac{1}{2}''$. It is inscribed with the subject's name, age and title: '*Arabella Comitessa Levinox. Ætae sue 23 Mensis. A.DÑI. 1577.*' It has been painted to show the Countess of Lennox and possibly is not a true likeness of the child. The portrait was probably commissioned to promote the claim for the Lennox earldom and designed to influence the queen and gain her support.

The second portrait of Arbella is a full-length study with the standard studio props of draped curtain, patterned carpet and table covered with a cloth on which Arbella rests her right hand. It carries the inscription in a cartouche: '*Arbella Stuarta, Comitessa Levinæ. Ætatis sua 13 et $\frac{1}{2}$. Anno Dñi 1589.*', also the unidentified monogram 'C.V.M.' The painting has been executed on a panel $63\frac{1}{2}'' \times 33''$. There is a later copy on canvas at Welbeck Abbey in the style of Rowland Lockey. The Hardwick portrait has been so badly restored and overpainted that it is difficult to say anything about its quality or lack of it. The date of 1589 is perhaps significant as that was the year in which Bess completed the little gallery in old Hardwick Hall and the portrait may have been commissioned by her to hang in the new room. The portrait brings to the fore the Lennox claim and it would have been typical of Bess, the only member of her family left with the motivation to keep the claim warm so long after it was a dead issue, to have commissioned it. Lord Hawkesbury, in a 'Catalogue of Pictures at Hardwick Hall' (*Derbyshire Archaeological Society Journal* (1903), vol. XXVIII) says of the portrait: 'This picture was given by the sixth Duke to 'Mr Cribb the picture cleaner, from whom it was bought by the ... seventh Duke.' It was lent for the Scottish Exhibition of 1888 and restored and reframed by Mr Haines, who no doubt was responsible for the present state of the painting.

There is a large full-length painting at Marlborough House called *Ara-*

bella Stuart after the style of Marcus Gheeraerts the younger, of which the well-known painting at Longleat is a copy; both are on canvas. A second copy on a panel is at Syon.

From the costume and hairstyle the Marlborough painting has been dated as *c.* 1605. If this is in fact Arbella, then the date falls in a period when there seems to have been no reason for having the portrait commissioned. Earlier in 1591, when the Parma marriage was being discussed, there would have been a need for a miniature by Hilliard, perhaps, or a full-length portrait by Lockey. Or later in 1610, when Arbella was about to marry William Seymour, one might have expected to find a full-length by Van Somer. The Marlborough House portrait will have to remain a doubtful attribution.

INDEX

Abrahall, Mrs, servant to A., 65, 80, 82
Abrahall, Richard, servant to A., 82
Adams, Mrs, wife of A's chaplain, 191–2, 198
Albert, Archduke of Austria, Duke of Brabant, Governor of Spanish Netherlands, 85, 201
Alexander brothers, 134
Alleyn, Edward, master of the Bear Garden, 134
Angus, 6th Earl, *see* Douglas, Archibald
Anne of Denmark, Queen of England, 41, 57, 122, 125, 130, 132, 133, 136, 137, 138, 139, 140, 142, 143, 147, 155, 156, 166, 178, 181, 184
Aremberg, Count d', 127, 133–4, 143
Arundel, 2nd Earl, *see* Howard, Thomas
Aubespine de Chateauneuf, M. de l', 50
Ault Hucknall, Derbyshire, 111

Babington, Anthony (d. 1586), a plotter, 39, 61
Bainton, Anne (b. Cavendish), 98
Bainton, Sir Henry, 98
Bancroft, Richard, Archbishop of Canterbury (1604–10), 151
Barley, Robert (1530–44), first husband of Bess, 2
Barnes, Thomas, a spy, 61–3
Batten, Thomas, servant to W. Seymour, 196, 198
Beale, Robert, Clerk to the Council, 34–5
Beaulieu, James, a correspondent, 172
Beaumont, M. de, French ambassador, 107, 114
Bedford, Countess of, *see* Russell, Lucy
Bertie, Mrs Catherine, 5–6, 9
Bertie, Peregrine, Lord Willoughby d'Eresby (1555–1601), 6
Bertie, Richard (1517–82), 6
Betoun, James, Bishop of Glasgow (1552–1603), 12, 20
Biron, Mrs, servant to A., 180
Blague, John, minister who married A., 180, 183

Blount, Charles, 1st Earl of Devon (1563–1606), 131
Bogden, Stephan, *see* Janiculo, Stephano
Bond, Sir William, 188
Bothwell, James, 4th Earl (1535?–78), husband of Scots Queen, 28
Bowes, Lady Isobel (d. 1622), 166, 167, 171
Bowes, Sir William (d. 1611), 167
Bowyer, Sir William, teller of King's Receipts, 150, 202, 203
Bradshaw, Mr, servant to Bess, 103
Bradshaw, Mrs Anne, servant to A., 180, 192, 194, 199, 200, 202, 207
Brandon, Charles, 1st Duke of Suffolk (1484?–1546), 5
Brandon, Frances, Duchess of Suffolk (1523–59), 2, 22, 76, 95, 97
Bridges, John, a trumpeter, 83
Britton, Eleanor, servant to George Talbot, 45
Bronker, Sir Henry, Queen's Commissioner (d. 1607), 99–102, 103, 106, 108–9, 110–11, 114–16, 119
Brooke, Catherine (b. Cavendish), 98
Brooke, George, 127, 129
Brooke, Henry, 11th Baron Cobham (1564–1619), 127–9
Brooke, Thomas, 98
Bruce, Christian, *see* Cavendish, Christian, Countess of Devonshire
Bruce, Edward, 1st Baron Kinloss, 160
Burghley, 1st Baron, *see* Cecil, William
Burghley, 2nd Baron, *see* Cecil, Thomas
Butler, Thomas, 10th Earl of Ormonde (1532–1614), 157
Buxton, Derbyshire, 165, 169
Bye Plot (1603), 127–9, 204

Caithness, Bishop of, *see* Stuart, Robert, 1st Earl of Lennox
Canterbury, Archbishop of, *see* Bancroft, Richard
Carleton, Sir Dudley, later 1st Baron Carleton and 1st Viscount Dorchester (1573–1631), a correspondent, 154, 208

Carr, Robert, 1st Viscount Rochester, 1st Earl of Somerset (d. 1645), 191, 204

Cavendish, Anne, *see* Bainton, Anne

Cavendish, Anne (b. Keighley), wife of Sir William Cavendish, 1st Baron Cavendish and 1st Earl of Devonshire, 59, 65, 84

Cavendish, Sir Charles, third son of Bess (1553–1617), 9, 11, 24, 27, 31, 37, 45–6, 59, 65, 83, 141, 144, 145, 161, 164, 168, 206, 210

Cavendish, Christian (b. Bruce), Countess of Devonshire, 160

Cavendish, Elizabeth, *see* Stuart, Elizabeth

Cavendish, Grace (b. Talbot), wife of Henry Cavendish, 16, 108, 141, 144, 157

Cavendish, Henry, eldest son of Bess (1550–1616), 9, 16, 24, 27, 47, 59, 69, 94, 96, 105, 108, 111, 112, 113, 115, 116, 140–1, 144, 152–3, 157, 160–1, 168, 206, 210

Cavendish, Henry, illegitimate son of above, 111, 115, 210

Cavendish, Mary, *see* Talbot, Mary

Cavendish, Sir William, second husband of Bess (d. 1557), 2, 5, 98

Cavendish, Sir William, 1st Baron Cavendish, 1st Earl of Devonshire, second son of Bess (1551–1626), 2–3, 5, 9, 24, 27, 31, 37, 45, 58, 65, 70, 79, 84, 90–1, 92, 99, 114, 141, 143–4, 145–6, 149–50, 157, 160 161, 167, 168, 209–10

Cavendish, William, 2nd Earl of Devonshire, 90, 160, 161

Cavendish, William, 6th Duke of Devonshire, 58

Cecil, Sir Robert, 1st Baron Cecil, 1st Earl of Salisbury (1563–1612), 54, 61, 68, 80, 85, 86, 88, 89, 99, 101, 104, 105, 106, 108, 109, 110, 114, 116, 117, 118, 119, 123, 126, 127, 128, 129, 131, 132, 137, 139, 143, 147, 150, 152, 154, 159, 160, 161, 165, 169, 171, 175, 179, 181, 185, 200, 201, 203

Cecil, Thomas, 2nd Baron Burghley, 1st Earl of Exeter (1542–1623), 150

Cecil, William, 1st Baron Burghley (1520–98), 9, 15, 16, 17, 23, 29, 42, 45, 46, 53, 54, 55, 60, 61, 62, 63, 64, 68, 70, 71, 72, 73, 86

Chamberlain, John (d. 1628), a correspondent, 154, 204, 206, 208

Chandos, Lady, Baroness Chandos, *see* Grey, Lady

Charles, Prince, later Charles I (1600–49), 124, 178

Chatsworth, Derbyshire, 5–6, 14, 21, 30, 31, 33, 34, 35, 36, 46, 73, 82, 95, 160, 168, 216

Chaworth, George, servant to Bess, 109

Chaworth, Mrs, servant to A., 202

Cheney, Lady Joan (d. 1614), 166

Cheney, Sir Thomas (d. 1558), 163

Chesterfield, Derbyshire, 167, 168

Christian IV, King of Denmark (d. 1648), 153–5

Clay, Hercules, servant to Bess, 103

Clifford, George, 3rd Earl of Cumberland (1558–1605), 45, 134

Cobham, 11th Baron, *see* Brooke, Henry

Condé, Henry II, Prince of, 88

Conference by R. Dolman, 75–6, 86

Conyers, Mr A., 189

Cook, Thomas, servant to Gilbert Talbot, 140

Cope, Sir Walter, Chamberlain of Exchequer, 153

Corvé, Captain Tassin, 199

Crocket, Captain, 198

Croft, Sir James (d. 1590), 53–4

Croft, Sir James, son of above, 166, 190–1, 198, 201

Crompton, Hugh, servant to A. (d. 1645), 172, 174, 180, 181, 192–4, 196, 198, 199, 200, 201, 206, 209

Cumberland, 3rd Earl of, *see* Clifford, George

Cutting, Thomas, lutanist, 155

Daniel, Edward, servant to Earl of Hertford, 96

Daniel, Samuel, masque composer (1562–1619), 137, 178

Darnley, Lord, *see* Stuart, Henry

Denbigh, Lord, *see* Dudley, Robert

Denmark, King of, *see* Christian IV

Devereaux, Robert, 2nd Earl of Essex (1567–1601), 47, 52, 54, 63, 83, 89, 111, 123

Devereaux, Walter, 1st Earl of Essex (1539–76), 32

Devon, 1st Earl of, *see* Blount, Charles

Devonshire, Countess of, *see* Cavendish, Christian

Devonshire, 1st Earl of, *see* Cavendish, Sir William

Devonshire, 2nd Earl of, *see* Cavendish, William

Digby, Mrs E., servant to Bess, 69

Dingley, George, S.J., a foolish priest, 71, 72–3, 75

Dodderidge, Francis, son of John, 92

Dodderidge, John, alias John Good, servant to Bess, 82, 83, 91–6, 99, 100, 104, 107, 165, 183, 200

Doleman, E., *see* Verstegan, Richard

Dorset, 1st Earl of, *see* Sackville, Thomas

Douglas, Archibald, 6th Earl of Angus (1489?–1557), 8, 76

Douglas, Margaret, Dowager Queen of Scots (1489–1541), 8, 17, 76

Douglas, Margaret, *see* Stuart Margaret, Countess of Lennox
Drake, Sir Francis (1542–96), 47, 55
Drummond, Lady Jane, 135, 184, 185, 200
Dudley, Robert, 1st Earl of Leicester (1532–88), 3, 9, 13, 14, 17, 20, 28, 29, 32, 33–4, 44, 47, 53, 54, 75, 86, 123, 151
Dudley, Robert, Lord Denbigh, son of above (d. 1584), 33–4, 36, 41, 86
Dudley, Sir Robert, 141, 151
Durham, Bishop of, *see* James, William

Elizabeth I, Queen of England (1533–1603), 1, 5, 8, 10, 13, 14, 15, 16, 17, 18, 20, 21, 23, 29, 30, 31, 32, 33, 36–7, 39, 40, 41, 42, 43, 44, 45–6, 47, 48, 52, 53, 54, 55, 57, 63, 64, 66, 70, 74, 75, 76, 83, 85, 86, 87, 88–9, 92, 93–4, 97, 99–100, 102, 103, 110, 114, 115, 116, 117–18, 119, 122, 130, 137, 156, 178, 239, 247, 266–7
Elizabeth, Princess, later Queen of Bohemia (1596–1662), 124, 178, 205
Elwes, Sir Gervase, Lt of the Tower (d. 1615), 204
Epicoene, see Janiculo, Stephano
Erskine, Thomas, 1st Viscount Fenton (1566–1639), 173, 202, 210
Essex, 1st Earl of, *see* Devereaux, Walter
Essex, 2nd Earl of, *see* Devereaux, Robert
Exeter, 1st Earl of, *see* Cecil, Thomas

Farnese, Alexander, Duke of Palma (d. 1592), 41, 42–3, 45, 53–4, 60–1, 62, 63, 64, 68, 70, 73, 74, 166
Farnese, Cardinal, 85
Farnese, Rainutio (d. 1622), 41, 42, 43, 46, 54, 57, 58, 60, 61, 63, 64, 66, 68–9, 73, 85, 86, 166
Farnham Castle, Surrey, 125
Felton, Dr, 206
Fénelon, La Mothe, French ambassador, 5, 9, 12
Fenton, 1st Viscount, *see* Erskine, Thomas
'Fines', 51
Fitton, Mary, 144
Fletcher, Richard, Bishop of Bristol (1589–93), 70
Foljambe, Godfrey, 167
Fotheringhay Castle, Northants, 39–40, 49
Fowler, Thomas, servant to Countess of Lennox (d. 1590) 9, 18, 58, 130
Fowler, William, son of above, 130–1, 144
Frank, Edward, 103
Freake, Old, embroiderer to A., 111, 121, 165, 183

Garnet, Father Henry, S.J. (1555–1606), 152, 153
Gesling, Charles, 164

Gib, Sir John, 135
Gifford, Gilbert, 39
Good, Francis, *see* Dodderidge, Francis
Goodrich Castle, Herefordshire, 35
Gosson, Richard, a goldsmith, 184
Greenwich Palace, 52, 55, 70, 122, 123, 150, 180, 193, 197
Greville, Sir Fulke (1554–1628), secretary of the Navy, 141
Grey, Catherine (1538?–1568), 8, 76, 93, 95, 97–8, 180, 183, 185, 208
Grey, Elizabeth (b. Talbot), Countess of Kent, 35, 118, 121
Grey, Henry, 6th Earl of Kent (1541–1615), 117, 118, 121, 122, 145, 170
Grey, Henry, 8th Earl of Kent (1583?–1639), 118, 121
Grey, Jane (1537–54), 22, 95, 97
Grey, Lady, Baroness Chandos, 189
Grey of Wilton, Thomas, 15th Baron (d. 1614), 127, 129, 204
Gunpowder Plot, 152

Hacker, John, servant to Bess, 103
Hammond, Dr, physician to James I, 189
Hampton Court Palace, 125, 136, 153
Hardwick, Bess of, Countess of Shrewsbury, grandmother of A. (1527?–1608), 2–3, 5–7, 8, 9, 11, 12, 13–14, 15–17, 19, 20–1, 22, 23, 24–5, 27, 28, 29, 30, 31, 33, 34, 35, 36, 37, 44, 45, 46, 48, 50, 51, 52, 55–6, 57, 58, 59, 64, 65, 66, 67, 68, 69, 70, 71, 72–3, 77, 78–80, 81, 82, 83, 84, 85, 87, 88, 89–90, 97–8, 99–104, 105–6, 108, 109, 110, 111, 112–13, 114–15, 119–20, 121, 124, 141, 145, 146, 149, 150, 153, 157–8, 159, 161, 167, 168, 188, 200, 207
Hardwick Hall, Derbyshire, 31, 32, 35, 48, 55–6, 57, 58–9, 72–3, 77, 81, 82–3, 84, 86–7, 90, 92, 99, 102, 104, 106, 108, 109, 110, 111, 112, 114, 115, 116, 117, 119, 121, 132, 149, 159, 160, 161, 168, 175
Hardwick, James, brother of Bess (1526–81), 32, 57, 58
Harington, Sir John (1561–1612), 47–8, 163
Hartington, Derbyshire, 141
Hastings, Henry, 3rd Earl of Huntingdon (1535?–95), 83, 141
Heneage, Sir Thomas, Vice-Chamberlain, 62–3
Henri III, King of France (d. 1589), 46
Henri IV, King of France (d. 1596), 74, 88, 107
Henry, Prince (1594–1612), 86, 124, 127, 142, 151, 154, 155, 176, 177–8, 181, 191, 200, 204, 208
Herbert, Henry, 2nd Earl of Pembroke (1538?–1601), 83

Herbert, Mary (b. Talbot), Countess of Pembroke (1580–1649), 51, 144–5, 148, 151

Herbert, Philip, 1st Earl of Montgomery (1584–1650), 134, 147–8, 150, 151

Herbert, William, 3rd Earl of Pembroke (1580–1630), 51, 144–5, 148

Hertford, Earl of, *see* Seymour, Edward

Hicks, Sir Michael, 141, 169

Hilliard, Nicholas (1547?–1619), court painter, 62, 63, 68, 70

Holles, Sir John, 153

Holstein, Duke of, *see* Joachim, Ernest

Hood, Thomas, servant to A., 80

Hooker, Nicholas, a goldsmith, 207

Howard, Alathea (b. Talbot), Countess of Arundel (d. 1654), 157, 158, 163, 165, 178, 191

Howard, Charles, 1st Earl of Nottingham (1536–1624), Lord High Admiral, 128, 132, 152, 198

Howard, Henry, 1st Earl of Northampton (1540–1614), 184

Howard, James, 157

Howard, Katherine, Countess of Suffolk, 131, 137

Howard, Mary (b. Stuart), Countess of Nottingham, 131–2, 152

Howard, Thomas, 3rd Earl of Arundel (1585–1646), 157

Howard, Thomas (d. 1536), 17–18

Huntingdon, 3rd Earl of, *see* Hastings, Henry

Hunton, Dr, physician to Bess, 159

James I, King of Great Britain (1566–1626), 5, 8, 11, 12, 13, 18, 19, 20, 30, 36, 40, 41, 57, 58, 76, 86, 87, 89, 109, 116, 117–18, 119, 120, 121, 122, 123, 124, 125, 126, 127, 128, 130, 131, 133, 134, 135, 136, 137, 139, 143, 147–8, 149, 150, 152, 154, 156, 158, 161, 172, 173, 178, 180, 181, 188, 189, 190, 193, 197, 198, 199, 200, 201, 202, 204, 205, 207, 208

James, William, Bishop of Durham (1606–17), 187, 190

Janiculo, Stephano, alias Bogden, a montebank, 172–4

Joachim, Ernest, Duke of Holstein-Sunderberg (d. 1658), 150

Jones, Inigo (1573–1662), 135, 148–9

Jonson, Ben (1572–1637), 135, 142, 148–9, 158, 163–4, 173

Keighley, Anne, *see* Cavendish, Anne, wife of Sir William Cavendish

Kent, 6th Earl of, *see* Grey, Henry

Kinloss, 1st Baron, *see* Bruce, Edward

Kirton, Edward, servant to W. Seymour (1654), 180, 192, 209

Kirton, Mr, a solicitor, 92, 94, 98–9

Kniveton, Jane, half-sister of Bess, 70, 90

Knollys, Lettice (1540–1634), 28, 32–3

Knyvet, Sir Thomas, 1st Baron, 172, 176

Leake, Sir Francis (d. 1626), 141, 149

Lee, Sir Henry, 134

Leicester, 1st Earl of, *see* Dudley, Robert

Lennox, Earls and Dukes of, *see* Stuart

Lockey, Rowland, a painter, 68

London, City and Town: Blackfriars, A's house at, 162, 163, 172; Broad St, 140, 141, 164, 220; Coleman St, 55; Hackney, 4, 9, 10, 17; Shrewsbury House, Chelsea, 65, 67, 69; Tottenham, 94; Tower, 9, 17, 18, 22, 54, 61, 62, 93, 98, 106, 124, 126, 129, 134, 137, 142, 181, 182, 183, 186, 187, 195–6, 201, 202, 204, 205, 207, 208, 209; Westminster, 69, 97, 116, 178, 198, 208; Whitehall, 52, 67, 116, 125, 142, 143, 148, 158, 164, 165, 178, 203

Lucien, Sir John, 154–5

Main Plot (1603), 127–9, 135, 141

Manners, John, 4th Earl of Rutland (d. 1587), 34

Manners, Roger, 5th Earl of Rutland (1576–1612), 83, 167

Markham, Sir Griffen (1564?–1644), a plotter, 127, 128

Markham, William, servant to A., 191–2, 198, 199

Mary, Queen of Scots (1542–87), 2, 3, 5, 8, 12, 16–17, 18–19, 20, 23, 25–6, 30, 31, 35–7, 38, 39–40, 42, 44, 48, 49, 56, 59, 61, 62, 94, 126, 141, 160, 168, 188, 189, 205, 208

Mary, Princess (1605–7), 150

Masques: *The Masque of Beauty* (1607), 158; *The Masque of Blackness* (1605), 148; *The Masque of Tethys' Festival* (1610), 178; *The Masque of the Queens* (1609), 163–4; *The Vision of the Twelve Goddesses* (1604), 137

Mathias, Archduke (d. 1619), 85

Mauvissière, Michele de Castelnau, Seigneur de la, French ambassador, 36, 37

Mendoza, Bernadino de, Spanish ambassador, 43

Moldavia, Duke of, *see* Janiculo, Stephano

Molin, Nicholo, Venetian ambassador, 156, 158

Monson, Sir William (1569–1643), 198

Montague, Dr Edward, Dean of the Chapel Royal, 149, 150, 151

Montgomery, 1st Earl of, *see* Herbert, Philip

Moody, Thomas, secret agent, 62–3

Morley, Thomas, agent for Cecil, 61–2

Moundford, Dr, President of Coll. of Physicians (1550–1630), 186, 188, 189, 190, 198, 207

Nassau, Maurice, Prince Stadholder of, 144
Nevers, Carlo Gonzaga, Duke of, 88–9
Newark, Nottinghamshire, 6, 117
North, Dudley, 3rd Baron, 134
Northampton, 5, 6
Northampton, 1st Earl of, *see* Howard, Henry
Northumberland, Earls of, *see* Percy
Nottingham, 1st Earl of, *see* Howard, Charles

Ogle, Cuthbert, 7th Baron, 83, 108
Orlando Furioso, Trans. by J. Harington (1591), 47
Ormonde, 10th Earl of, *see* Butler, Thomas
Overbury, Sir Thomas (d. 1613), 204, 205, 207
Owen, David, servant to Bess, 101–2
Owen, Hugh, 102
Owen, John (1560?–1622), epigrammatist, 155
Owen, Richard, page to A., 102, 111, 121, 122
Owlcotes, Derbyshire, 84, 92, 108
Oxburgh Hall, Norfolk, 191

Paget, William, 1st Baron (1505–1603), 33
Palavicino, Sir Horatio, a financier (1540–1600), 141
Palmer, Dr, a divine, 206
Parker, Francis, servant, 83
Parma, Duke of, *see* Farnese, Alexander
Parry, Sir Thomas (d. 1616), 181, 182, 183, 188
Parsons, Father Robert, S.J. (1546–1610), 75, 118
Paulet, Sir Amias, 39
Pembroke, Earls of, *see* Herbert
Percy, Dorothy, Countess of Northumberland (d. 1619), 151
Percy, Henry, 2nd Earl of Northumberland (1532?–1585), 33
Percy, Henry, 3rd Earl of Northumberland (1564–1632), 58, 83
Percy, Thomas, 1st Earl of Northumberland (1528–72), 14, 18
Phelippes, Thomas, 61, 62, 63
Philip II, King of Spain (1527–98), 36–7, 41–2, 46, 47, 53, 60, 73, 74, 75
Pierrepont, 'Bessie' (1568?–1621), 35–6
'Poly', a code name, 63
Pusey, Timothy, servant to Bess, 104

Raleigh, Sir Walter (1554?–1618), 45, 47, 126, 127–9, 143

Ratcliffe, Alexander, servant to Gilbert Talbot, 141
Reeves, Edward, servant to W. Seymour, 180, 181, 183, 192, 194, 195, 199, 201, 206
Rich, Lady Penelope (1562?–1607), 131
Rich, Robert, 3rd Baron, later 1st Earl of Warwick (d. 1619), 131
Richmond Palace, Surrey, 20, 69, 108, 116
Ricroft, John, agent to Cecil, 62
Rivers, Father Anthony, S.J., a correspondent, 88, 118
Robsart, Amy, wife of R. Dudley (d. 1560), 32
Rochester, 1st Viscount, *see* Carr, Robert
Rodney, Edward, friend of W. Seymour, 176, 180, 195, 196, 198
Roulston, Anthony, a kidnapper, 71
Royston Park, Hertfordshire, 148, 187, 190
Rufford Abbey, Nottinghamshire, 1, 6, 169
Russell, Lucy, Countess of Bedford (d. 1627), 131, 140
Ruthven, Patrick, Lord, 12
Rutland, Earls of, *see* Manners

Sackville, Thomas, 1st Earl of Dorset (1536–1608), 161
St Loe, Sir William, second husband of Bess (d. 1565), 3, 24
St Paul, Sir George, 168, 171, 176
Salisbury, 1st Earl of, *see* Cecil, Sir Robert
Saville, Sir George, 169
Saville, Lady Mary (b. Talbot), 169
Savoy, Duke of, Charles Emmanuel (d. 1603), 128
Scaramelli, Giovani, Venetian secretary, 52, 54, 118, 119, 122, 125
Scriven, Thomas, servant to Gilbert Talbot, 186, 187
Seymour, Edward, 1st Earl of Hertford (1537–1621), 8, 76, 92, 93–6, 97–8, 100, 102, 118, 119, 174, 175, 176, 198, 205, 209
Seymour, Edward, Lord Beauchamp (1561–1612), 8, 76, 93, 94, 119, 174, 208
Seymour, Edward, son of Lord Beauchamp (1587–1618), 93, 95, 100
Seymour, Francis (1590–1664), 197
Seymour, Thomas (1563–1600), 8
Seymour, William, later 1st Duke of Somerset (1588–1660), husband of A., 174–6, 179, 180–3, 186, 187, 188, 191, 192, 195–8, 199, 201, 205, 207, 208, 209
Shakespeare, William (1569–1616), 82, 135
Sheen Park, Surrey, 122, 123, 125
Sheffield, Lady Douglas, 32, 151
Ships: *Adventure*, 198–9; *Charles*, 197; *Talbot*, 55
Shirland, Bridget, servant to A., 103
Shrewsbury, Earls of, *see* Talbot
Simple, John, a kidnapper, 71

Sinclair, Sir Andrew, 154
Skinner, Lady, 163, 172
Skipworth, Sir William, 166
Smith, Samuel, servant to A., 185, 207
Smythson, Robert, architect, 58
Society of Jesus, 71, 74–5, 152
Somerset, 1st Earl of, *see* Carr, Robert
Somerset, Edward, 4th Earl of Worcester (1553–1628), 131, 132, 149
Somerset, Elizabeth, Countess of Worcester, 131
Southampton, 3rd Earl of, *see* Wriothesley, Henry
Southwell, Elizabeth, 151.
Stafford, Sir Edward, 62–3
Stanhope, Sir John, 1st Baron (1545?–1621), 104, 105, 106, 110, 132, 200
Stanhope, 1st Baron, *see* Stanhope, Sir John
Stanley, Sir William, 6th Earl of Derby (1561–1642), 71
Stapleton, Henry, a misguided Catholic, 111, 112, 113, 115
Starkey, James, household chaplain to Bess (d. 1603), 82, 83, 90–2, 107
State of England 1600, 86
Stewart, Sir William, 132
Stuart, Arbella: Parentage, 1–2, 3, 4, 17, 156; Death of father, 11; Death of mother, 28; Birth, 10; Claim to succession, 2, 7–8, 17, 36, 40, 76, 156; Character, 11, 51; Appearance, 50–1, 107, 156; The Lennox claim, 12–14, 18, 21, 30, 58, 124; Portraits of, 50–1, 234–5, (1577) 13–14, (1589) 58; Jewellery, 18–19, 58, 67, 79, 80, 130, 137, 158, 183–4, 202, 203, 204; Finances, 21, 66, 78–80, 121, 122–3, 125, 147, 150, 153, 156–7, 161, 165, 171, 174, 183–4, 191, 202, 203–4; Education, 21–2, 51, 69, 72, 87, 107; Influence of Virgin Queen, 26, 27, 28, 38; Betrothal to R. Dudley, 33–4; Marriages proposed and rumoured before 1603, 33–4, 41, 52–3, 58, 69, 85, 86, 88; First Court visit (1587), 41, 44–8; Plate, 48, 88, 150; Second Court visit (1588), 52–3; Hardwick Hall not built for, 58–9; Third Court visit (1591), 65–71; Religion, 69, 173; Clothes, 67, 69, 70, 71, 177; Portrait for Parma, 68–70; Kidnap plot, 71–2; New Year gifts, (1600) 88, (1604) 135–7, (1609) 174; Remembers Essex, 89, 111; Proposed marriage with E. Seymour, 91–6, 98–104; Secret lover, 105–9; Views on men, 109–10; Attempts escape from Hardwick, 111–13; Refuses to attend Queen's funeral, 117–18; To Wrest Park, 117–18; To Sheen Park, 122, 123; Marriages rumoured after 1603, 127, 144, 150; Cecil an ally, 129; Returns to Court, 130–8; Health, 132, 137, 147, 163,

187, 188–9, 202; Peerage for W. Cavendish, 149–50; Visits Bess 1605, 150; Death of Bess 1608, 159–60; House in Blackfriars, 162–3; Midlands progress, 165–70; Licence for sale of oats, 161–2; Licence for Irish wines and spirit, 165, 168, 169, 170, 171, 176; Before Council, 173; In masques, 158, 178; Marriage to W. Seymour, 180–1; Arrested and confined, 181–5; To be sent to Durham, 186–91; Believes herself pregnant, 186–7; Escape, 191–4, 198–9; Capture, 199; The Tower, 201, 202; Mental state, 208; Death, 1615, 207; Post mortem, 207
Stuart, Charles, 1st Earl of Lennox (1555–76), father of A., 1, 3, 4, 6–7, 8, 9, 11, 12, 13, 18, 27
Stuart, Elizabeth, Countess of Lennox (1555–82), mother of A., 1, 3, 4, 5–7, 8, 9, 14, 15, 18, 21, 28–9, 44, 79, 102, 132
Stuart, Esmé, 1st Duke of Lennox (1542–83), 30, 41, 86
Stuart, Henry, Lord Darnley (1545–67), 4, 18, 26
Stuart, Ludovic, Duke of Lennox (1574–1624), 57, 86
Stuart, Margaret, Dowager Countess of Lennox (1515–1578), 1, 4–5, 6–10, 11–12, 14, 15, 17, 18, 20, 27, 28, 58, 87, 94, 130, 173, 200
Stuart, Princess Mary (b. 1605), 194–5
Stuart, Mary, Countess of Nottingham, *see* Howard, Mary
Stuart, Matthew, 13th Earl of Lennox (1516–71), 18
Stuart, Robert, Bishop of Caithness (1542–86), 1st Earl of Lennox, 1st Earl of March (1517?–86), 20, 30
Suffolk, Countess of, *see* Howard, Katherine
Suffolk, Duchess of, *see* Brandon, Frances
Suffolk, 1st Duke of, *see* Brandon, Charles
Suffolk, Duchess of, fourth wife of C. Brandon, *see* Bertie, Mrs Catherine
Sutton-in-Ashfield, Nottinghamshire, 103

Talbot, Alathea, Countess of Arundel, *see* Howard, Alathea
Talbot, Edward, 8th Earl of Shrewsbury (1561–1617), 108, 141
Talbot, Elizabeth, Countess of Kent, *see* Grey, Elizabeth
Talbot, Francis, Lord (1550?–82), 35, 59
Talbot, George, 6th Earl of Shrewsbury (1528–90), fourth husband of Bess, 2, 3, 6, 14–15, 16–17, 23, 24–5, 28, 29–32, 34, 35, 40, 45, 49, 55, 56, 58, 59, 60, 79, 141, 168
Talbot, George (1575–7), 25, 30

Talbot, Gilbert, 7th Earl of Shrewsbury (1552–1616), 11, 16, 32, 35, 45, 47, 48, 51–2, 55, 57, 59–60, 66, 79, 84, 117, 118, 122, 123, 124, 125, 130, 131, 132, 133, 135, 136, 137, 140, 143, 144, 145, 149, 151, 153, 155, 156, 157–8, 159, 160, 163, 164, 167, 168, 169, 170, 171, 183, 186, 188, 189, 191, 198, 200, 203, 206, 209

Talbot, Grace, *see* Cavendish, Grace

Talbot, John (b. 1583), son of Gilbert, 35

Talbot, Mary (b. Cavendish), Countess of Shrewsbury (1556–1632), 11, 16, 32, 35, 45, 47, 48, 50, 51, 55, 57, 69, 79, 84, 103, 117, 118, 119, 123, 124, 125, 126, 131, 132, 137, 140, 141–2, 143, 144, 151, 155, 157–8, 159, 160, 161, 163, 164, 169, 172, 179, 190, 191, 198, 200–1, 202, 203, 205, 206, 207, 209

Talbot, Mary, *see* Herbert, Mary, Countess of Pembroke

Taxis, de, Spanish ambassador, 142

Temple Newsam, Yorkshire, 5

Theobalds, Hertfordshire, 45, 46, 48, 154

Throckmorton, Lady, 71

Tudor, Princess Margaret (1489–1541), 1–2, 8, 76, 156

Tudor, Princess Mary (1498–1533), 8

Velasco, Don John de, Constable of Castille, 142–3

Vere, Sir Francis, 154

Vere, Susan, Countess of Montgomery, 147

Verstegan, Richard, exiled Catholic (1548–1641), 75–6, 86

Waad, Sir William, Lt of the Tower (1546–1623), 181, 197, 204

Walsingham, Sir Francis (1532?–90), 17, 21, 25, 28, 29, 30, 36, 37, 39, 42, 53–4, 60–2, 130

Walsingham, Lady, wife of Sir Thomas, 131, 137

Willoughby, Sir Francis, 77–8

Winchester, Hampshire, 128, 133

Windsor Castle, Berkshire, 124, 127, 149

Wingfield, Manor, South, Derbyshire, 45, 48–9, 56, 57, 60, 82, 159, 164, 169

Winwood, Sir Ralph (1563–1617), 204, 205, 208

Woodstock, Oxfordshire, 134

Worcester, 4th Earl of, *see* Somerset, Edward

Worksop Manor, Nottinghamshire, 58, 117, 123, 168, 209

Wray, Isobel, *see* Bowes, Lady Isobel

Wrest Park, Bedfordshire, 117–18, 119, 121, 122, 170

Wriothesley, Henry, 3rd Earl of Southampton (1573–1624), 126

Yelverton, Sir Christopher (1535?–1612), 170

Yelverton, Henry (1566–1629), 170, 176